NACUBO Guide to Issuing and Managing Debt

George A. King
Richard E. Anderson
David M. Cyganowski
Patrick J. Hennigan

National Association of College and University Business Officers

Library of Congress Cataloging-in-Publication Data

NACUBO guide to issuing and managing debt / George A. King . . . [etc.].
   p. cm.
   ISBN 0-915164-93-0
   1. Education, Higher—United States—Finance.
2. Universities and colleges—United States—Business
 management. 3. Debt—United States. I. King, George A.
II. National Association of College and University Business Officers.
LB2342.N17 1994   94-7163
  378'.02'0973—dc20   CIP

Edited by Anne Kendrick

Cover design by Stacey Trey

Contents

Part III: Structuring a Financing

Foreword

The *NACUBO Guide to Issuing and Managing Debt* is a comprehensive sourcebook with two essential purposes: to provide executive-level decision makers with the information they need to determine whether borrowing is in the best interest of their institutions, and to assist administrators who are actually going through the process of issuing debt in developing the most appropriate capital financing strategy for their needs.

Because today's financing decisions require careful evaluation as well as sophisticated analysis, this publication has been developed to provide a thorough examination of the factors involved in deciding whether to borrow, and to give presidents, business officers, trustees, and other institutional administrators the knowledge and skills needed to gain the most benefit from the debt market.

Issuing debt is a complex decision with long-term implications. For this reason, the *Guide to Issuing and Managing Debt* stresses the importance of assessing and preserving debt capacity for the institution's future, including evaluation of excessive and risky levels of debt, existing debt and new money, and tax-exempt financing.

Once the decision to issue debt has been made, a complex process begins that is both time-consuming and costly. The guide navigates the reader through the process of issuing debt, the participants involved, and all of the steps involved from start to finish in issuing a bond. It also emphasizes the importance of developing a capital plan, which necessarily involves risks that must be managed, and discusses allocating and utilizing the limited financial assets of the institution.

As a resource, the *Guide to Issuing and Managing Debt* contains market statistics that we believe are not available elsewhere or have never before been accessible through a single source. As a reference, it includes listings of individuals in the higher education community who have expertise in debt financing, facilities authorities, ratings agencies, and many other areas.

We are confident that you will find this book to be an important tool in your assessment of your capital structure—a tool through which you will discover how careful debt issuance can help you fulfill your institution's educational mission. NACUBO is grateful to the authors for this thorough, valuable, and unique contribution to the field of higher education debt financing.

Caspa L. Harris, Jr.
President

Alice W. Handy
Chair, Higher Education
Finance Committee

Authors

George A. King is a vice president in the public finance department of CS First Boston. Prior to joining CS First Boston, Mr. King was an attorney with the law firm of Mudge Rose Guthrie Alexander & Ferdon, where he participated in higher education financings in several capacities, including counsel to the institution, bond counsel, underwriter's counsel, disclosure counsel, bond insurer's counsel, and special counsel for derivative product transactions. Mr. King has written several monographs on higher education finance and is a co-author of *A Guide To Municipal Official Statements: Disclosure and Tax Requirements* (Prentice Hall, 1990). Mr. King is a Trustee of Wagner College, Staten Island, New York.

Richard E. Anderson is vice chancellor for finance at Washington University in St. Louis. He has written or edited numerous books and monographs on higher education finance including *Finance and Effectiveness* and *The Costs and Finance of Adult Education and Training*. Mr. Anderson was a co-founder of the Forum for College Financing and a Professor of Higher Education at Teachers College, Columbia University.

David M. Cyganowski is a director in the public finance department of CS First Boston and the head of the firm's higher education financing group. Mr. Cyganowski also specializes in health care finance and has completed numerous financings for teaching hospitals affiliated with large universities and university systems.

Patrick J. Hennigan is a vice president in the public finance department of J.P. Morgan Securities Inc., where he specializes in higher education finance. Mr. Hennigan was a higher education credit analyst at J.P. Morgan prior to joining the investment banking group and was twice selected as the outstanding higher education credit analyst in the industry through a survey of institutional investors. Prior to joining J.P. Morgan, Mr. Hennigan was a faculty member at Columbia University and the University of Virginia.

Acknowledgements

The *NACUBO Guide to Issuing and Managing Debt* was created through the efforts of a diverse group of higher education finance professionals and college and university business officers.

The book has been a project of the NACUBO Higher Education Finance Committee, including commentary and reviews. The input and support of its members has been essential to its completion. In addition to Messrs. Anderson, Cyganowski and King, the committee is comprised of Alice W. Handy (Chair) of the University of Virginia; Edward J. Bambach, formerly of the New Jersey Educational Facilities Authority; Robin Jenkins, NACUBO Center for Institutional Accounting, Finance, and Management; Stanford G. Ladner of Mudge Rose Alexander & Ferdon; Louis R. Morrell of Rolllins College; Joseph P. Mullinix of Yale University; Joan A. Panacek of the New Jersey Educational Facilities Authority; Joseph A. Pastrone, retired from the University of California; Michael O. Stewart of Marian College of Fond du Lac; and Farris W. Womack of the University of Michigan. Anna Marie Cirino, associate director of NACUBO's CIAFM, served as project director for the guide. Bradley Meeker, program assistant of product development; and Anne Kendrick, editor, provided invaluable staff assistance and support at NACUBO.

The authors, the committee, and the staff at NACUBO also wish to acknowledge the contributions of the following persons to the progress of this book:

- Philip L. Cifarelli, director of financial services and assistant treasurer of Skidmore College, who contributed the case study of the Skidmore College's 1993 bond issue included in chapter 1.

- Lisa Danzig, director, Standard & Poor's Corporation, who provided the compilation of the list of higher education institutions with outstanding rated indebtedness included in chapter 17.

- Parker W. Duncan, senior partner of the Public Finance Department of Wyatt, Tarrant & Combs of Kentucky, who assisted in the review process.

- Charles Ellinwood, managing director of A.H. Williams & Co., Inc.

- Joe E. Forrester, director of CS First Boston, who provided input on federal tax considerations.

- Robert Kay, financial analyst at CS First Boston, particularly with respect to the financial information provided in chapter 17.

- Paul J. Lawler, vice president for finance, Rensselaer Polytechnic Institute, who contributed the case study of the general obligation student loan bonds included in chapter 1.

- Susan A. McMillan, vice president of CS First Boston, particularly with respect to credit enhancement considerations included in chapter 12.

- Michael McTague, executive assistant to the president of Dowling College, and formerly vice president for administration and finance of The Sage Colleges.

- Clifford Nancarrow, vice president of business affairs at Western State College, particularly with respect to the case study of Western State College's 1992 bond issue included in chapter 1.

- Richard T. Nolan, of McCarter & English of New Jersey, particularly with respect to the various financing vehicles described in chapter 10.

- Bernadette O'Connell, associate in public finance at J.P. Morgan Securities Inc., who prepared updates of market statistics.

- Joan A. Panacek, deputy executive director, New Jersey Educational Facilities Authority, particularly with respect to the National Association of Higher Educational Facilities Authorities included in chapter 19.

- Sebastian T. Persico, vice president for administration of Lehman College, and formerly vice president of administration of Wagner College.

- Richard J. Reilly, attorney at Mudge Rose Guthrie Alexander & Ferdon.

- Christian Stewart, of CS First Boston, particularly with respect to the focus on investors included in chapter 3 and the market statistics included in chapter 17.

- M. Lee White, senior vice president and manager of Higher Education Finance at George K. Baum & Company, particularly with respect to the case study of Western State College's 1992 bond issue.

- Gary D. Wolf, vice president of Chemical Securities Inc., particularly with respect to student loan financing matters included in chapter 7.

- Joanne Wuensch, associate in public finance at J.P. Morgan Securities Inc., who updated market statistics.

Introduction

This book is about debt financing for higher education institutions. College and university business officers need to be knowledgeable about debt financing because a combination of circumstances have come together to make tax-exempt financing available for higher education institutions and this tool can be of great benefit to institutions in fulfilling their educational missions. Today's financing decisions require much more than simply deciding whether or not to borrow. Such decisions involve sophisticated analysis to determine how to allocate and utilize the limited financial assets of an institution.

Financing decisions cannot be avoided. Even deciding to forgo a project altogether has academic and financial consequences. Paying for a project with endowment or fund raising or from annual cash flow is a decision to choose one financing technique over other available options. The decision to use external financing introduces its own additional choices and decisions for colleges and universities. All choices come with opportunity costs, and often identifiable dollar impacts as well.

The objective of this guide is to provide the reader with a combination of information needed to actively participate in the financing process; ask the questions necessary to facilitate decision making; and contact individuals in the higher education community who can assist in the process of arriving at decisions.

Higher education finance is characterized by the same rapid change as many other aspects of our economy and society. Neither this guide nor any other similar source can substitute for the current expertise of business officers and higher education finance professionals. This is particularly applicable to references to laws, regulations, and policies, which are always subject to change. References to market-driven prices and practices also are only reflections of various individual markets. Financing decisions cannot be made on the basis of this guide because the information is continuously changing. When used with this perspective in mind, this publication approaches higher education finance with a combination of scope and measured detail that will offer valuable assistance to all colleges and universities that may use the capital markets to further their academic missions.

Why Finance? Why Borrow?

The primary external financing tool available to higher education institutions is debt financing in one of many forms. Unlike other corporations, independent colleges and universities, as nonprofit corporations, and public colleges and universities, as governmental entities or public benefit corporations, cannot sell equity or their assets. Instead, ownership vests in the public domain in one of several ways. Even the disposition of assets of nonprofit corporations eventually is subject to review by a court of law if the independent college or university ceases to exist. Therefore, the equity markets and all the variations on equity securities and other securities convertible to equity securities do not exist for colleges and universities. The focus for higher education is the debt market. Fortunately, the sophisticated debt capital markets available to colleges and universities today makes debt a generally satisfactory alternative.

A variety of internal financing techniques also are available to higher education institutions. In using these techniques, colleges and universities must make an assessment concerning their internal cost of capital.

Higher Education Sector of the Capital Markets

During the past 10 years, the volume of debt issued in the capital markets by colleges and universities has increased dramatically from an annual volume of less than $2 billion in the late 1970s and early 1980s. Universities became more active in the markets in 1983, signaled by Harvard's $229 million issue sold in December 1982. That issue was one of the first higher education bonds with a variable interest rate that was reset periodically. Peak issuance occurred in 1992 and surpassed $10 billion.

During the three years from 1990 to 1992, the higher education sector has ranged from 4 to 5 percent of the total municipal market. As figure 17-6 on page 140 indicates, issuance declined after the enactment of the Tax Reform Act of 1986, which set a $150 million cap on the amount of tax-exempt bonds outstanding for independent, nonprofit universities. The number of higher education issues has increased steadily since 1987, however, and the numbers and types of institutions raising capital through tax-exempt financings continues to expand. Recently, public universities have become more active in the public markets and issue a larger proportion of new volume each year.

Not only has volume increased in the higher education sector during the past decade, but the variety of issues and types of security structures also have broadened beyond fixed rate bonds to include variable rate bonds, commercial paper, and lease-rental bonds. In the 1970s and early 1980s, universities sold bonds typically secured by specific revenue streams from dormitories, parking systems, student centers, or other revenue-generating operations. These were traditional revenue bonds with all of the standard legal provisions for rate covenants, additional bonds test, flow of funds, and debt service reserve requirements. Rarely, with these issues, was it necessary to assess the overall creditworthiness of the institution or of a system of campuses because the revenue pledge was very narrow and credit analysis focused on the specific revenue stream.

Today, more university issuers are pledging their full faith and credit, which is usually defined as a pledge of all available unrestricted revenues. These revenues include tuition and fees, investment income, federal indirect cost recovery, enterprise revenues, and other unrestricted moneys. This broader pledge has been used particularly for lease-rental issues and for projects that are not revenue generating, such as academic buildings and research laboratories. Academic facility financing is relatively recent for some public institutions because of past limitations of financing to revenue-producing facilities. The lifting of these statutory restrictions and the market acceptance of public college general obligation pledges have supported the growth of public college academic facility financings. As a result, investors often must analyze the financial operations of a university and its capacity to carry additional debt.

The use of mortgages in higher education financing structures varies across the country as a result of the different requirements of investors and the assorted state higher education financings authorities. In general, however, investor requirements for mortgages have decreased over time as the emphasis has shifted toward covenant protection, including a negative covenant not to create or allow to be created a mortgage on certain or all of the property of the institution unless the bondholders receive an equal interest in the property. Public institutions often are restricted by statute from mortgaging their land and buildings, but there are also variations among states with respect to techniques for using the property of the institution to buttress the cash flow security for the bond issue.

The higher education sector, after tax reform, consists not only of tax-exempt bonds but also of a small and growing amount of taxable issues. Large independent research institutions that have more than $150 million in debt outstanding have been issuing taxable securities as alternatives to tax-exempt debt. For example, the University of Chicago and Columbia, Cornell, Georgetown, Princeton, Stanford, and Yale universities each exceeded the $150 million limit and have issued taxable debt. Until the $150 million cap is lifted, a few large independent institutions may sell tax-exempt issues to refinance outstanding bonds. Washington University, in anticipation of the possible removal of the cap, has used a repurchase agreement to access low-cost capital on an interim basis. For the immediate future, new issue volume in the tax-exempt market will consist mainly of large public university and smaller independent college issues.

For investors who are considering adding

higher education bonds to their portfolios, the federal tax code's $150 million cap provides a constraint on the supply of quality tax-exempt higher education bonds. This restriction becomes more significant each year because the amount of the cap has never been increased since it was imposed in 1986 and is not indexed to inflation. Investor demand for higher education bonds has remained strong since 1987.

In the past few years, and particularly in 1993, serious consideration has been given to lifting the $150 million cap on higher education bonds, and also to making other adjustments to their tax treatment under the Internal Revenue Code. These proposals would assist colleges and universities greatly without having a significant effect on the costs to the federal government of having a larger amount of tax-exempt bonds in the market. While no business or financial officer can assume passage of the provisions, many institutions have developed tentative plans for utilizing the proposed tax code provisions.

Credit Perspectives

As a sector of the municipal market, the credit quality of higher education bonds is strong, with approximately 80 percent of the issues rated "A" or better. Figure 17-7 on page 141 indicates the distribution of ratings for independent and public university issues as assigned by Standard & Poor's Corporation. These ratings incorporate an assessment of each university's financial performance, demand for services, selectivity, matriculation rates, debt burden, and quality of management. The role of management in implementing an effective strategic planning process has been given even greater weight in the rating process during the volatile 1990s. With many colleges and universities facing reduced enrollments, slower revenue growth, aging facilities, and increasing competition for research grants and gifts, buyers of university bonds will remain comfortable with the credit quality of an institution if the administration has a strong plan to maintain institutional stability. This positive perception of higher education debt generally is reenforced by the historically low rate of default for bonds issued by universities and by the essen-

tial nature of higher education for regional economic development.

Formulating a ratings strategy is one of the most important steps in planning and structuring a financing. Most purchasers of higher education securities will want to know of the rating before making their investment decision, but a variety of rating agencies and approaches to the rating process can be taken by colleges and universities. The absence of a rating is not a bar to carrying out a financing, but nonrated transactions are developed, structured, and marketed differently from rated financings. If bonds are sold with a rating, that rating will be continuously evaluated by the rating agency throughout the life of the bond. If the credit supporting the bond changes, there could be a rating upgrade or downgrade, either of which would be expected to affect the market value of the bond in the hands of the investor, but neither would change the interest rate on the bonds (unless the bonds were variable rate bonds). Ratings strategies also need to consider that new financings may have an effect on outstanding issues. A current action by the institution that directly causes a rating downgrade for outstanding bonds will damage the institution's reputation in the market and hinder sales for the current bond issue.

Debt Capacity

Determination of debt capacity is a function of the parameters used in making an assessment of the institution's resources. For example, the debt capacity of a medical school that is part of a larger university depends on whether the medical school is analyzed as a stand-alone revenue source, as part of the hospital to which it is related, or as part of the larger university of which it is a component. In addition, business officers must recognize that the assessment of debt capacity will be influenced by external parties and their perspective on what is proper debt capacity for the institution. For example, the assessment of the rating agencies is critical in achieving the most advantageous rating for a bond issue; the evaluation of investors is important in structuring an issue that will attract buyers; the assessment of credit enhancers will control whether credit enhancement can be used in achieving the most efficient structure for the offering; and the assessment of a governmental issuing agency is significant in securing the issuer's approval allowing the bond offering to proceed.

When balancing the different perspectives that each of the internal and external evaluators bring to the debt capacity question, business officers will have some (but often limited) latitude to modify the evaluator's standard policies by explaining the institution's business objectives for the offering. For example, the institution may need to take a "leveraged" position in terms of theoretical debt capacity, but if the proceeds of the issue are applied to a revenue producing purpose that is also a key strategic project, the leverage often will be viewed in a much more sympathetic light than would normally be the case. Dormitories and parking garages can fit this profile. If the institution can show that an academic facility is strategically essential, nonrevenue producing facilities may fit this profile also. There are limits to the strategic argument, however, because most market participants have institutional policies concerning tolerable debt capacities. Business officers should make their case strongly, but should keep their expectations controlled when a strategic argument is aligned against rating agency, credit enhancement, or investor policies.

Business officers also should consider the structure of bond issues as a variable that can be used to influence the debt capacity analysis. Variable rate issues require more institutional reserves or the demonstrated capacity to carry the debt if the maximum interest rate is applicable. At the same time, the purchase of an interest rate cap, interest rate swap, or other derivative product can enable an institution to gain a portion of the benefits of a variable rate issue without bearing the full impact of the risks associated with variable interest rates. On the other hand, while a fixed rate issue usually will have a higher initial interest rate than a variable rate security, rating agencies, credit enhancers, investors, and the governing board of the institution often look favorably on the certainty and reduced risks associated with a fixed rate issue.

As a practical matter, business officers faced with determining their debt capacity must make certain critical assumptions before they can perform any calculations. As long as those assumptions are clearly stated, the analysis can later be modified with various scenarios if there is an interest in taking on or eliminating certain risks.

Financing as a Management Tool

Financing can provide both programmatic and financial benefits. The use of debt can enable an institution to engage in educational and research activities that it would otherwise have to postpone or abandon. A traditional approach would dictate that the necessary capital be accumulated before expenditures are made. However, in some settings this may be inappropriate or impossible. There may be no alternative source of capital. Projects may need to be self-financed with debt repaid from the cash flows of the project. If there is sufficient demand for a prospective program, the cost of borrowed funds can be paid from operating revenues of the program. Further, even if funds can be accumulated, the delay may bring other unacceptable costs. If a program is postponed until it is financed with equity, some students will not receive the benefits of that program.

Borrowing may increase or decrease financial flexibility. An institution may have the capital to acquire the desired land or construct the building, but tying up the institution's liquid assets for such a project may not be in the institution's best interest. Dormitories, for example, can demonstrate a clearly defined income stream, and lenders may be inclined to provide market access more readily for such projects. However, if an institution uses its internal resources for dormitories, it may deprive itself of the ability to finance a necessary, but less marketable, academic building. In addition, if an institution has a limited borrowing capacity, a source of interim funding for nonanticipated expenses may be lost if a project is financed.

Managing Risks

The financing process necessarily involves risks that must be managed. If the benefits exceed the costs, the financing should be undertaken. Of course, in the real world, the process often involves subtle and complex evaluations. Because costs and benefits will be demonstrated differently, a comparative analysis also must evaluate the probability of the expected cost or benefit occurring.

Most obviously, principal and interest must be repaid. Repayment costs can be as fixed as absolute sums payable on fixed dates until the final maturity of the debt, or payments can vary with swings in interest rates using variable rate debt. Repayment risk can be managed but never eliminated.

Financing poses organizational risks to the extent that a legal obligation to repay borrowed funds often places the lender in a priority position ahead of routine operating expenditures with respect to the institution's income stream. If the income stream is growing, these claims may not pose a problem. However, if the income stream shrinks, the role of debt service can become a major burden. Eventually, debt service payments could adversely affect an institution's ability to carry out its business. Organizational risk can be managed by avoiding the over-leveraging of the institution's assets, particularly with respect to debt service as a percentage of gross income and net income after mandatory transfers other than debt.

A less measurable risk is that access to borrowed capital may encourage an institution to implement projects with less care and discipline in the project approval process than should be applied. Access to debt financing may make the short-term cost attractive without sufficient critical evaluation of the intrinsic merit of the project and the conservation of resources for unforeseen future use. Such policy risks can be managed only with a disciplined and merit-based approach to financing and project approvals.

Capital Planning

The first and most important plan an institution must establish is its long-term strategy. Top managers must know where an institution is going before they can evaluate the benefits of specific programmatic expansion. In the absence of a strategic vision, many new programs will be perceived to be of equal value, or priorities will be distorted by the degree of attention generated by interest groups. A strategic plan will delineate accurate institutional priorities.

After a strategic plan is in place, the institution should have both a capital plan and an operating plan. The operating plan should include:

- trends and projections of operating income and expenses with appropriate details — tuition, state support, gifts, research funding, etc.;
- comparative data with other institutions;
- an estimate of deferred maintenance by type (e.g., cosmetic, structural, and health and safety threat); and
- a specific list of assumptions about the operating environment.

The capital plan will concentrate on data and trends that most directly affect the capital budget. The capital plan should include:

- a catalog of plant facilities by type of construction, age, and use;
- a discussion of relevant local and national economic and demographic trends;
- trends in space per user (e.g., classroom space per student);
- outstanding debt with relevant details;
- available capital;
- appropriate comparative data; and
- a plan to issue and repay debt.

It is important to articulate a detailed context for these plans. This gives all constituencies a practical opportunity to question the assumptions and to understand why, for example, the business school needs a new building. It is also important that the capital and operating plans be fully integrated. Future operations not only determine the capital needs, but will also provide a large share of the capital funding. Similarly, the operating cost of new buildings must be integrated into future budgets.

The capital plan will start with an extended list of capital projects in some priority ranking. Associated with each project will be its cost and designated capital and income. The shortfall between costs and designated sources must be filled with unrestricted income and capital. This apportionment is the heart of the capital plan.

It is important that all assumptions are conspicuously displayed and that the capital plan tests alternatives to the chosen assumptions. For example, a plan to construct dormitories might assume an increase in enrollment. The institution must be confident that this growth will materialize or have plans to support the project if enrollment falls short. Even more important, a worst-case scenario should be simulated for the full operating and capital budget. This test need not be draconian. No construction would be implemented if it had to stand up against a 1930s style depression with a simultaneous World War II enrollment slowdown. But it is not unreasonable to plan for enrollment stagnation and a capital market like those experienced during the 1970s. Admittedly, such modeling will dampen expansionist plans, but going forward and being wrong may cost an institution its stability or, in the extreme case, its existence.

Capital financing demands planning. The capital planning process must balance a merit-based choice of project priorities with the institution's strategic plan. Such projects must be measured against available resources. The commitment of payment streams to repay debt service over periods as long as 20 or 30 years is not a decision to be taken lightly. The proper implementation of a financing plan also requires a great deal of "context." Financings do not occur in a vacuum. Constant issuance of small amounts of debt can be a costly process in terms of time as well as expenses of issuance. Integrated financial programs are more appropriate for higher education institutions, particularly since refunding, refinancing, early redemptions, tender offers, and other opportunities in the market make it costly to issue debt and put it on the shelf for 20 or 30 years until it is paid in the regular course of business. Finally, the market will penalize institutions that attempt to raise money in the capital markets in the absence of a coherent financial plan. Such institutions will be perceived as less well managed and therefore a greater credit risk.

The Role of Governing Bodies

Each business officer and president will have their own type of relationship with their governing board, and this relationship will shape the role of the governance body in the capital financing. This section will list a number of governance issues that business officers should consider in the course of planning and implementing a capital financing activity.

Legal Authority. Business officers should review the articles of incorporation, charter, and bylaws of their institutions to gain informal assurance that the financing concept or proposed financing technique is authorized. Public institutions will be directed by statutory and regulatory directions more than their independent counterparts. Legal opinions eventually will be needed to close the transaction, but business officers should have a working knowledge of these documents regardless of their reliance on counsel at a later date.

Legal Role of the Full Board and Committees. It is common for the bylaws, in particular, to specify which committees are involved in the issuance and management of debt. Frequent reviewers of capital financing activities will be the business and finance committee, the executive committee, and the full board. The approval process for public institutions is likely to be more individualized depending on the laws of each state as well as political custom and policy in the state. For example, some states require approvals from the legislative branch as well as the executive branch before a financing is approved. It is important to include the process for meeting governance body review requirements as a part of the financing planning phase. Putting together a financing team will involve several outside parties, and board members should be informed of contemplated financings in a timely manner. Business officers should avoid situations that could allow board members to hear first from an outside source that a project or financing is under consideration or review.

Policy Role of the Full Board, Committees, and Certain Individuals. In addition to legal requirements for particular governance procedures, most business officers and presidents will have relationship and policy reasons for adding formal or informal events to the governance body review process. These events should be identified early in the process.

Typical Board Meetings. To the extent that it is

possible to generalize about board procedures for independent colleges and universities, most institutions will have two board meetings, one with the full board and one with the executive committee. The order of the meetings usually will be determined by regular meeting schedules, as special meetings for financings are relatively rare.

At the first meeting, the board or committee usually adopts a reimbursement resolution (to fulfill a federal tax law requirement as explored in chapter 8) and directs the institution's management to proceed with investigating and structuring the financing.

At the second meeting, the substantially final forms of the financing documents normally are available and the board or committee will approve the documentation. In addition, the board or committee normally will set parameters for the principal financial terms such as interest rate, final maturity, and total principal amount of borrowing. These parameters make it possible for the board or committee to delegate the determination of the final terms of the transaction to senior management, usually the president and the business officer. In addition, senior management, and sometimes certain board officers, will sign the financing documents, subject to specific instructions contained in the bylaws.

Public institution governance bodies will operate with varying procedures and time requirements, some of which may be set by statute (e.g., notice of meeting procedures). The business officer must be proactive in researching the various requirements and should be cautious in assuming that all of the approvals will come from the same agency.

Avoiding Timing Delays. The capital markets require rapid and decisive actions, even for routine transactions. For example, even the most routine bond issuance has a "pricing" period on a particular day when either the underwriter takes orders during a negotiated sale or the bids are opened during a competitive sale. Business officers, on behalf of their institutions, need to be able to accept proposed interest rates at the bid opening of a competitive sale or within a matter of a few minutes or hours during a negotiated sale. Experience will dictate that it is simply not practical to expect to convene a committee or another gov-

erning body for the bond sale unless legal requirements afford no choice. There is not enough time for this formality. Inclusion of certain trustees in an informal way permits flexibility of timing and also allows the business officer to benefit from the experienced perspective of the board.

Getting Started

The business officer's decision about how to begin the process will greatly influence the way in which the higher education financing is put together. Typically, the choices available for the initial contacts include colleagues from other institutions who have financing experience; the applicable state higher education financing authority for independent or public institutions or the state treasurer's office for public institutions; counsel to the institution if counsel is experienced in financing matters; or an investment banker for securities if the institution is in a position to make a knowledgeable decision about contacting an investment banker. The case studies in chapter 1 provide three separate examples of how institutions can get started. There is no uniform best approach, however, and business officers should begin the financing process by speaking with individuals who have their trust and confidence.

Post-Closing Responsibilities

The successful closing of any financing is the conclusion of one phase of the financing process and the commencement of others. The most apparent obligation, of course, is to operate the institution so that the debt service payments can be made when due. Compliance with covenants and reporting requirements will be required in all cases. Periodic disclosure of information concerning the credit status of the institution is currently an informal activity and is expected to be formalized very soon by various regulatory bodies. Certain financing techniques also require active post-closing involvement of the institution or its agents, such as the resetting of variable interest rates.

Business officers should consider the post-closing implications of their decisions during the financing process. Covenants are a particularly important obligation of the institution and can greatly affect the ability of the institution to engage in various activities in the future. Failure to comply with covenants with respect to arbitrage and other tax considerations could result in interest on tax-exempt bonds being retroactively declared to be taxable. Chapter 9 addresses covenants. Care should also be taken to fully understand the limitations of the amendment process with respect to financing documents. Requirements for bondholder consent reduce the likelihood of being able to use an amendment provision, yet there are certain covenants over which investors will insist on holding a veto. Decisions to involve credit enhancers in the financings will generate additional covenants and restrictions, but these parties often hold the consent powers for amendments while the credit enhancement is in effect. This section cannot anticipate all of the individual issues that may arise for each institution, and business officers should work with their financing teams to explore the post-closing implications for the institution.

PART I

Overview of Higher Education Capital Markets

❖ O N E ❖

Coming to Market

There is, of course, no simple way for colleges and universities to access the debt markets. Many complicated factors must be considered and decisions made. However, once institutional leadership determines to consider the issuance of debt, many of the decisions will fall into place. Although this guide is not intended to minimize the complexity of the process, presidents and business officers should not be dissuaded from considering public debt because they are new to the game.

Participants in the financing process who are external to the institution (e.g., consultants, underwriters, bond counsel, issuing authorities, and others) have a stake in carrying out the issuance of debt. Institutions must be certain that external debt is the proper way to proceed. Under certain circumstances, internal borrowing by appropriating money from endowments and charging implicit interest to the project may be a more reasonable approach. Perhaps the project should not be financed with debt at all. The institution's board and the issuance requirements of state authorities will provide a natural check on over-eager issuance. Institutional decision-makers also can expect bond counsel, rating agencies, and underwriters to warn them about excessive and risky levels of debt. These experts, however, may be less likely to advise leaders about preserving debt capacity for future projects, and the value of advice in this area will vary greatly depending on the scope of information concerning future institutional plans available to the advisors. In general, these professionals can provide advice, but only the institution's top leadership can balance present and future needs.

Furthermore, institutions must be prudent in issuing debt that they expect to support with a future campaign for endowment. In general, it is easier to locate major donors for a building than for creating endowment to help support debt. In addition, use of an endowment to directly support tax-exempt debt often presents insurmountable difficulties under the arbitrage rules.

The chapter begins with three case studies, each intended to add some context and institutional dimension to the process of debt financing. The first two case studies are of small independent and public colleges, respectively. They were purposely chosen to take some of the mystique out of the issuance of bonds. Although both institutions had issued debt before, neither could be considered a seasoned issuer in all respects.

All three case studies illustrate that outstanding debt and new debt issues need to be considered as a totality. With interest rates being historically low in the early 1990s, it makes good sense to refinance older debt when issuing new debt. Combining the older issues with new project funding can lead to considerable cost savings.

The Skidmore College case study explains how derivative products (see chapter 11) can be combined with traditional debt to provide a more effective financing package. The Western State College case study shows the importance of considering political cycles when thinking about issuing debt. The Rensselaer Polytechnic Institute case study is a compelling example of how colleges and universities can use higher education finance as a powerful and innovative management tool.

Case Study of an Independent Institution: Skidmore College

Skidmore College, Saratoga Springs, New York
Dormitory Authority of the State of New York
Skidmore College Insured Revenue Bonds, Series 1993
by Philip L. Cifarelli

Skidmore College is a highly selective, predominantly residential, independent, coeducational college located in Saratoga Springs, New York. The college offers more than 60 degree programs in the traditional liberal arts disciplines and various preprofessional areas to an enrollment of approximately 2,100 full time students. The student-faculty ratio is 11:1. The college's annual operating budget for its fiscal year ended June 30, 1993, was approximately $60 million, and the market value of its endowment fund was approximately $50 million. The comprehensive fee (tuition, room, and board) for the 1992–1993 academic year was $21,920. More than 80 percent of the college's revenue is derived from tuition and student fees.

Tax-exempt financing plays an integral role in the capital structure of the college. Since the 1960s the college has utilized tax-exempt financing on five occasions for facilities totalling approximately $70 million (1963—$5.6 million, 1968—$6.4 million, 1983—$5.8 million, 1987—$11.7 million, and 1993—$40.4 million) and participated in one pooled financing for equipment totalling approximately $2.1 million (1985). In addition, the college has participated in two bond issues where general obligation bond proceeds of the college were used to fund student loans directly to students totalling approximately $8 million (1992—$2.3 million and 1993—$5.7 million).

The following case study discusses the key issues involved in the most recent facilities financing for $40,445,000, which closed on July 22, 1993. The proceeds of the 1993 bonds were used (i) to finance the construction, expansion, or equipping of several different facilities of the college as described below, (ii) to fund the implementation of various energy conservation upgrades campuswide, (iii) to refinance $10,650,000 outstanding principal amount of the college's 1987 facilities bonds, (iv) to purchase a surety bond from the

1993 bonds' bond insurer to fund the debt service reserve fund for the 1993 bonds, and (v) to pay the costs of issuance of the 1993 bonds.

Evolution of the 1993 Capital Financing

In December 1992, Skidmore College was less than a year away from the start of the largest capital campaign in its history. The feasibility study was not yet completed, but the goal for the four to five year campaign was projected at that time to be in the range of $75 million. Each of the last two capital campaigns had necessarily been "bricks and mortar" efforts, but now the focus had shifted to endowment. Based on the college's strategic plan, not less than $50 million would be raised for endowment. The only "bricks and mortar" project contemplated for this campaign would be an addition to and renovation of the Scribner Library at a cost of approximately $12 million. While several other important building needs still existed, the library was the only building project to be included in the campaign because of the overriding importance of the endowment objective.

Karl Broekhuizen, Skidmore's vice president for business affairs and treasurer, and Philip Cifarelli, Skidmore's director of financial services and assistant treasurer, discussed moving the library project forward at a faster pace. According to board of trustees policy, major construction projects could begin only after half of the funding is in hand and the other half has been identified. That would mean that the library project would not begin until 1995 or 1996, and would not be completed until 1998 or 1999. Both the pressing academic needs of faculty and students and the favorable market for construction costs in upstate New York during 1993 were strong incentives for accelerating the project. Further, debt financing was especially attractive at this time because of historically low interest rates. The financial officers decided to investigate the alternative plans of finance available from external capital markets sources. The review naturally focused on the tax-exempt securities market, which offered the potential for the college to benefit from tax-exempt interest rates. (The college's eventual interest rates are listed on the cover page to the official statement, which appears on the last page of this case study.)

The college's initial plan was to use short-term variable rate revenue notes that could be repaid as proceeds from the campaign were received. The revenue note approach evolved into a permanent financing approach of issuing long-term bonds to build the library, reinstating $12 million back into the unrestricted endowment portion of the campaign. The investment earnings from the $12 million of incremental endowment funds could be used to bolster the college's revenues and keep the institution's debt service ratios within the college's budget guidelines. For tax reasons, the incremental endowment could not be raised for library construction or allocated to secure the library bond issue—but for internal budgeting ratios, the college's annual revenues would in fact be stronger with the additional endowment earnings. Therefore, the presence of the additional endowment earnings was an important element in the college's business decision to pursue the bond issue. To the extent that the decision incorporated an expectation of fund raising not yet completed, the financing plan differed from the general rule of having such funds in hand. This is only partially accurate, however, because the case for the campaign was a mature concept for both Skidmore's management team and broader leadership group and estimates of campaign goals were based on thorough preparation and research.

This strategy had four additional benefits. The college had approximately $10.6 million of bonds outstanding that were issued in 1987 and bore an average coupon of 7.47 percent and final maturities of 25 years (2012). To date, rates had not yet fallen enough to make a stand-alone refunding of this issue economically feasible. On a stand-alone refunding, the issuance costs would cancel too much of the savings, but by combining the refunding with a new money issue, some savings could be realized (approximately $300,000). In addition, there were several computer and

telecommunication equipment needs as well as some energy conservation projects, together totalling approximately $3.5 million, that the college had been contemplating financing. Again, these smaller projects would benefit from the economies of scale of a larger bond issue. The college also had been seeking an optimal financing technique for a portion of planned capital expenditures (e.g., roof replacements, residence hall renovations, etc.) totalling $3 million. The college had measured its various costs of capital and found its internal cost of capital to be more costly than accessing the external capital markets for these projects. The college was careful to schedule the maturity of bonds supporting each phase of the project to the appropriate economic life of the financed expenditure.

Presentation to Senior College Management

After considerable deliberation, the strategy was presented to the senior management of the college shortly before the December 1992 holidays. The general response was cautious optimism. As a result of these discussions, senior management decided to potentially add two more major construction projects to the issue, a $3 million addition to the science center and a $2 million addition/renovation to the athletic facilities. Both of these projects would benefit greatly from the economies of scale of the group of projects, and neither would present an undue management burden in terms of implementation.

Debt service for the additional projects included approximately $475,000 built into the current operating budget for debt service on existing debt that would mature within the next 24 months. The total issue size exclusive of issuance costs and reserve funds was expected to be approximately $34.1 million (including the refunding of the 1987 facilities bonds), which was well within the college's overall debt capacity. Total debt service after the issue would represent approximately 5 percent of current fund expenditures and mandatory transfers, approximately 70 percent of the median measure for Standard & Poor's "A" rated institutions. Further, this percentage of current fund expenditures and mandatory transfers would decline rapidly over the short-term (less than five years) as the overall institutional budget grew (by 1997 total debt service would be approximately 3.7 percent of current fund expenditures and mandatory transfers). Total debt after the issue would equal approximately 80 percent of the total endowment, equal to the S&P median for "A" rated institutions. Allowing for conservative appreciation and assuming the success of the capital campaign, this ratio of debt to endowment also would decline rapidly within five years (to approximately 50 percent by 1997).

Senior management gave their approval to proceed. The following preliminary timetable covering key items was prepared:

Select Financing Counsel	Early January 1993
Select an Underwriter	Late January 1993
Present the Financing Strategy to the Board of Trustees and Obtain Approval to Proceed	Mid February 1993
Meet with the Issuer	February 1993
Develop the Plan of Finance	March 1993
Meet with Rating Agencies and/or Credit Enhancers	March 1993
Obtain Board of Trustee Approval for Transaction	March 1993
Obtain Issuer Approval for Transaction	April 1993
Mail Preliminary Official Statement	April 1993
Price the Issue	May 1993
Close the Issue	June 1993

Forming a Financing Team

The first step in the process was to secure the services of financing counsel. The college had recently issued student loan bonds with a consortium of New York colleges and universities, and the members of the consortium had been represented by a financing counsel. Having financing counsel involved in that transaction was a very positive experience. Including financing counsel was a prudent step, as this would be the largest tax-exempt financing in the history of the college by at least a factor of three. Interviews were held with attorneys from two prominent firms with excellent municipal finance departments. The college's general counsel actively participated in the interview and selection process, and the college selected financing counsel on schedule in January 1993.

While the financing counsel was being selected, requests for proposals were sent out to five investment banking firms. Three of the firms were large national firms; the other two were regional firms with a strong presence in the upstate New York market. Each firm was asked to summarize its qualifications, credentials, and higher education references. Further, each firm was asked to prepare some rough bond sizings and present some preliminary ideas on a plan of finance. Interviews were held with all five firms with financing counsel in attendance. The firms were judged on the strength of their presentations, the care they took to understand the issues facing the college, the creativity of their ideas, and the personal chemistry they generated with the college's team. Because the sale of the bonds were negotiated with the assistance of the Dormitory Authority of the State of New York (DASNY), fees were not a strong consideration in the selection process. The college had an understanding with the underwriters that the college expected to pay underwriting fees analogous to comparable issues financed through DASNY. Fee negotiations would take place prior to pricing the issue after the issue size and plan of finance were determined.

With only one exception, all the firms made strong presentations. Because it was such a close competition among the four remaining firms, it was not so much a matter of finding reasons to choose one firm over the others, but of finding reasons to narrow the consideration. The first choice was whether to go regional or national. The regional firm offered solid investment banking services and had an unparalleled retail sales capability in the upstate New York market, but it did not have a lot of experience in derivative products or the institutional sales capability of the national firms. It was uncertain whether derivatives would play a role in the plan of finance, but since this was a possibility under active consideration, the decision was made to choose a national firm. To preserve the retail sales capability, the regional firm would be named as a comanager. Of the national firms, one was facing the prospect of an ownership change. While it was unlikely that such a change would affect the college's financing, it was enough of a concern to distinguish the firm from the other national firms and eliminate them from consideration. Of the two remaining firms, it was almost a coin toss. After much deliberation, the firm with slightly more experience dealing with small to mid-size independent colleges and universities was selected as lead senior managing underwriter.

Structuring the Bond Issue—Part A

With the college's team of internal personnel and external advisors assembled, the financing schedule accelerated. Discussions immediately centered on the plan of finance and obtaining the board of trustees' approval to proceed. The first two critical issues to be faced were the choice of an issuer for the tax-exempt bonds and the decision to proceed with a fixed rate or variable rate financing. Based on preliminary discussions with key trustees, it was clear that there would be little or no support for a variable rate issue. The decision was made to proceed with a fixed rate, but to hold in reserve a strategy of entering into an interest rate swap to create synthetic floating rate debt. The ability to customize the characteristics of size and term for such a swap would allow the college to create the floating rate obligations on a smaller scale than a traditional variable rate bond issue for the total principal amount of the 1993 bonds.

The college had two choices of issuers for the tax-exempt bonds, DASNY or the Saratoga County Industrial Development Agency (IDA). For many years DASNY (the state-wide educational finance agency) was the only choice available, but legislation passed in the late 1980s allowed IDAs in New York to serve as conduit issuers for qualified Section 501(c)(3) organizations. IDAs have become active issuers of higher education debt in New York, in part because of lower fees, the absence of certain state-level credit-based issuance restrictions, and the ability to proceed on rapid financing schedules. The IDAs do not offer DASNY services such as prepar-

ing the official statement, preparing loan documents, negotiating with underwriters, serving as a liaison with the trustee, preparing the annual arbitrage rebate calculations, etc. These services can be very helpful, especially for small colleges that operate thinly staffed or those in the market for the first time.

The college selected DASNY after careful consideration that included a legal review by financing counsel. The main reason for the decision not to use IDAs was that, while IDAs in New York can serve as a conduit issuer under most circumstances, they cannot issue debt related to housing. Since the college's 1987 facilities bonds financed a residence hall, this portion of the financing plan could not have been included as part of an IDA issue. While this did not automatically preclude using the IDA as an issuer, the college team considered the economics of the IDA fee savings compared to the additional cost of implementing the refunding as a separate issue with DASNY. The economics did not support two separate issues. The combination of economic issues and the availability of other DASNY services led the college to select DASNY as the issuer.

The college financing team met with DASNY in mid-February shortly before meeting with the board of trustees. It was important to meet with the issuer early in the transaction to initiate matters that have a longer lead-time. DASNY has two basic tracks for its higher education clients. The first is a "plain vanilla" fixed rate master resolution insured program, under which the master resolution and loan documents have been standardized by DASNY and approved by the major municipal bond insurers. Such standardization is designed to build in efficiencies and reduce costs. As an alternative to this program, a college or university can do a "stand alone" financing whereby the bonds are sold on the strength of the institution without credit enhancement. In New York, for an institution to sell bonds through DASNY on its own credit, the institution's bond issue must have a rating of A+ or A-1. This rule is set by the Public Authorities Control Board (PACB), which must approve all DASNY financings. (Note: The PACB does not have jurisdiction over IDA financings.)

The choice of financing track was a major decision. Skidmore College does not have a public bond rating because its outstanding issues all have been credit-enhanced. Obtaining a rating is a time-consuming process that would not be undertaken unless it provided an economic benefit. Accordingly, the question to be answered was, if the college pursued a rating, would it receive an A+ or A-1, and if so, would this rating provide an economic benefit in the marketplace? The investment banker viewed the college's credit as a solid A, bordering on A+ or A-1. However, based on the current market, even with the A+ or A-1 rating, municipal bond insurance would still add incremental savings as compared to a stand-alone issue. The decision was made to insure the issue.

Board of Trustees Deliberations

The next step was obtaining approval to proceed from the board of trustees. Up to this point, key trustees were kept fully briefed on the progress of the issue. The trustee meeting in late February was the first occasion to make a formal presentation to the board as a whole. Despite efforts to educate individual board members prior to the full board meeting, there were many questions on the plan of finance (which was not yet finalized due to flexibility built into the plan to allow for responses to market changes). Other board members discussed the prudence of adding additional debt, the risks involved if the capital campaign was not successful, and the institutional need for the underlying projects (with the exception of the library). After considerable discussion, the board granted approval to proceed subject to final approval from the executive committee. It was clear that the executive committee would grant final approval for the transaction only after all of the board concerns were thoroughly addressed. Eventually, the executive committee approval was granted based on a later version of the plan of finance that incorporated final institutional decisions on several issues that had been held open as long as possible to retain flexibility.

Structuring the Bond Issue—Part B

After the February board meeting, the college's financing team devoted its efforts to assembling a credit review package to send to prospective bond insurers. The 1987 facility bonds were insured by a leading national bond

insurer. Since this put the current insurer in a position to grant a rebate credit on the refunding portion of the 1993 bond issue, this insurer was the favorite to insure the new issue. Nevertheless, the goal was to create a competitive atmosphere among the insurers that would allow all interested firms to put forward their best proposal without conceding the outcome in advance. Putting together a quality credit review package was the key to attracting aggressive bids because the college had to be able to make a very favorable impression on the bond insurers other than the current insurer within a very short period of time.

The "Description of the College" section of the credit package also served the important purpose of providing the basis for the college description section of the DASNY preliminary official statement. Although the bond issue would be insured, the investment banker believed that investors currently were looking beyond the insurance to the quality of the underlying credit. Skidmore College had a good story to tell, and it was important to communicate it effectively in order to gain the potential economic benefit in the form of aggressive investor bidding for the bonds.

It was at this point in the transaction that the timetable was amended to delay the process approximately 30 days. The revised objective was to price the issue in late June. This delay was necessary for several logistical reasons. Discussions among the senior management of the college over which projects to include in the issue were taking more time than expected, the DASNY's board meeting to approve the bond issue was delayed, and given the college staffs' day-to-day responsibilities, it took longer than anticipated to complete the "Description of the College" section of the credit package. This delay was not a concern because it integrated well with some expected marketplace developments. A large amount of tax-exempt issues were maturing or were to be redeemed (as a result of prior advance refundings) on July 1, 1993, which meant that there would be a strong demand for new issue tax-exempt bonds in late June. The college team was hopeful that this would result in lower interest rates.

The credit review package was sent to prospective municipal bond insurers at the end of April. The investment banker planned to request bids as soon as the college's board approved the issue and plan of finance. After considerable deliberation, the senior management of the college made final adjustments to the project list. The most significant change was the decision to add one more major construction project to the issue, a $4.5 million art gallery and museum of which $3 million would be financed. The remaining $1.5 million would be added to the campaign goal. Despite the endowment focus of the campaign, the development staff had identified several prospective major donors who conditioned their gift to support of an art gallery and museum. Adding the gallery and museum to the science center and athletic facilities projects would nearly complete the original campus master plan, and all of the projects could be accommodated within the basic financing strategy. Based on consultations with the college's architects, some adjustments were made in the project budgets, and the total issue size, exclusive of issuance costs and reserve funds, now stood at $38.1 million, still well within the college's debt capacity.

With the projects finalized, the plan of finance could be more fully developed. The college would issue a combination of serial and term bonds at a fixed rate of interest with the final maturity set at 30 years. The refunding portion of the issue would mature as originally scheduled in the year 2012. The cash flow on the refunded issue would be structured so that 100 percent of the net present value savings (which had increased to $800,000 due to declining interest rates) would be captured within the first two years. Accordingly, the annual debt service on the refunded portion would be approximately the same as it was prior to refunding after the first two years. This captured savings would be added to the endowment fund to augment the investment earnings available to be considered in budget ratios to satisfy management guidelines as to acceptable debt levels for the college. The new construction would be amortized over 30 years, while the computer and telecommunication equipment purchases and the energy conservation projects would be amortized over 10 years. Finally, the $3 million of scheduled capital projects would carry a bullet maturity of 10 years. A small portion of interest would be capitalized to the extent necessary until the various sources of funds identified by the college to pay

the debt service became available. Principal amortization would begin immediately after the capitalized interest period (i.e., the new money would not "wrap" the refunding). Accordingly, the college's annual debt service would decrease significantly after 2012 when the refunding portion matures. The issue would have an average life of approximately 16 years. The bonds would carry 10 year call protection. They would be secured by municipal bond insurance, and the college would pledge to DASNY tuition and fees equal to the annual debt service and grant a mortgage to DASNY on certain properties.

The plan was presented to the board in mid-May. Two questions framed much of the board's discussion: (1) were all the projects necessary to support the academic mission and/or financial strategy of the college, and (2) were the various risks in such a financing limited where possible and otherwise acceptable to the college? The academic leadership presented the detailed case for each of the construction projects, and then the financing plan and an analysis of the risk parameters was presented, with assistance from the investment banker and financing counsel. The academic basis for each of the projects was clearly documented. In terms of risk, three factors were identified as significant: a decline in student enrollment, an unsuccessful capital campaign, and falling short of the endowment investment assumptions. The combined presentation of historical trends, measurements against various benchmarks (internal and external), sensitivity analyses, and a "likely worst-case scenario" contingency plan ultimately persuaded the executive committee that the bond issue was prudent. The plan of finance was approved after extensive discussion.

Shortly after the board's approval, the prospective insurers made site visits to the college. During the visits, the senior managers of the college made presentations on their respective areas of responsibility and the investment banker discussed the plan of finance. When the bids were received a few days later, it was clear that the hard work had paid off. The winning bid, submitted by a bond insurer other than the current insurer of the refunded 1987 facility bonds, was $150,000 below the investment banker's estimate, and $75,000 below the current insurer's bid.

NEW ISSUE

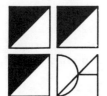

$40,445,000
DORMITORY AUTHORITY
OF THE STATE OF NEW YORK
SKIDMORE COLLEGE
INSURED REVENUE BONDS, SERIES 1993

Dated: June 15, 1993   Due: July 1, as shown below

Payment and Security: The Skidmore College Insured Revenue Bonds, Series 1993 (the "Series 1993 Bonds") will be special obligations of the Dormitory Authority of the State of New York (the "Authority"). Principal and redemption price of and interest on the Series 1993 Bonds are payable solely from and secured by a pledge of certain payments to be made under the Loan Agreement (the "Loan Agreement"), dated as of June 23, 1993, between Skidmore College (the "Institution" or the "College") and the Authority and all funds and accounts (except the Arbitrage Rebate Fund) authorized under the Authority's Master Insured Revenue Bond Resolution, adopted October 25, 1989, as amended and supplemented (the "Master Resolution") and established under the Authority's Series Resolution Authorizing Up To $45,000,000 Skidmore College Insured Revenue Bonds, Series 1993, adopted June 23, 1993 (the "Series 1993 Resolution").

Payment of the principal and Sinking Fund Installments of and interest on the Series 1993 Bonds when due will be guaranteed by a municipal bond insurance policy to be issued simultaneously with the delivery of the Series 1993 Bonds by FINANCIAL SECURITY ASSURANCE INC. (the "Insurer" or "Financial Security").

The Loan Agreement is a general obligation of the College and requires the College to pay, in addition to the fees and expenses of the Authority and the Trustee, amounts sufficient to pay the principal, Sinking Fund Installments and Redemption Price of and interest on the Series 1993 Bonds, as such payments become due. The obligations of the College under the Loan Agreement to make such payments will be secured by a pledge of certain revenues of the College. At the time of delivery of the Series 1993 Bonds, a portion of the bond proceeds will be used to purchase a surety bond for the Debt Service Reserve Fund in an amount equal to the Debt Service Reserve Fund Requirement. The College is also obligated to make deposits to the Building and Equipment Reserve Fund, as described herein.

The Series 1993 Bonds will not be a debt of the State of New York nor will the State be liable thereon. The Authority has no taxing power.

Description: The Series 1993 Bonds will be issued as fully registered bonds in denominations of $5,000 or any integral multiple thereof. Interest (due January 1, 1994 and each July 1 and January 1 thereafter) on the Series 1993 Bonds will be payable by check or draft mailed to the registered owners of the Series 1993 Bonds at their addresses as shown on the registration books held by the Trustee or at the option of a holder of at least $1,000,000 in principal amount of Series 1993 Bonds, by wire transfer to the holder of such Series 1993 Bonds, each as of the close of business on the fifteenth day of the month next preceding an interest payment date. The principal and Redemption Price of the Series 1993 Bonds will be payable at the principal corporate trust office of United States Trust Company of New York, New York, New York, the Trustee and Paying Agent or, with respect to Redemption Price, at the option of a holder of at least $1,000,000 in principal amount of Series 1993 Bonds, by wire transfer to the holder of such Series 1993 Bonds as more fully described herein.

Redemption: *The Series 1993 Bonds are subject to redemption prior to maturity as more fully described herein.*

Tax Exemption: In the opinion of Bond Counsel, under existing law and assuming compliance with the tax covenants described herein, interest on the Series 1993 Bonds is excluded from gross income for federal income tax purposes and is not a specific preference item for purposes of the federal alternative minimum tax. Bond Counsel is further of the opinion that, by virtue of the Act, interest on the Series 1993 Bonds is exempt from personal income taxes of the State of New York and its political subdivisions, as described more fully herein. See however, "PART 11 - TAX EXEMPTION" herein regarding certain other tax considerations.

$19,700,000 Serial Bonds

Due July 1	Amount	Interest Rate	Price or Yield	Due July 1	Amount	Interest Rate	Price or Yield
1997	$ 860,000	3.90%	100 %	2003	$4,595,000	4.70%	4.85%
1998	1,295,000	4.10	100	2004	1,325,000	4.80	4.95
1999	1,350,000	4.25	4.30	2005	1,390,000	4.90	5.05
2000	1,410,000	4.40	4.50	2006	1,450,000	5.00	5.15
2001	1,430,000	4.50	4.65	2007	1,490,000	5.10	5.20
2002	1,545,000	4.60	4.75	2008	1,560,000	5.10	5.25

$8,045,000 5.25% Term Bonds Due July 1, 2013 to Yield 5.40%
$12,700,000 5.375% Term Bonds due July 1, 2023 to Yield 5.50%
(Accrued interest from June 15, 1993 to be added.)

The Series 1993 Bonds are offered when, as and if issued. The offer of the Series 1993 Bonds may be subject to prior sale or withdrawn or modified at any time without notice. The offer is subject to the approval of legality by Nixon, Hargrave, Devans & Doyle, Rochester, New York, Bond Counsel and to certain other conditions. Certain legal matters will be passed upon for the College and the Underwriters by Counsel to the College, Mudge Rose Guthrie Alexander & Ferdon, New York. New York. The Authority expects to deliver the Series 1993 Bonds in definitive form in New York, New York, on or about July 22, 1993.

The First Boston Corporation First Albany Corporation	Bear, Stearns & Co. Inc. Lehman Brothers

July 1, 1993

The transaction priced as planned on June 30, 1993. The college sold $40,445,000 of bonds at a true interest cost of 5.58 percent. The net present value savings on the refunding of the 1987 facility bonds was $800,400 or 7.5 percent of the refunded debt. The issue closed on July 22, 1993, and from there the project implementation phase moved ahead quickly, marking the beginning of an exciting new chapter in the college's history.

Conclusions and Lessons

Skidmore College learned many lessons from its capital financing experience; three are basic and can be applied to other colleges and universities. First, it is important to assemble a strong working team. This team will not only make sure that obvious questions are asked but that more subtle and perhaps more important issues are reviewed. A strong college financing team also is essential to stay on top of events and resolve unanticipated matters as they arise. Second, detailed planning is critical. Leaving matters unresolved or failing to plan effectively can cause delays at critical points in the process, which in turn can increase the costs of borrowing. It is important, for example, to carefully evaluate the benefits of refinancing existing debt and incorporating this refinancing into a prospective new issue. Effective planning also requires building some flexibility into the timetable. It's a rare financing that does not experience some delays. Perhaps the most important thing to do is just get started. There is no perfect time in the academic calendar to begin planning to issue debt. The college or university cannot control the market, but it can control how quickly it is ready to go to market.

Although the 1993 bond issue is now complete, the issue will not sit on the shelf for the next 30 years. Skidmore College's next step is to formulate a strategy to realize additional value from the current opportunities available in the capital markets through the employment of a fixed to variable interest rate swap. The college will formulate such a strategy in 1994.

Case Study of a Public Institution: Western State College

Western State College
Trustees of State Colleges of Colorado, Gunnison, Colorado
Series 1992 Student Fee and Housing Revenue Auxiliary Bonds
by Cliff Nancarrow and Lee White

Western State College is a moderately selective residential, coeducational, public college located in the heart of the Colorado Rockies in Gunnison, Colorado. The college is an undergraduate institution with degree programs in traditional liberal arts disciplines and various preprofessional areas. Approximately 2,350 full-time students attend the college. The college's annual operating budget for the 1992–1993 fiscal year was approximately $19 million. The comprehensive fee for Colorado residents (tuition, room and board), for the 1992–1993 academic year was $3,900. Thirty percent of the college's revenue is derived from state appropriations, 25 percent from tuition and student fees, and 25 percent from auxiliary revenues.

This financing was the institution's first tax-exempt financing. The case study describes the key issues involved in planning and executing a plan of finance for the $12,975,000 bond issue that closed on November 1, 1992. The proceeds from the 1992 bonds were used to (1) finance the remodeling of two of the college's three major dormitories, remodel the college's student union, and build a courtyard as a focus of campus outdoor life; (2) retire $1.2 million of a Department of Education loan that had been outstanding since 1965; (3) fund a debt service reserve fund for the 1992 bonds and a capitalized interest fund; and (4) pay the costs of issuance of the 1992 bonds. The bonds received an underlying rating of "Baa1/BBB+" (Moody's/Standard &

Poor's) and were sold as a "AAA" rated (Standard & Poor's) bond by virtue of a bond insurance policy.

Identifying an Institutional Need

In the spring of 1992, Cliff Nancarrow, vice president for business affairs at Western State College, faced a difficult challenge—finding a way to revitalize student satisfaction with the daily living conditions at the college. It wasn't going to be easy.

The student dormitories, examples of the worst institutional architecture of the 1950s, were in deplorable condition. They had critical health and safety problems and did not conform to the requirements of the Americans with Disabilities Act. Furthermore, the college union and bookstore building—a focal point of on-campus living—was embarrassingly small, unattractive, and outdated. Though the campus was set in some of Colorado's most beautiful mountain valleys, Nancarrow knew that scenery alone would not satisfy the type of more discriminating and sophisticated student that could be attracted by the college.

Nancarrow assembled the list of projects that would be necessary to bring the campus up to the standards demanded by students: remodeling of the two major dormitories, college union expansion and renovation, and the addition of an adjacent plaza or courtyard assembly area. He estimated the construction costs at almost $9 million. The auxiliary financial statements reflected only $300,000 in the repair and replacement fund, not enough to properly maintain the dorms or represent a substantial down payment on a $9 million construction program.

Nancarrow knew he would have to seek external sources of funds. He had never done a municipal bond transaction and did not know whether his college was creditworthy. It was also unclear what additional student fee and dormitory fee revenue would be necessary to amortize even a modest amount of new debt. It was obvious to him that he needed to develop a plan of finance for the project, and that he would need specialized help.

Forming a Finance Team

After obtaining the approval of the Trustees of the State Colleges in Colorado to explore various financing alternatives, Nancarrow initiated a search for professional assistance. Like most public colleges, Western is required to obtain goods and services through a competitive bidding process under the state procurement code. On June 22, 1992, the college's Director of Purchasing issued a request for proposal (RFP) "seeking to obtain the expert assistance of an investment banker to serve as financial advisor/underwriter for evaluating and obtaining . . . the financing required. . . ." Since the upcoming November 1992 Colorado general election included a proposed State Constitutional Amendment that would affect the ability of state colleges to issue debt, the college was careful to specify that the development of an acceptable plan of finance and the consummation of the financing transaction was expected to be completed no later than mid-October, only four months away.

The RFP stated that all underwriter reimbursement would come from proceeds of the financing transaction, if the transaction was consummated. If a transaction did not proceed to closing for any reason, the trustees would disclaim any responsibility for any costs incurred by the financial advisor/underwriter.

The RFP required the financial advisor/underwriter to:

- provide recommendations on the structure and security of the proposed financing based on a comparative analysis of the associated costs and relative advantages of each alternative;
- participate in the development of necessary documentation to include maturity schedules, redemption schedules, redemption features, interest rates, basic security provisions, and other covenants, as well as prepare the preliminary official statement and official statement;
- prepare recommendations on the most favorable time for the sale of securities and appropriate terms and conditions to be used in connection with the sale of securities in order to achieve the most favorable overall cost to the trustees over the period of financing;
- prepare materials for and make presentations to secure ratings and bond insurance or other credit enhancements, should such be deter-

mined to be in the best interest of the trustees; and

- execute the plan of finance.

In addition to the standard provision of references and description of experience with similar financing projects, each investment banker was asked to specify the fees the firm would charge per each $1,000 bond for services as financial advisor/underwriter for various types of transactions. Evaluation criteria and the relative weighing of each were established as follows:

1. Overall quality of content—25 percent
2. Proposed underwriter's discount—25 percent
3. Experience and expertise of firm and personnel assigned by firm—25 percent
4. Proposed methods of funding projects and restructuring existing securities issues—25 percent

An internal team was formed to evaluate the RFP responses. Members included Cliff Nancarrow and the following Office of State Colleges staff members: Juan Garcia, vice president for administration and finance; Bruce Pech, director of legal affairs and personnel; Melodie Christal, director of planning and budgeting; and Andy Rodriguez, director of purchasing at Mesa State College. Rodriguez had recent experience in analyzing investment banking proposals related to a Certificate of Participation financing completed for his campus the previous year. With the exception of Rodriguez, each member of the committee would continue to be actively involved with the selected banker in developing and executing the plan of finance.

Qualified proposals were received on July 17, 1992, from seven investment bankers and were routed to each committee member for initial review, analysis, and scoring. The committee convened via teleconference on July 23, 1992, to discuss the proposals and to compare scores. The successful bidder received the highest weighted average score and was rated as the most responsive bidder by four of the five committee members. In addition, the proposed fee was considered reasonable. The committee was able to recommend to the board of trustees a banker with whom each member of the committee felt professionally comfortable.

Creating a Plan of Finance

The investment banker now had just six weeks to prepare a plan of finance to present to the president of the college, Dr. Kay Howe, and the board of trustees on September 10, 1992.

The first step in creating the plan of finance was to examine the cost and timing of the project, which included the renovation of two dormitories (Mears Hall Complex and Chipeta Hall), the college union, and construction of a new adjacent courtyard. The breakdown was as follows:

	Cost	Start Date	Completion Date
Mears Hall	$3,000,000	Spring 1993	Fall 1994
Chipeta Hall	$3,700,000	Fall 1994	Fall 1995
College Union	$2,600,000	Spring 1993	Fall 1993
Courtyard (Phase 1)	$500,000	Spring 1993	Fall 1993

The investment banker examined student enrollment trends, dormitory occupancy rates, and student fee pricing ability. The revenue sources available to meet debt service requirements included student fees and all of the cash flows generated by the college's auxiliary enterprises, including income from rental of residential units, operations of the student dining facilities, and the college union.

The student FTE count was growing modestly. The college drew its students not only from Colorado, but attracted about one-third of its student population from other states. The dormitory occupancy was 90 percent, and freshmen were required to live in the facilities. In 1992, student fees were $230.50 per semester and dormitory charges were $806 per semester.

The primary goal of the plan of finance was to secure at least a minimum investment grade rating from one of the primary rating agencies. The minimum investment grade rating—"Baa" from Moody's Investor's Service or "BBB" from Standard & Poor's Corporation—was crucial to allowing the college access to the favorable interest rates available in the tax-exempt bond market. The key issue for the rating agencies is the viability of projected revenues generated by increased student fees and dormitory fees. It was critical to show coverage of future maximum debt service by proposed fees and charges by a coverage factor of 1.25x. The assumptions used were conservative—FTEs were held constant and dorm occupancy was projected at only 85 percent.

It was determined in the plan of finance that student fees would be used to finance the college union and the courtyard renovations, while dormitory revenues would cover the debt service requirements for the Mears Hall and Chipeta Hall renovations. To minimize the impact of fee increases on students or "fee shock," it was determined that all fee increases would be phased in over several years. Student fees would have to be increased approximately 10 percent per year for three years beginning in 1994. Dormitory fees were estimated to increase 7.7, 6.4, 10.0, 11.8, and 6.6 percent each year from 1994 to 1998, respectively. To accommodate this phase-in of fees, capitalized interest from bond proceeds for 18 months was included in the plan of finance. This would pay interest on the bonds for the first year and a half the bonds were outstanding.

The college also had $1.2 million outstanding from a 1965 Department of Education (ED) loan, that was being paid with student fees. The covenants on this ED debt precluded the issuance of new bonds, so a refunding of the debt was incorporated into the finance plan. This small refunding also allowed the college to reallocate existing student fees from payment of ED debt on dormitories to payment of the new debt for the college union. This would reduce the needed increase in student fees for the college union project and slightly increase the dormitory fees. Such a reallocation of fees seemed to make the plan of finance more equitable for students and reduced the cross subsidy among the auxiliary activities.

Several factors affected the timing of the transaction, including:

Amendment One: This tax and spending limitation amendment was on the general election ballot in November 1992. The amendment, which passed in the election, carried far-reaching consequences for all government entities in Colorado. Completing the financing before the November election was a critical part of the fi-

nance plan. Had the financing been delayed until after the election, the project would have been bogged down in the legal confusion that followed implementation of Amendment One, and financing would have been delayed for at least two years.

Approval Process: The program approval process for Colorado higher education institutions required the plan of finance to be presented to the Colorado Commission on Higher Education as well as the legislature's Capital Development Commission.

Interest Rate Market: Market conditions were favorable for tax-exempt bonds in the summer of 1992, with rates dropping below 7 percent for the first time in 10 years. The college wanted to take advantage of these low rates.

Issues for Approval of Plan of Finance by Board of Trustees

When Nancarrow presented the plan of finance to the board of trustees at its September meeting, board members were most concerned with the following issues:

- Use of coverage revenues for deferred maintenance and increase in current repair and replacement funds.
- Student's perception of and reaction to the project, as well as their ability to pay the fee increases.
- The project's applicability to other institutions in the board's system (e.g., aversion to the cross pledging of the revenues of other colleges governed by the board of trustees) was an important objective.

Structuring the Bond Transaction

The bond indenture—the loan contract between the college and the bondholders—was one of the primary documents in the transaction. Creating the indenture was the primary job of the board of trustees' bond counsel. In this case, bond counsel also was assigned to prepare the official statement, that is the disclosure document sent to prospective investors.

Once drafts of the bond documents were prepared, college officials, a member of the board of trustees, an Office of State Colleges staff member, and representatives of the investment banker traveled to New York to meet with the rating agencies. The group presented extensive data on the college and the financing. Nancarrow asked Gary Reiff, chairman of the board's finance committee, to go on the trip to express the board's support for the project. The group met with representatives of the Moody's and Standard & Poor's rating agencies in New York. They described the proposed financing, the debt service coverage projections, and the bond covenants, and supplied information about the need for the projects, the college's financial history, the market for the college, and enrollment trends. The presentations resulted in a "Baa" rating from Moody's and a "BBB+" rating from Standard & Poor's.

To obtain the most favorable interest rates for the college, the financing team also pursued municipal bond insurance and was successful in this effort. With the bond insurance, the bonds were upgraded to a rating of "AAA" from Standard & Poor's. This provided for lower interest rates and reduced the college's overall debt service cost. Although the bond insurer charged a one-time, up-front fee of 1.2 percent of total debt service, the insurance still provided a net financial benefit for the college.

An initial sticking point in discussions with the bond insurer was the requirement to create a repair and replacement fund in addition to a fully funded debt service reserve fund of maximum principal and interest. After negotiation, this was funded at $250,000.

Marketing the Bond Transaction

In October, all of the pieces were in place to bring the college's new bond issue to market. The documents had been agreed to and included all of the appropriate covenants required by the bond insurer, the rating agencies, the trustees, the college, and the investment banker. Market conditions were favorable, and it was time to establish interest rates and sell the bonds to the marketplace.

The key objective of the investment banker was to find as many large investors as possible to generate competition for the $12.9 million bond issue. This would help create the conditions necessary to obtain as low an interest rate as possible.

The bond issue had a 20-year amortization schedule with a final maturity of 2015. The bond issue had a number of small annual principal payments beginning in 1997 through 2004 known as serial bonds. The serial bonds would be sold principally to retail investors. Most of the principal amount of the bonds was established in the late maturities of 2008 and 2015. These bonds, known as term bonds, are sold to large institutional investors such as mutual funds and insurance companies.

This type of bond sale was a negotiated transaction in which an investment banker is selected and interest rates are established by the firm selling bonds directly to final investors. Prior to the day of pricing, the investment banker's sales staff had been "premarketing" the bonds to get potential investors acquainted with the issue. Since this was the college's first bond issue, investors had to be educated about the college and its plan of finance. All potential institutional investors must first approve a new credit for purchase before interest rates are established. Only then does the investor decide if the proposed level of interest rates on the bonds are attractive enough to actually place an order with the investment banker for a particular principal amount of the bonds.

On the day of pricing, representatives of the investment banker met with Nancarrow to discuss market conditions and specific interest rates for each maturity of bonds. With Nancarrow's approval, the bonds were marketed over a three-hour time period. At the end of the day of marketing, Nancarrow agreed that the actual interest rates were satisfactory and signed the bond purchase agreement with the investment banker. The final true interest rate of the bonds, including all costs of issuance, was 7.01 percent.

The bonds were then on schedule to be officially closed on October 29, 1992. On this day the investment banker wired the proceeds of the bonds to the bond trustee to be held for the benefit of the college, the bonds were officially issued to the investors, and the bond insurance policy took effect.

Conclusions and Lessons

The college began moving rapidly forward on the renovation of two dormitories and on the transformation of its student union, thanks to the successful completion of the financing. While

In the opinion of Bond Counsel, assuming continuing compliance with certain requirements described herein, under the statutes, regulations, published rulings and judicial decisions existing on the date of the original delivery of the Bonds, amounts representing interest on the Bonds, to the extent paid by the Trustees, are not includable in gross income for purposes of federal or State of Colorado income taxation and are not treated as a specific preference item for purposes of the federal alternative minimum tax imposed on individuals and corporations. See the caption "TAX EXEMPTION" herein.

$12,975,000

BOARD OF TRUSTEES OF THE STATE COLLEGES IN COLORADO
AUXILIARY FACILITIES SYSTEM REVENUE BONDS
(WESTERN STATE COLLEGE OF COLORADO PROJECT)
SERIES A 1992

Dated: October 1, 1992 **Due: May 1, as shown below**

The Series A 1992 Bonds will be issued as fully registered bonds in the denomination of $5,000 or any integral multiple thereof. Interest will be payable on May 1 and November 1 of each year, commencing May 1, 1993. Principal of and interest on the Series A 1992 will be paid by check or draft of The Bank of Cherry Creek, N.A., as Paying Agent, mailed to DTC or its nominee, as described below.

MATURITY SCHEDULE

Due (May 1)	Principal Amount	Interest Rate	Yield	Due (May 1)	Principal Amount	Interest Rate	Yield
1997	$330,000	5.20%	5.20%	2001	$475,000	5.90%	6.00%
1998	390,000	5.40	5.40	2002	505,000	6.10	6.15
1999	425,000	5.60	5.60	2003	535,000	6.15	6.25
2000	450,000	5.70	5.80	2004	565,000	6.25	6.35

$2,655,000 Term Bonds Due May 1, 2008 Interest Rate 6.60% Price or Yield 6.70%
$6,645,000 Term Bonds Due May 1, 2015 Interest Rate 6.625% Price or Yield 6.77%

(Plus Accrued Interest from October 1, 1992)

Payment of the principal of and interest on the Bonds when due will be guaranteed by a municipal bond insurance policy to be issued simultaneously with the delivery of the Bonds by Connie Lee Insurance Company.

ConnieLee

The Bonds are subject to optional, extraordinary optional and mandatory redemption prior to maturity under the circumstances and at the prices more fully described herein. See "THE BONDS — Redemption Provisions."

The net proceeds from the issuance of the Bonds will be used to finance the renovation, construction and/or equipping of certain dormitory, student center and other facilities (the "System Improvements") at Western State College of Colorado in Gunnison, Colorado ("Western"), to fund certain reserves and other amounts as described herein, and to pay costs of issuance associated herewith. In addition, a portion of the proceeds will be used to finance the retirement of certain bonds held by the United States Department of Education ("DOE") in connection with certain loans previously made by DOE to Western.

The Series 1992 Bonds, when issued, will be registered in the name of CEDE & Co., as nominee of the Depository Trust Company, New York, New York ("DTC"). DTC will act as securities depository of the Series 1992 Bonds. Individual purchases will be made in book-entry form only in the principal amount of $5,000 and integral multiples thereof. Purchasers will not receive certificates representing their interest in the Series 1992 Bonds purchased. The principal of and interest on the Series 1992 Bonds are payable by the Paying Agent to DTC (or its nominee as the Registered Owner), which will in turn be responsible to remit such principal and interest to its Participants, which will in turn be responsible to remit such principal and interest to the Beneficial Owners of the Series 1992 Bonds as described herein. See "THE SERIES 1992 BONDS — Book-Entry Registration."

The Series A 1992 Bonds are limited obligations of the Board of Trustees of the State Colleges in Colorado (the "Board") payable solely from certain revenues of the Board which are pledged to the payment of the Series A 1992 Bonds under the Resolution, which sources of payment are described in this Official Statement. The issuance of the Series A 1992 Bonds shall not directly, indirectly or contingently obligate the State of Colorado or any agency, instrumentality or political subdivision thereof to levy any form of taxation therefor or to make any appropriation for their payment.

The offering of the Bonds to potential investors is made subject to this entire Official Statement. Each prospective investor in the Bonds should read this Official Statement in its entirety.

The Series A 1992 Bonds are offered, subject to prior sale, when, as and if issued by the Board and accepted by the Underwriter named below, subject to the receipt of an approving opinion from Kutak Rock, Denver, Colorado, as Bond Counsel and Disclosure Counsel. Certain legal matters will be passed upon for the Board by Bruce Pech, Esq., Director of Legal Affairs for the State Colleges in Colorado. Certain matters will be passed upon for the Underwriter by Powers & Phillips, P.C. It is expected that the Series A 1992 Bonds in definitive form will be available for delivery in Denver, Colorado on or about October 29, 1992 against payment therefor.

GEORGE K. BAUM & COMPANY   STERN BROTHERS & CO.

The date of this Official Statement is October 22, 1992.

reducing the inventory of neglected maintenance actions and correcting the health and safety deficiencies proved beneficial, of even greater value has been the impact these undertakings have had on generating momentum over a broad spectrum of campus activities. By financing this project, the college has communicated to students that it values them and is committed to providing them with quality living quarters and activity areas. The college sent a message to its faculty and staff that thoughtful change can occur and agreed-upon objectives can be achieved in compressed time frames when will is wedded to focused activity.

The finance team formed to complete this project was successful because it was committed to a common goal with a firm deadline. At the college, the bond project was assigned "drop everything" priority. Telephone calls were promptly returned, and documents and schedules were completed on time and accorded detailed review. Team members backed one another up with "logic, clarity, and consistency" checks of accounting schedules and legal text. This preparedness made the initial meeting of the entire team invaluable.

Knowing that there would only be one oppor-tunity to secure the board's approval of the plan of finance, the Office of State Colleges staff members kept members of the board of trustees personally informed of the team's progress. President Howe met personally with student leaders to secure their endorsement of the projects and to reassure them that required fee and rental increases would be reasonable. A letter written by the president of the student government association to the members of the board expressed mild student concern over increased costs of attendance, but nonetheless supported the project. This student endorsement was instrumental in obtaining trustee approval of the plan of finance.

On November 3, 1992, the Colorado electorate passed Amendment One, which has dramatically and adversely impacted the financing of state-supported higher education. Had the college not acted when it did, the project would have been delayed at least two years while the legal implications of Amendment One were sorted out. Fortunately, however, on November 3, the college had $13 million in the bank. The "drop everything" priority of the financing had happily now shifted to the phone calls of architects and engineers.

Case Study of an Innovative Student Loan Financing with College General Obligation Debt

Dormitory Authority of the State of New York
College and University Education Loan Revenue
Bonds, 1992 Issue
by Paul J. Lawler

Rensselaer Polytechnic Institute is a comprehensive research university located in Troy, New York. The institute offers 121 degree programs in engineering, science, architecture, management, and the humanities to an enrollment of approximately 6,500 full-time students. The student-faculty ratio is 12:1. The institute's annual operating budget for its fiscal year ended June 30, 1993, was approximately $182 million, and the market value of its endowment fund was approximately $296 million. The comprehensive fee (tuition, room, and board) for the 1993–1994 academic year is $23,000. More than 47 percent of the institute's revenue is derived from tuition and student fees.

Tax-exempt financing plays a major role in the capital structure of the institute. Since 1991 the institute has used tax-exempt financing on four occasions totaling approximately $91 million (1991: $38 million, 1992: $16 million, and 1993: $37 million). The institute has participated in two bond issues where general obligation bond proceeds of the institute were used to fund student loans directly totaling approximately $19 million (1992: $16 million, and 1993: $3 million).

The following case study discusses the key

issues involved in the 1992 student bond issue that was structured to include borrowings for several institutions in addition to Rensselaer: Columbia University, Cornell University, the College of St. Rose, Skidmore College, and Union College.

Background

Over the past decade, as the real cost of education has increased and competition for students has heightened, financial aid has become one of the most important issues facing colleges and universities. Loans are often overlooked, but are a critical component within the pricing structure for students and their families. Traditionally, consumer credit for the education sector has been supplied (or supported) by the federal government, related semi-autonomous agencies, and the commercial banking industry. The following case study suggests that selected and careful employment of university resources and credit support can yield important benefits to an institution's enrollment base and financial health.

Within the span of a single generation, the real, inflation-adjusted price of a high quality college education within the private sector has doubled. During this same period, median family income has remained essentially flat. (See figure 1-1.)

On top of this discouraging news, the U.S. savings rate has remained at a very low level (compared to our international competitors). As a consequence, college attendance constitutes the largest capital expenditure that many working and middle class families will face over their working lives.

Unfortunately, continuing federal deficits and constrained state budgets have precluded necessary public sector support for student financial aid. Significant increases in institutionally funded scholarships and grants have offset these shortfalls to some degree (and, as a consequence, have grown at a faster rate than most other expenses at many universities), but internal budgetary and financial pressures faced by universities in the 1990s are placing severe restraints on internal aid resources as well.

The net result has been shrinking affordability and limited resources with which to respond. Colleges and universities are facing the dual pressure of a reduction in the ability of most families to pay and a clear limitation of university financial support. The challenge facing higher education

Figure 1-1

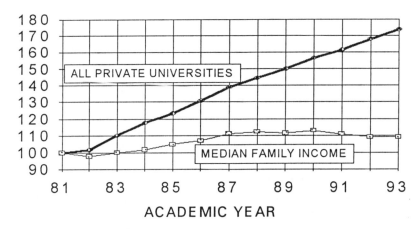

TUITION & FEES vs MEDIAN FAMILY INCOME
INFLATION ADJUSTED
1981 = 100

is to provide low cost, low-term financing acceptable to potential customers in order to make a high quality educational experience affordable once again.

Market

The market providing capital for student loans is enormous, and includes large federally supported programs such as Perkins (formerly NDSL), Stafford (formerly GSL), Supplemental Loans to Students (SLS), and Parental Loans to Undergraduate Students (PLUS). Some programs such as Perkins are provided through the institution, while others such as PLUS and Stafford are offered through the network of commercial banks throughout the United States.[1] The Student Loan Marketing Association (Sallie Mae) provides capital for loans directly to universities, and also purchases large blocks of federally sponsored student loans from banks, that are in turn financed through the national capital markets. Money centers and regional and local banks also provide important additional sources of capital for students loans without federal guarantees.

A review of the annual volume of student loans from selected federal sources, shown in figure 1-2, is indicative of the enormity of the market.

Colleges and universities have used these federal and private programs to provide the nongrant portion of financial aid, which is generally based upon the "federal" or "institutional methodology" (formerly known as the "congressional methodology").

While these loan programs have provided essential and invaluable support to students, they do not address the need for credit to finance the required family contribution portion of college costs, or the credit needs of middle class families not typically eligible for federally supported grant or loan programs.[2] This need has typically been met by commercial banks via either the federally sponsored PLUS program or through consumer lending programs. Only a very small fraction of these needs are met directly through college and university sponsored loan programs; in 1992, for example, less than one-half of one percent of Sallie Mae's loan volume financed student loans originated at educational institutions.

Informal surveys of students and their families

conducted at Rensselaer suggested that many families are intimidated and confused by the complexity of aid and loan packages. Furthermore, even comfortable upper-middle class families do not necessarily have the cash resources readily available to pay as much as $100,000 per child in college costs.

In order to accommodate perceived customer need, Rensselaer decided to explore the feasibility of developing a low cost, affordable, and user-friendly college payment program.

Program Design

A necessary precondition for the entire program was the development of a student loan program offering low cost and affordable payments. The use of tax-exempt financing through the state authorizing agency (in this case, the Dormitory Authority of the State of New York) brought access to low cost capital. The creation of a mortgage-backed option to permit consumer deductibility of interest against taxes further reduced the net interest cost to the borrower. Low interest costs were wrapped around a 15-year term in order to ensure that monthly payments were stable and affordable to most families. The endorsement of both parents and students on the note would permit additional flexibility for the family in determining future payment obligations. (The dual signatures also provided credit enhancement.)

To ensure that the program would meet student and family needs, a consumer survey was conducted. Based on the results of the survey, a customer assurance package was developed to meet the following criteria:

- Loan amounts covered up to 95 percent of total college costs
- Program incorporated in financial aid packaging
- Minimal credit checks to ensure customer availability

The credit risks attendant upon this plan design (i.e., high loan to cost ratio and de-emphasis of credit review) were considered acceptable because of the following credit protections incorporated into the program:

Figure 1-2

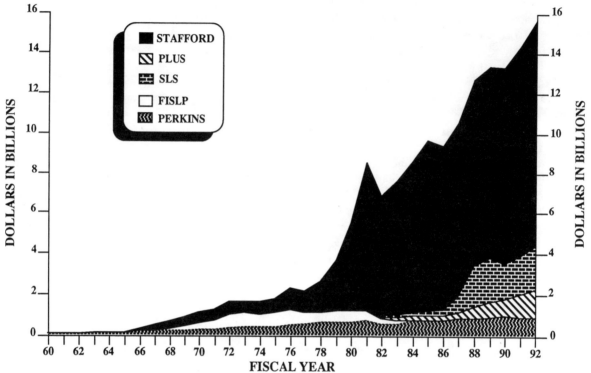

| ANNUAL LOAN VOLUME, TITLE IV PROGRAMS |
| FY 1960 - FY 1992 |

Note: Loan volume for Stafford, PLUS, SLS and FISLP are loan guarantees, some of which are ultimately cancelled; Perkins loan volume refers to actual dollars disbursed.

Prepared by: U. S. Department of Education, OPE/SFAP/PTAS, Analysis and Forecasting Division, Loans Branch

- Loans cosigned by parents and students. Rensselaer students (a large proportion of whom graduate in engineering and the sciences) have an exemplary loan repayment record, with historical default rates below 4 percent.
- Interest rate on loans adjusted to incorporate higher than projected default rate.
- Capital invested in program from internal sources totaling approximately 10 percent of loans against unanticipated losses and defaults. The interest rate on loans was adjusted to generate a market rate of return on this investment.

The resulting financing design had the advan-

tage of lowering the cost of education by as much as 25 percent when compared with conventional financing. These savings were considered significant enough to proceed with a detailed implementation plan.

Implementation of the Financing Plan

Implementing a new, complex, and rather sophisticated financing program required the close cooperation and support of a number of key administrative units within the university, including the offices of finance, admissions, financial aid, public relations, and government relations. Close working relationships were also necessary with the state issuing agency (the Dormitory

Authority of the State of New York), legislative staff, and institute trustees. Prior state legislation authorized the issuance of up to $200 million in student loan bonds by the authority, of which $90 million had already been used. In addition, the bond issue had to be incorporated into the overall state volume cap for tax-exempt bond issues.

Discussions initiated by Rensselaer amongst financial officers of selected independent colleges and universities within the state indicated a wide interest in a new student loan program, and a number of schools elected to participate. Since student loan bonds are not included in the calculation of the $150 million federal limit on tax-exempt bond issuance, some institutions previously excluded from tax-exempt financing could also participate. Broad institutional participation carried a number of advantages, including economies of scale (including a wider distribution of legal, underwriting, and distribution costs), enhanced credit, and broader geopolitical support. It also necessitated close cooperation within the consortium and a flexible financing arrangement in order to accommodate the individual institutions' particular needs.

Discussions were held on the effect of the program on institutional debt capacity, financial condition, and administrative resources. It was imperative that the program be self-supporting and neutral to institutional balance sheets. This was achieved by structuring the loan rate to meet not only the debt service obligations on the bonds, but also the cost associated with assumed loan defaults, servicing costs, administrative expenses, issuance costs, and negative arbitrage (a surcharge for these costs is limited by tax law to no more than 2 percent per annum). Each participating institution was able to lend to students within these parameters and provide additional reserves to the program.

Of equal importance was the attention devoted to the cash flow structures of the bond issue. The bond cash flows had to mirror the relending pattern of the institutions to minimize loan rates and negative arbitrage, and prevent early redemption. Each participating institution developed careful assumptions concerning the loan demand and timing of origination; average, minimum, and maximum loan size; repayment options (immediately repay or deferral); loan term;

and loan prepayments. Maximum flexibility was built into the program; for example, loan prepayments could be recycled to new borrowers with approval by the Dormitory Authority of the State of New York for a period of up to five years.

Further parameters such as application and/or origination fees and borrower insurance were also stipulated. Loan servicing was contracted to a third-party servicer by all participants except for one who serviced all loans in-house. Institute counsel developed a promissory note and appropriate disclosure according to consumer lending laws.

Effective marketing was critical to the program's success. As noted previously, customer needs were identified early. This allowed the plan to be constructed for easy accessibility and consistency with other financial aid elements, with a goal of simple "one-stop shopping" for all college financial needs. The plan was patterned on successful and well-established consumer lending operations (such as auto retail financing), with an emphasis on the unique college affordability benefits.

A disciplined approach for the many required authorizations was also necessary, particularly in light of the number of institutions involved. Authorizations included university finance committees and trustee boards; public oversight agencies and the tax-exempt issuing agency; underwriters; and bond counsel. To coordinate these activities, a working group consisting of members from each participating institution, the Dormitory Authority, the lead bond underwriter and institutions' counsel met regularly. This group formulated the borrowing plan, addressing administrative and legal issues. The use of an underwriter experienced in student loan lending and counsel knowledgeable of both tax and consumer credit proved invaluable. Of equal importance was the use of an experienced student loan servicing and originating organization.

Results

Careful staff work and close adherence to scheduled deadlines resulted in successful implementation of the program. Highly rated tax-exempt bonds were issued to fund educational loans at competitive, below-market rates and to cover

NEW ISSUE

$44,999,629.71
DORMITORY AUTHORITY
OF THE STATE OF NEW YORK
COLLEGE AND UNIVERSITY EDUCATION LOAN
REVENUE BONDS, 1992 ISSUE

Dated: April 1, 1992
(except for Capital Appreciation Bonds
which are dated their date of delivery)

Due: July 1, as shown
on the inside cover

Payment and Security: The College and University Education Loan Revenue Bonds, 1992 Issue (the "Bonds") are special obligations of the Dormitory Authority of the State of New York (the "Authority") payable solely from and secured by a pledge of certain payments to be made under the Loan Agreements between the respective Institutions and the Authority and all funds and accounts (except the Arbitrage Rebate Fund) authorized and established under the Resolution.

Payment of the principal of and interest on the Bonds when due will be guaranteed by a municipal bond insurance policy to be issued simultaneously with the delivery of the Bonds by Municipal Bond Investors Assurance Corporation (the "Insurer" or "MBIA").

MBIA

Each Loan Agreement is the general obligation of the respective Institution and requires the Institution to pay, in addition to a portion of the fees and expenses of the Authority and the Trustee, amounts sufficient to pay such Institution's allocable share of the principal and Redemption Price of and interest on the Bonds. Such payments by all of the Institutions will be sufficient in the aggregate to pay the principal and Redemption Price of and interest on the Bonds, as such payments become due. The obligation of each Institution under its Loan Agreement to make such payments is secured by a pledge of certain revenues of such Institution, which pledge may be subordinate to certain Prior Pledges of such revenues made by such Institution. A default by one Institution under its Loan Agreement will not, in and of itself, be a default under the Loan Agreement of any other Institution, and remedies may only be taken against an Institution which is in default under the terms of its Loan Agreement. At the time of delivery of the Bonds, Bond proceeds will be deposited in the Debt Service Reserve Fund in an amount equal to the Debt Service Reserve Fund Requirement.

The Bonds will not be a debt of the State of New York nor will the State be liable thereon. The Authority has no taxing power.

Description: The Bonds will be issued as fully registered bonds in denominations of $5,000 or any integral multiple thereof except that the Bonds maturing on July 1, 2003 through and including July 1, 2013 (the "Capital Appreciation Bonds") will be issued in denominations of $5,000 aggregate principal and interest payable at maturity, or any integral multiple thereof. Interest (due January 1, 1993 and each July 1 and January 1 thereafter) on the Bonds, except for the Capital Appreciation Bonds, will be payable by check or draft mailed to the registered owners of the Bonds at their addresses as shown on the registration books held by the Trustee or at the option of a holder of at least $1,000,000 in principal amount of Bonds, by wire transfer to the holder of such Bonds, each as of the close of business on the fifteenth day of the month next preceding an interest payment date. Interest on the Capital Appreciation Bonds will be compounded on each January 1 and July 1, commencing on July 1, 1992, but will be payable only at maturity, or upon redemption or acceleration in the manner set forth herein. The principal and Redemption Price of the Bonds will be payable at the principal corporate trust office of Manufacturers and Traders Trust Company, Buffalo, New York, the Trustee and Paying Agent or, with respect to Redemption Price, at the option of a holder of at least $1,000,000 in principal amount of Bonds, by wire transfer to the holder of such Bonds as more fully described herein.

Redemption: *The Bonds are subject to special redemption prior to maturity as more fully described herein.*

Tax Exemption: In the opinion of Bond Counsel, based upon an analysis of existing laws, regulations, rulings and court decisions and assuming (among other things) compliance with certain covenants, interest on the Bonds is excluded from gross income for federal income tax purposes. In the opinion of Bond Counsel, interest on the Bonds is a specific preference item for purposes of the federal individual and corporate alternative minimum taxes. Bond Counsel is further of the opinion that interest on the Bonds is exempt from personal income taxes imposed by the State of New York and any political subdivision thereof (including The City of New York and the City of Yonkers). Bond Counsel expresses no opinion regarding any other tax consequences caused by the ownership or disposition of, or the accrual or receipt of interest on, the Bonds. See, however, "PART 9 - TAX EXEMPTION" herein regarding certain other tax considerations.

The Bonds are offered when, as and if issued and received by the Underwriters. The offer of the Bonds may be subject to prior sale or withdrawn or modified at any time without notice. The offer is subject to the approval of legality by Orrick, Herrington & Sutcliffe, New York, New York, Bond Counsel, and to certain other conditions. Certain legal matters will be passed upon for the Institutions by their Counsel, Nixon, Hargrave, Devans & Doyle, Rochester, New York. Certain legal matters will be passed upon for the Underwriters by their Counsel, Mudge Rose Guthrie Alexander & Ferdon, New York, New York. The Authority expects to deliver the Bonds in definitive form in New York, New York, on or about May 14, 1992.

Smith Barney, Harris Upham & Co. Incorporated	**First Albany Corporation**	**Morgan Stanley & Co.** Incorporated
J. P. Morgan Securities, Inc.		**PaineWebber Incorporated**

April 3, 1992

program expenses. All authorizations and approvals were received and the bonds were issued within nine months of the initiation of discussions, permitting time for marketing and distribution of loan funds.

A thoughtful and determined marketing plan tailored for our institution resulted in:

- a high level of interest amongst the inquiry pool and applicants;
- a significant, 10 percent increase in enrollment, exceeding both budget targets and prior years results; and
- a higher level of satisfaction with the financial aid packages provided to students and families.

Conclusion

While a wide variety of federally sponsored loan programs are available to students and their families, the higher education sector nevertheless appears to be behind consumer durable goods industries in offering accessible, affordable, and easy-to-understand financing to their customers. There are likely a number of reasons for this, including the traditional access to federally sponsored, subsidized loans, and the typical administrative separation of admissions/financial aid and finance within the university.

Joint cooperative initiatives undertaken by colleges and universities have the potential of providing important credit support to students and their families.

List of Colleges and Universities with Outstanding Publicly Held Indebtedness

Figure 17-8 on page 142 presents a listing of higher education institutions with Standard & Poor's Corporation (S&P) rated debt issues outstanding as of July 9, 1993. In many cases, the actual issuer of the debt is a higher education authority issuing on behalf of a college or university. The Connecticut Health and Educational Facilities Authority, for example, issues on behalf of Trinity College. The list includes schools that have issued:

- unenhanced debt (issues sold and rated on the basis of the institution's own creditworthiness);
- insured debt (sold and rated on the basis of a municipal bond insurance policy);
- bank or letter of credit-backed debt (rating based on bank enhancement); and
- collateralized debt (rating based on the institution's creditworthiness and enhancement in the form of collateral—generally investments).

The list does not include higher education debt rated "AAA" based on escrow structures (refunded bonds) or community college ratings. In addition, an institution with only bank-backed debt rated and outstanding may not appear on the list, as these issues are analyzed by S&P's bank group and not the higher education group.

In many cases, an institution will have several different types of debt and ratings outstanding. For example, Loyola University of Chicago, which issues through the Illinois Educational Facilities Authority, has unenhanced, insured, and bank-backed debt outstanding. Nearly 500 different institutions are represented, with an almost even breakdown between independent institutions (242) and state-supported colleges and universities (230). The states with the highest concentration of rated independent institutions are Massachusetts (26), New York (46), and Pennsylvania (34). California (22) and Texas (20) have the greatest number of rated public institutions.

Notes

1. Legislation enacted in 1993 directs an increasingly larger proportion of Stafford and PLUS Loans directly through colleges and universities. See chapter 7 for a discussion of student loan financing.
2. The Federally supported PLUS Loans offered through commercial banks are not need-based, but until recently were restricted as to amount.

TWO

Capital Finance Market Segments and Participants

The higher education capital finance market includes individuals and entities that can be best organized in chronological order for a financing process and by function at each specific point in time. (See figure 2-1.) Later chapters will examine these participants in more detail, but this section will introduce a basic framework to the discussion as well as some vocabulary with respect to the participants.

Colleges and Universities

There are 2,157 four-year (599 public and 1,558 independent) and 1,444 two-year (999 public and 445 independent) higher education institutions in the United States, according to the United States Department of Education as reported in the August 25, 1993, *Chronicle of Higher Education Almanac*. The degree to which one can generalize about the common characteristics and common interests of higher education institutions varies with the topic at issue. With respect to capital financing, the differences between categories of institutions are extraordinary.

This section provides a general analytical framework for dividing consideration of higher education financing into just four categories. This categorization, while not wholly adequate, represents a workable compromise. The selected categories are public institutions, independent institutions, large institutions, and small institutions.

Public Institutions

Public institutions are legally classified most often as either governmental entities or public benefit corporations, and it is this legal character that drives their approach to and treatment by the capital markets. Public institutions often raise their capital by means of a state or local government general obligation borrowing backed by the

taxing power of the governmental issuer. Therefore, the investors in such bonds are taking the credit risk that tax revenues will be available to pay the debt service. The operating results of the public college or university are of interest to the government because the government is not inclined to subsidize the debt service, but legally, even a total failure to achieve any operating income from the public college or university would not remove the governmental payment obligation for the debt.

Such general obligation bonds normally are received well in the capital markets and qualify for among the lowest available interest rates.

Independent Institutions

Independent institutions are legally classified as nonprofit corporations under Section 501(c)(3) of the Internal Revenue Code of 1986, as amended. Independent institutions receive certain governmental benefits, but such institutions are not governmental by nature. In the field of financing, therefore, independent higher education institutions cannot issue debt through the vehicle of state and local general obligation tax-backed bonds as described above for public institutions.

Independent institutions issue debt in the public capital markets through a public financing authority or agency or directly under the institution's own legal authorization. Most nonprofit institutions have available a statewide higher educational facilities authority that is a governmental entity which serves as a financing vehicle to issue tax-exempt debt, the proceeds of which are then loaned (usually simultaneously) to the independent college or university. The loan repayments coincide in time and amount with the funds necessary for the authority to repay the authority's bondholders and to cover administrative expenses of issuing the bonds and maintain-

Figure 2-1. The Higher Education Capital Financing Process

PHASE ONE: PLANNING

Business officers; institution's strategic planning team
Governing board committees and the full board
Investment banker/underwriter
Financial advisors
College general counsel
College financing counsel

PHASE TWO: PREPARATION AND STRUCTURING

All of Phase One, plus:

Issuing authority
Bond counsel to the issuing authority
Investment banker/underwriter's counsel
Verification agent
Derivative product participants
Credit enhancement providers
Rating agencies
Bond trustee
Bond trustee counsel
College auditors
Market regulators: the Internal Revenue Service, the
    Municipal Securities Rulemaking Board, the Securities
    and Exchange Commission, and others

PHASE THREE: MARKETING AND SALE

All of Phases One and Two, plus:

Investment banker's trading desk
Primary market investors: institutional and other (retail)
  investors

PHASE FOUR: CLOSING

All of Phases One, Two, and Three, plus:

Depository Trust Company
CUSIP Bureau
Escrow agent

PHASE FIVE: POST-CLOSING AND ADMINISTRATION

Various participants, including:

College or university business officer
College or university auditor
Issuing authority
Bond trustee
Escrow agent
Depository Trust Company
Credit enhancement provider
Rating agencies
Market regulators
Primary market investors
Secondary market investors

---

ing the authority's existence. Many colleges and universities have a choice of several state and local governmental entities or agencies that can serve as conduits for the financing.

The second alternative available to nonprofit institutions is to issue debt into the market directly, without the benefit of the educational facilities authority. Such debt is not tax-exempt because only the authority's participation in the transaction conveys the governmental benefit of tax-exempt income to the purchasers of the authority bonds.[3] Such direct debt does enjoy favored treatment under the federal securities laws, however, because Section 3(a)(4) of the Securities Act of 1933 provides an exemption from the registration provisions of the securities laws that otherwise are applicable to most nongovernmental securities. Section 12(g)(2)(D) and Section 13(a) of the Securities Exchange Act of 1934 contain a similar exception from the reporting requirements of the 1934 act. Such registration and reporting requirements are a mainstay of the corporate debt market, but represent an ongoing legal reporting and disclosure system that increases the costs of those who use the capital markets without an exemption. As a general matter, only certain classes of securities have an exemption. This is a valuable asset that many independent colleges and universities do not use to their best advantage.

Large Institutions

The public capital markets are generally more comfortable financing credit risk with respect to a larger institution. No absolute delineation of a larger institution exists, because size can be measured in several ways, including enrollment, income, and even variety of program offerings of campus locations. A working threshold of 10,000 students would include the 412 largest institutions among the 3,541 institutions reporting enrollment to the U.S. Department of Education as of fall 1991. A threshold 20,000 students would include 103 institutions. It should be noted that "size" in higher education finance is principally determined by enrollment, a recognition of the tuition-dependent nature of all but a small number of independent colleges and universities in the country. In contrast, the corporate market may consider size in several categories such as sales, market share, profits, assets, number of locations, and number of employees. Even the nonprofit community will rank foundations as large on the basis of assets. Yet a college or university most often will be grouped as large or small based principally on enrollment.

Size is relevant most often in independent college credit markets because, as mentioned above, public colleges generally raise capital using the tax-based security of general obligation state or local government securities. Larger independent colleges have a greater percentage of their category that can be characterized as established, solid institutions with a stable identity in the market, predictable student demand, historical alumni support resulting in an adequate endowment, and an experienced management team, particularly in the presidential and chief financial officer positions. In addition, the nation's elite independent college and university research institutions are concentrated in the larger institution category.

Small Institutions

Smaller institutions defy broad categorization, but certain profile characteristics can be described based on the history of institutions that have used external financing. A class of elite smaller institutions of high quality, very strong student demand, and large endowments enjoy ease of access to the capital markets. A second class of smaller institutions is characterized by strong quality and student demand, but does not have the comparable depth of endowment. A third class can be grouped as those that are maintaining an equilibrium of student demand without the benefit of a significant endowment to cushion student demand or mitigate high tuition dependency. Finally, a significant number of smaller institutions have not historically been able to (or perhaps sought to) gain public capital market access due to an excessively narrow market for student demand, lack of financial reserves, or insufficient financial performance.

Credit Quality

Rating Agency Groups

Three principal nationally recognized credit rating agencies publish independent credit ratings of higher education debt securities. Investors seriously consider both the rating itself and the contents of the rating reports when making their own investment decision with respect to individual higher education bonds.

Credit rating agency bond ratings are not ratings of the college or university itself. Rather, a rating applies to the particular bond issue rated. Financing structure and the nature of the pledged revenues are critical factors to a rating. The same college or university thus can have different ratings outstanding for different issues of securities if there is a difference in the security

or structure of the issue. In addition, the inclusion of credit enhancement such as bond insurance or a letter of credit in the financing structure usually will result in an upgrade of the rating on the issue to the higher rating of the credit enhancement provider.

Credit ratings are explored further in chapter 13.

Nonrated Issues

Receipt of a credit rating is not a condition to gaining access to the capital markets. Credit ratings can be divided into "investment grade" and "non-investment grade." In the absence of being able to obtain a rating, a bond issuer may sell what is known as "nonrated" bonds.

Nonrated bonds became a prominent part of capital markets history in the 1980s. Market access for nonrated bonds reached new levels, but the nonrated bonds became popularly characterized as "junk bonds," in many cases unfairly. Nevertheless, any higher education institution interested in issuing nonrated debt should expect to address and overcome the implication that its securities are deficient "junk bonds" to some degree. As a general matter, in the absence of a solid rationale for forgoing a rating, issuing debt without a rating will carry a meaningful interest rate penalty for the college or university.

Certain investors, particularly some mutual funds and other institutional investors, are prohibited by law or investment policy from purchasing nonrated securities, further contributing to the market penalty for these securities.

Overview of Investors Who Participate in Higher Education Financings

Chapter 3 is a particular focus on investors in higher education securities. In general, however, tax-exempt higher education securities rated in the "A" category or higher do not exhibit investor characteristics markedly different from other tax-exempt securities. As the rating category moves into the "BBB/Baa" category, including variations as low as "BBB-," the investors become more specialized. The most specialized category of higher education investors is found for taxable higher education bonds, which are classified in the "taxable municipal" category.

Participants

The capital financing process involves many players, from the institutions themselves to financial advisors, auditors, and ratings agencies. Each of these participants and its role in the financing process is described below.

Colleges and Universities

The degree to which one can generalize about the common characteristics and common interests of higher education institutions varies with the topic at issue. In the area of capital financing, the differences are significant. Chapter 1 covers some parameters for distinguishing among these institutions. The great majority of higher education institutions in the United States have not used the tax-exempt market for financing legally available to them.

A definitive database of higher education financing activity presently does not exist. Most measurements of "education bonds" include elementary and secondary school districts with higher education securities. Further, public institutions that issue their debt through the vehicle of state or local tax-based general obligation bonds are not adequately distinguished in existing databases. Therefore, it is not possible to state exactly how many higher education institutions have raised capital through the public tax-exempt or taxable markets.

Rating agencies are one available measure. As of January 1994, Standard and Poor's Corporation maintained credit ratings on nearly 500 higher education credit ratings (excluding state or local general obligation bonds that are not identified as a higher education purpose). As of December 1993, Moody's Investors Service maintained approximately 400 higher education rating, and Fitch Investors Service maintained 35 higher education ratings.

State and Local Issuing Authorities

Many states have created state-wide or local authorities or agencies to issue tax-exempt securities and loan the proceeds to higher education institutions. Loan repayments are set at the amount sufficient to allow the authority or agency to make timely payment of principal and interest on the securities and pay the administrative costs of operating the agency or authority.

State and local issuing authorities make varied contributions to the higher education financing market. All authorities serve as a legal entity, which by state legislation is either a governmental instrumentality or a public benefit corporation and is authorized to issue tax-exempt securities under federal tax law. Some authorities provide a comprehensive range of services from the earliest stages of planning a project and structuring a financing to the final stages of construction and facility maintenance. Other authorities function more in the model of passive conduits. Issuing authorities and agencies can be critical resources to assist colleges and universities in the state or commonwealth in navigating the financing process, but this is not universally the case and some agencies and authorities provide minimal services. College financial officers should consult their respective educational facilities financing authority in the process to ascertain that assistance is available. See appendix B for a listing of the members of the National Association of Higher Educational Facilities Authorities.

Investment Bankers

The investment banker is a key participant in a higher education financing. His or her primary function is to raise the capital required for a college or university to complete its project. This is most commonly achieved by purchasing securities for the college or university through a conduit issuer and subsequently reselling them to investors. A college or university's interaction with the investment banker will be based primarily on the method of sale selected to issue the bonds, either a negotiated sale or a competitive sale. In a negotiated sale, the institution (directly and through the conduit issuer) works directly with one or more investment banks in structuring the financing. The institution then sells the securities to such investment bank(s) for resale to investors pursuant to the terms and conditions of a bond purchase agreement (which recites the interest rates, maturities, call provisions, legal covenants, etc.) among the college or university, the issuer, and the investment banker(s). In a negotiated sale, an investment banker is retained early in the process to assist in the structure of the transaction and participates in virtually all other facets of the financing as well (e.g., credit ratings, municipal bond insurance, disclosure documents, legal covenants, etc.).

The other method of sale is a competitive sale in which a college or university (through the conduit issuer or directly) invites financial institutions to submit bids to purchase the securities at a specific date and time in the future. In a competitive sale, a college or university is interested primarily in an investment bank's underwriting and distribution capabilities rather than its structuring expertise. The structuring aspect is usually handled by an independent financial advisory firm, which cannot be part of any underwriting syndicate competing to buy the securities. Consequently, in a competitive sale, there would be little, if any, interaction between the college or university and the investment bank until the time of sale.

Financial Advisors

The role of a financial advisor in a higher education financing is to provide advice on all financial matters relating to the proposed transaction. Whether a college or university should retain a financial advisor depends on the magnitude and complexity of the institution's long-term capital financing plan and the method of sale employed to sell the bonds. If a college or university is to embark upon a long-term capital financing program, a financial advisor is commonly retained at the outset to provide expertise on a continuous basis and assist the institution in formulating and implementing the most suitable plan of finance. Since colleges and universities are relatively infrequent issuers of debt, a financial advisor can provide valuable insight into the overall financing process that will, among other things, give comfort to an institution's financial staff. In many cases, the conduit issuer of the bonds (either a state or local agency) already retains a financial advisor for the benefit of its college or university clients, which would preclude the need for the institution to have a financial advisor of its own. An institution may also elect to use an investment bank's public finance department instead of a financial advisor and work directly with the investment banker on a negotiated sale basis.

Method of sale is also an important factor in the decision to retain a financial advisor. As mentioned above, there are two methods of sale available to a college or university when issuing its bonds through a conduit issuer: negotiated or competitive. While it is not uncommon for a financial advisor to be retained on a negotiated sale (especially in the context of a major long-term capital financing program as described above), the majority of negotiated sales involve the institution and its investment banker, which, in all probability, was retained in the initial stages of the financing. In a competitive sale, on the other hand, financial advisors are a necessity. They work with the institution and other members of the financing team to provide advice on a variety of matters, including the evaluation of structuring alternatives, credit ratings, credit enhancement, negotiation of business terms, and timing, all of which are crucial elements in securing the lowest cost of funds for the institution upon the most flexible terms.

While each institution will have its own opinions and preferences regarding investment bankers and financial advisors, one of the keys to a successful financing program is a fair and thorough evaluation of financial firms that may potentially participate in the transaction with particular emphasis on its experience in the increasingly specialized area of higher education finance.

Bond Counsel to the Governmental Issuing Entity (in Tax-Exempt Bond Financings)

Bond counsel is an unusual legal role that exists in the structure of tax-exempt financings. Bond counsel delivers an independent legal opinion with respect to the authorization of the securities under applicable laws; the nature of the federal and state tax exemptions of the interest payable on the securities; and the legal, valid and binding nature of the critical financing documents that make up the legal structure and form the basis for the pledge securing the securities.

Bond counsel is selected by the issuer or the higher education institution, depending on particular custom and practice. The independent status of bond counsel is critical to the securities issuance process, however, and bond counsel does not represent any party's interest as counsel other than the bondholders' interest in structuring a legal, valid, and binding transaction in all respects. The governmental bond issuer typically will have a general counsel and the college or university will have counsel, each of whom will fulfill certain responsibilities with respect to the bonds separate from the matters undertaken by bond counsel.

General Counsel to the College or University

College general counsel usually will review the documentation in the financing process. College general counsel will have certain areas of existing expertise that will be the subject of legal opinions at the time of the closing of the bond issue, such as the status of any litigation.

Financing Counsel to the College or University

Higher education institutions often will retain a financing counsel as a special counsel to assist the college general counsel in the review of the structure of the transaction and the documentation associated with the financing. In addition, financing counsel may take a significant role in the preparation of the college or university section of the disclosure document associated with the sale of the bonds. Utilization of financing counsel has increased in conjunction with the sophistication of the financing techniques that have gained market acceptance in the investor community for higher education securities. The financing counsel normally will deliver one or more legal opinions in connection with the completion of its role.

College financing counsel usually is essential rather than optional if a tax-exempt financing is not involved. In this event, financing counsel will fill the financial document drafting and coordination role played by bond counsel in a tax-exempt financing.

Underwriter's Counsel

The investment banker/underwriter usually retains an outside counsel for its municipal finance transactions, which are negotiated rather than competitively bid. Underwriter's counsel will review the financing documents generally and will play a leadership role in designing and implementing the diligence process that is required in connection with the issuance of public securities. Underwriter's counsel normally is called upon to deliver a "due diligence" legal

opinion as well as certain federal securities laws opinions to its client, the investment banker. In the absence of an experienced financing counsel representing the institution, underwriter's counsel also may take a leadership role in assisting the institution in preparing the college and university section of the disclosure document associated with the delivery of the securities.

Bond Trustee (and Escrow Agent)

The bond trustee is appointed by the issuer of the bonds pursuant to the bond indenture or bond resolution. The bond trustee functions as the representative of the bondholders and, as such, enforces the remedies of the bondholders in the event of a default under the financing documentation. In addition, the bond trustee normally functions as the paying agent for the bonds, receiving the total amount of all debt service payments from the issuer of the bonds and then dividing and distributing such debt service payments to the bondholders.

An additional trustee-type role, the escrow agent, is present in an advance refunding financing. In many refinancings, an escrow fund is set up sufficient to pay principal and interest due on the refunded bonds until the first call date (generally, 10 years after issuance). The escrow agent, who is almost always required to be the trustee for the refunded bonds, holds these funds and administers the payouts to the holders of the refunded bonds at the proper times and in the correct amounts.

Bond Trustee Counsel

The bond trustee usually retains a regular counsel for its municipal finance transactions. Bond trustee counsel will review the financing documents to identify the obligations of the bond trustee and satisfy the bond trustee that the procedural aspects of the securities issue are in accordance with the bond trustee's operating capabilities and procedures.

Auditors

A fundamental aspect of disclosure of significant information to potential investors is the disclosure of financial information in the form of audited financial statements. Business officers should anticipate the inclusion of from two to five years of audited financial statements as an appendix to the official statement disclosure document relating to higher education debt securities.

In most financings, audited financial statements are supplemented by unaudited stub financial information that is compiled by the institutions's auditor, but that is not the subject of a formal audit opinion. Higher education financings are the exception to the rule in most cases, however. Interim higher education financial information often is not required for disclosure because the irregularity of income as compared to the year-round incurrence of expenses can make mid-year financial statements confusing with respect to year-end results. Rather, the accuracy of budget projections is handled as a diligence matter, but one that does not become a disclosure matter in the official statement.

Business officers should be aware that comfort letters, representing a statement of certain diligence procedures undertaken by the auditors during a financing, have been a standard part of most public finance transactions. However, the American Institute of Certified Public Accountants (AICPA) issued a new policy position with respect to such comfort letters in 1993 and the municipal finance community has not developed a uniform response to the new policy. Nevertheless, negotiations with respect to comfort letters have become more pointed with each passing year and this trend appears to be continuing.

In certain cases, disclosure in the official statement of multi-year financial information will require the auditor to make adjustments to prior years' information. Such adjustments can be difficult and time-consuming and should be addressed early in the planning process for the financing.

Verification Agent

The verification agent plays a critical role in a refunding or refinancing unless the refunded debt is paid simultaneously with the issuance of the new debt. This often cannot be the case because many publicly offered securities, including tax-exempt bonds, have a feature known as "call protection." Call protection blocks out a period of time, usually 10 years, during which the issuer cannot retire the bonds early. In order to authorize the issuance of new debt or, sometimes, in

order to have the refunded debt "deemed paid as a legal matter," an escrow account is established using the proceeds of the refunding bond issue and other equity funds that may be contributed by the college or university. In order to accomplish a "legal defeasance," the investments in the escrow fund must be sufficient to pay all amounts remaining due on the refunded bonds at the time such amounts are due until the expiration of the call protection period, at which time the refunded (and escrowed) bonds are redeemed. The verification agent delivers a verification report in which the mathematical accuracy of the defeasance calculations, together with calculations designed to assure that the refunding bonds are not taxable arbitrage bonds, are confirmed.

Verification is a critical matter in refundings, and colleges and universities should take an active interest in the quality of the firm chosen to perform the verification. Most of the major accounting firms offer verification services, but some are more experienced than others, particularly when a complex verification is involved. Other firms, frequently staffed by former members of the national accounting firms, also are active in the verification service, and their experience can be verified if such a firm is under consideration. Because the cost of verification services is a small part of the financing budget, verification services should not be assigned on the basis of a price bidding unless all bidders are impeccably qualified as to credentials in advance. In addition, it is preferable to select a verification agent who has experience working with the institution's investment banker and the bond counsel in a tax-exempt issue, because all three parties will have to agree on the calculations required to be verified. The benefits of having an established working relationship based on prior experience among these parties will pay great dividends to the entire financing team in terms of both cost and time during the course of the complex task of structuring and verifying escrows and defeasances.

The concepts of refunding and defeasance are addressed in more detail in chapter 6.

Rating Agencies

Three principal nationally recognized credit rating agencies publish independent credit ratings of higher education debt securities: Standard

& Poor's Corporation, Moody's Investors Service, and Fitch Investors Service. Investors seriously consider both the rating itself and the contents of the rating reports in the course of making their own investment decisions with respect to individual higher education bonds.

Credit ratings are examined in more detail in chapters 2 and 13.

Credit Enhancers

Credit enhancements are available to strengthen the credit profile and credit rating of many higher education securities. The principal forms of credit enhancement are municipal bond insurance and letters of credit. Credit enhance-ment provides an additional layer of repayment assurance to the bondholders. There are important differences between the available types of credit enhancement.

Credit enhancement is discussed in more detail in chapter 12, including the advantages and disadvantages of municipal bond insurance and letters of credit.

Notes

3. A technical alternative exists pursuant to Revenue Ruling 63-20, but this is a highly complex financing technique that is rarely used and should be reviewed with counsel.

❖ THREE ❖

Investors

Investors in the tax-exempt debt securities most often used by higher education institutions generally fall into two groups: the institutions that buy securities in large blocks that are run by professional money managers and the individual investors. In the early 1980s a clear shift away from the retail investor segment to the institutional segment occurred. Most individual investors now buy tax-exempt securities through large institutions. As figure 3-1 illustrates, the magnitude of this shift is dramatic.

The Role of Investors in a Higher Education Debt Financing

Individual Investors

Individual investors dominate the buying side of the equation for municipal bonds by investing directly or through fiduciaries such as bond funds, trust departments, and investment advisors. Individuals tend to favor short and intermediate maturities of 10 to 12 years and prefer to purchase bonds priced at par.

Mutual Funds

Investment companies hold a diversified portfolio of municipal securities and sell "units" or "shares" to investors. Current holdings are in excess of $200 billion in long-term bonds and about $100 billion in short-term money market funds. Two basic types of bond funds exist:

Unit Investment Trust (U.I.T.)—A fixed portfolio of municipal securities sold to investors in trust units, which represent fractional undivided ownership interests in the portfolio. The same securi-

Figure 3-1

PURCHASERS OF TAX EXEMPT DEBT

1981

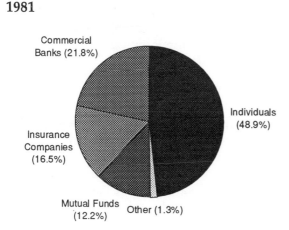

1992

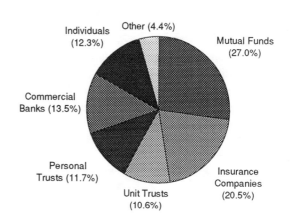

Source: Federal Reserve Flow of Funds, April 1993

43

ties are held in the portfolio until maturity or redemption. A U.I.T. is a "closed end" fund, with a fixed number of units available to investors.

Managed Fund—A portfolio of municipal securities sold to investors in shares. An investment advisor actively manages the portfolio in line with set investment policy. Managed funds continuously offer new shares to the public and are therefore called "open end" funds.

Commercial Banks

Since the Tax Reform Act of 1986, commercial bank portfolios consist primarily of "bank qualified" paper. Bank trust departments are active buyers on behalf of individual investors. The largest bank trusts also offer a pooled fund referred to as a common trust fund that allows individuals to invest in a diversified pool of municipal bonds similar to mutual funds. Trust buyers traditionally favor short and intermediate maturities that sell at par. In addition, they prefer high quality bond ratings of Aa/AA or Aaa/AAA.

Property and Casualty Insurance Companies

Currently, property and casualty insurance companies own approximately $150 billion of municipal bonds. These companies are extremely sensitive to changes in tax rates and traditionally purchase bonds with maturities ranging from five to 20 years. Typically, these companies are flexible about coupons and ratings; however, they rarely invest in bonds below investment grade.

Property and casualty companies also are affected by the occurrence of natural disasters. The recent series of natural disasters has cut heavily into insurance company profits, which has diminished their need for, and therefore their demand for, tax-exempt securities. As a result, some insurance companies recently have become net sellers of tax-exempt securities.

Corporations

Because corporations closely watch their after-tax revenues, corporations often trade between taxable and tax-exempt instruments, depending upon their effective tax rate. Corporate purchases of tax-exempt securities typically are confined to short maturity ranges (one to three years).

Objectives in Higher Education Bonds and Other Financing Vehicles

Investors (buyers) look for stable or improving credit quality in either independent or public college and university debt securities. Diversity and reliability of revenue sources is important given the impact of a recessionary economy along with declining state appropriations and federal grants. Investors examine the trends in applications, acceptances and matriculation over a three to five year period. Similarly, the levels of tuition and room and board should be adequate to fund programs and meet expenses, but must remain competitive. Investors get added comfort when the college or university maintains its bond rating with Moody's, Standard and Poor's, or Fitch. A further consideration is the institution's capital spending program. A burdensome program could prompt a rating downgrade.

How to Work with Institutional Investors

Disseminating information is crucial when working with institutional investors. These institutions employ research analysts to continually monitor issues in which they have invested. The key to developing a successful investor relations program is communication and willingness to provide up-to-date information.

Site Visits

Site visits are highly recommended and should be encouraged. While institutional research analysts clearly want to know the numbers to ascertain the financial strength of entities in which they invest, a working knowledge of the facilities and the management are key ingredients in formulating an opinion.

❖ F O U R ❖

Market Regulators and Legal Parameters

Higher education securities and financings are subject to various government regulations, from the federal to the state level. This chapter describes these regulatory forces, as well as the legal parameters with which business officers should be familiar before undertaking a capital financing.

Regulatory Forces and Legal Considerations

Federal Regulation of Higher Education Securities and Financings

The federal securities laws are designed to be generally inclusive in their governance of financial instruments unless an exemption can be identified. The types of securities issues issued by public and independent higher education institutions normally qualify for one or more exemptions, but these exemptions are a privilege rather than an entitlement. In the past, there have been constitutional arguments based on principles of federalism to support and strengthen the exemptions, but the United States Supreme Court decisions in recent years have strongly undercut those constitutional arguments and under present law, the concept of exemptions as a discretionary privilege prevails.

Two principal statutes frame federal securities law regulation. The Securities Act of 1933 is characterized by a system of registration, whereby nonexempted securities must be registered with the Securities and Exchange Commission (SEC) prior to the offering of the securities for sale. The Securities Exchange Act of 1934 is characterized by a system of "periodic reporting," whereby issuers of nonexempt securities must file quarterly, annual, and special event reports with the SEC. The SEC makes such reports available to the public. The 1933 act and the 1934 law also contain other provisions, including anti-fraud rules, from which no securities are exempt.

Municipal securities benefit from exemptions from the registration and reporting provisions of the 1933 and 1934 acts. However, Congress has established the Municipal Securities Rulemaking Board (MSRB), to provide separate regulation of the municipal securities market. The MSRB is discussed in more detail below.

Other significant federal securities laws include the Trust Indenture Act of 1939 and the Investment Company Act of 1940. Principles of securities law liability are found in several of the federal securities laws and include concepts of fraud and insider trading. As a general matter, actions relating to securities, including the distribution of information about upcoming or outstanding securities issues, should not be taken lightly by business officers. Do not make assumptions about what is permissible in this area. Counsel should be included in the capital financing planning team from the earliest stages. Business officers' objectives should be the prevention of legal problems. In the area of the federal securities laws, problems are relatively easily avoided, but are difficult and expensive to resolve when they occur.

The Municipal Securities Rulemaking Board

Congress created the Municipal Securities Rulemaking Board (MSRB) in 1975. The MSRB was formally established by the SEC's appointment of the first board (consisting of 15 members) pursuant to the 1975 Amendments to the Securities Exchange Act. Board members are equally divided among securities firm, bank dealer, and public representatives and are appointed to three year terms. New board members are chosen according to board rules and the public representatives are subject to SEC approval.

The board has a full-time staff, including an office of the general counsel. The board issues its rules in categories of administrative, definitional, and general, as well as interpretive letters and notices. The MSRB rules significantly influence the operations of the municipal securities market and from time to time business officers may become involved in areas where the MSRB rules are controlling or influential. For example, the MSRB underwriting assessment fee is a small element of the costs of issuance for municipal securities; certain MSRB rules apply to the distribution of an official statement disclosure document within proscribed time periods; advertising of municipal securities is governed by an MSRB general rule; and the role of financial advisors is regulated by an MSRB rule to avoid a conflict of interest with the issuer.

The MSRB is particularly interested in the subject of municipal securities disclosure, both in terms of the content of the disclosure and the timing and manner of distribution of disclosure information.

Disclosure

Historically, disclosure in college and university capital financings has taken the form of an official statement. Currently, however, the concept of secondary market disclosure is a vital issue in the municipal securities market. Secondary market disclosure is a variation on the theme of periodic reporting with respect to the Securities Exchange Act of 1934. Business officers should be aware that secondary market disclosure carries both legal liabilities and costs of compliance that are additional to those associated with the historical practice of disclosures made at the time of initial issuance of the securities. Disclosure and secondary market disclosure are areas that business officers should discuss with college financing counsel because the landscape of regulation and policy is in a period of rapid transition that has been ongoing and persistent since 1988. Issues of federal tax law applicable to municipal securities were the "issue of the 1980s" and issues of disclosure with its many variations appear to be the "issue of the 1990s."

In March 1994, the Securities and Exchange Commission proposed public comment amendments to Rule 15c2-12 under the Securities Exchange Act of 1934. These amendments would have the effect of creating a structure for mandatory secondary market disclosure utilizing a nationally recognized municipal securities re-

pository. The commission has allowed a substantial public comment period for these amendments to give municipal market participants the fullest opportunity to comment on these significant changes. Business officers should review the legal requirements, policy considerations, and investor relations aspects of secondary market disclosure with their counsel and investment bankers.

Figure 4-2 provides a representative listing of topics discussed in a representative independent college description to be included in an official statement or a credit review package to be sent to potential credit enhancers and the rating agencies for use during the rating process.

Disclosure has been the subject of many books and articles. Depending on the nature of your questions, NACUBO may be able to refer you to sources of additional information. See appendix D for a description of various NACUBO services.

State Regulation

Each state has its own state securities laws, referred to in the securities industry as "Blue Sky" laws. Most state laws interact efficiently with the federal securities laws, but any offering of bonds directly or indirectly by a higher education institution should include a review of applicable state securities laws during the financing process. In addition, business officers should note that individual state securities laws govern the offering and sale of securities within its borders, so the state securities laws of many more states than the state where the institution is located are likely to be relevant to a financing. The investment banker will arrange for a state securities law review to be performed (typically by underwriter's counsel).

Legal Opinions

Chapter 2 described the capital finance market participants, of whom several were counsel to the various parties to the transaction. In addition, bond counsel is an independent counsel whose role is to opine as to the legality and enforceability of the securities and the tax status of the interest paid on the securities under federal and state tax laws. The opinions listed in figure 4-1 are relatively standard in a higher education financing:

Legal opinions are not guarantees but opinions based on reasonable investigation and reasonable diligence. Opinions are subject to negligence and malpractice types of reviews in the event of negative developments with respect to the financing. It is important for business officers to appreciate that the legal opinion which is not given by an experienced and high-quality counsel is in some respects even more important than the legal opinion which is given because a financing that cannot gain the confidence of counsel should be seriously questioned. Business officers can play a crucial role in setting the tone and

Figure 4-1

BOND COUNSEL VALIDITY OPINION ADDRESSING

Due authorization of the issuer to execute an indenture or adopt a bond resolution as well as to issue the securities

Legal, valid, and binding nature (with respect to the issuer of the bonds or notes) of the indenture or resolution as well as the securities

The enforceability of the pledge made pursuant to the indenture or resolution, as well as the parity standing of the securities being issued with other applicable securities that are outstanding or that are authorized under the indenture or resolution

No conflict of the principal financing documents with other laws, regulations, or court decisions or other documents

Examination of one of the actual bonds or notes, as executed

Federal and state law tax opinions on tax-exempt treatment of the bonds

---

BOND COUNSEL SUPPLEMENTAL OPINION ADDRESSING

Due authorization of the issuer to execute other financing documents such as a loan agreement or some other agreement as well as the bond purchase agreement

Legal, valid, and binding nature (with respect to the issuer of the bonds of notes) of financing documents not covered by the bond counsel validity opinion

An opinion relating to the effectiveness of a legal defeasance in an advance refunding

A form of opinion with respect to counsel's participation in the due diligence review process and a related statement on the absence of material misstatements and omissions (subject to certain qualifications) in certain portions of the official statement disclosure document that were prepared by or derived from documents prepared by bond counsel

Opinion as to exemption from the Securities Act of 1933 and the Trust Indenture Act of 1939

COLLEGE COUNSEL OPINIONS (COMBINATION OF
GENERAL COUNSEL AND FINANCING COUNSEL) ADDRESSING

Due authorization of the institution to execute a loan agreement or a lease
agreement under an indenture or a resolution

Legal, valid, and binding nature (with respect to the college) of the loan agreement
or lease agreement

Opinions as to real estate matters customized to each transaction

Opinion that the Section 501(c)(3) standing of the institution is intact for an
independent college financing

Opinion as to no conflict of the principal financing documents (to which the
institution is a party) with applicable laws and regulations

A form of opinion with respect to counsel's participation in the due diligence
review process and a related statement with respect to the absence of material
misstatements and omissions (subject to certain qualifications) in the official
statement disclosure document

TRUSTEE COUNSEL OPINION ADDRESSING

Due authorization of the trustee to execute an indenture or accept the appointment
as trustee under a resolution

Legal, valid, and binding nature of the indenture or resolution with respect to the
trustee

CREDIT ENHANCEMENT COUNSEL OPINION ADDRESSING

Due authorization of the credit enhancer to deliver the credit enhancement
instrument

Legal, valid, and binding nature of the credit enhancement instrument with respect
to the credit enhancement provider

UNDERWRITER'S COUNSEL OPINION ADDRESSING

A form of opinion with respect to counsel's participation in the due diligence
review process and a related statement with respect to the absence of material
misstatements and omissions (subject to certain qualifications) in the official
statement disclosure document

Opinion as to exemption from the Securities Act of 1933 and the Trust Indenture
Act of 1939

boundaries of discussions and debates with respect to legal opinions.

As a general matter, legal opinions should address the authorization of each party to a major financing document to enter into the applicable agreement. In addition, the legal, valid, and binding nature of each party's critical agreements should be the subject of a counsel's opinion. Other important legal issues will vary with the identity of the financing participants and the structure of the financing.

Questions sometimes arise with respect to the distinction between internal counsel and independent external counsel. An attorney's standard of care and diligence in rendering a legal opinion does not vary, and attorneys are supposed to be independent in their review. Some parties will place importance on receiving an opinion of external counsel, but this point usually is subject to negotiation, particularly if internal counsel is clearly experienced and qualified in the area of law under discussion.

Over the course of a higher education financing, special situation legal opinions are likely to arise. Examples of such opinions could include the following:

Preference Opinions. Certain financing structures raise bankruptcy law questions. The rating agencies routinely seek preference opinions in structured financings such as asset-backed student loan financings. In addition, variable rate transaction structures raise preference issues. Preference opinions can be rendered by a counsel already involved in the transaction as a "special counsel."

Litigation "No Merit" Opinions. "No Merit" opinions can be among the most strenuous legal opinions arising in financing transactions. Situations arise where there is a legal challenge to a financing that is not concluded when the bond issue needs to proceed. To render a "No Merit" opinion, counsel must review the matter and declare that the challenge to the financing has no merit and that a court should rule in favor of the issuer of the securities. A "No Merit" opinion with sufficient credibility can provide sufficient comfort for investors to purchase the securities notwithstanding the ongoing dispute. "No Merit" situations are generally rare and less likely to arise in a higher education financing context than in a governmental issue where issues of taxing power and voting rights can be involved.

Reliance Opinions. Situations may sometimes arise where a counsel is unable to render a particular opinion, but is willing to accept and rely upon the opinion of another counsel. Counsel is entitled to rely on an opinion if he or she believes it is reasonable for the issuing counsel to deliver the opinion. The distinction between reasonable reliance as compared to delivery of the opinion oneself is a technical difference, but one that business officers may encounter from time to time. Reliance opinions are utilized regularly in complex areas of federal tax law, particularly advance refundings and issues involving new types of financing instruments or derivative products. Reliance opinions also can be used to resolve disputes between parties and their counsel as to legal issues that may be inhibiting the progress of a transaction.

Description of an Independent Institution for Various Disclosure Purposes

The following table is representative of the topics that an independent institution could discuss in a section of the official statement disclosure document entitled "Description of the College." This information would be used in disclosure documents prepared at the time of the initial issuance of the securities.

Issues of secondary market disclosure are the subject of a range of industry and regulatory viewpoints at this time. As contrasted with disclosure at the time of initial issuance of the securities, there is not yet a consensus on the proper content or timing of secondary market disclosure. Progress toward a consensus is likely to be made in 1994 as a result of several ongoing regulatory initiatives affecting the municipal securities market. (See figure 4-2.)

Description of a Public Institution for Various Disclosure Purposes

Disclosure for public institutions must be determined on a case-by-case basis and depends on

Figure 4-2

Sample Independent College Disclosure Description Topics

(1) General and Historical Information
(2) Governance
(3) Administration
(4) Institutional Plan
    (a)   *Academic Affairs*
    (b)   *Enrollment*
    (c)   *Facilities*
    (d)   *Development*
    (e)   *Finance*
(5) Academic Programs
    (a)   *General Study Programs*
    (b)   *Special Programs*
(6) Accreditations and Memberships
(7) External Support for Research and Instructional Development
(8) Faculty
(9) Students
(10) Enrollment and Admissions (fall semesters for past five years)
(11) Freshman Application and Enrollment (fall semesters for past five years)
(12) Transfer Application and Enrollment (fall semesters for past five years)
(13) Graduate Application and Enrollment (fall semesters for past five years)
(14) Freshman Geographic Distribution (fall semesters for past five years)
(15) SAT Scores of Entering Freshmen (fall semesters for past five years)
(16) Facilities
    (a)   *Overview*
    (b)   *Academic Buildings*
    (c)   *College Libraries*
    (d)   *Residence Halls*
    (e)   *Office Space*
    (f)   *Special Purpose Buildings*
    (g)   *Deferred Maintenance and Renovations*
(17)   Student Life
(18)   Tuition and Fees
(19)   Room and Board Charges
(20)   Financial and Governmental Aid
(21)   College Financial Information
    (a)   *Accounting Matters*
    (b)   *Management's Discussion of the College's Operating and Financial Performance*
    (c)   *Budgeting Procedures*
(22)   Outstanding Long-Term Debt
(23)   Endowment and Similar Funds
(24)   Fund Raising
(25)   Employee Relations
(26)   Pension and Retirement Programs
(27)   Insurance
(28)   Litigation
(29)   Future Plans of the College

the nature of the pledged security and the institution's financial position. In all cases, the financing team should review the role of state and other governmental appropriations to determine the appropriate disclosure approach. In extreme cases of dependence, a public college disclosure section could resemble that of a state general obligation bond. An extreme case of autonomy could result in a disclosure section that resembles that of an independent institution. Public colleges normally can expect to (1) include a section describing their relationship to the state; (2) disclose the level of state appropriations in the financial sections of the official statement; and (3) discuss the possibility of a reduction in state appropriations as a potential risk of investing in this security.

PART II

Financing Purposes

❖ FIVE ❖

New Money Projects

One of the most common purposes for undergoing a debt financing at a college or university is new money projects. Some examples of such projects are described below.

Academic Facilities and Libraries

Academic facilities and libraries represent the essence of the higher education institution. Without state-of-the-art academic facilities, neither the large research university nor the small liberal arts college can justify its costs to students in the current education market. Capital financing for academic facilities can enable an institution to compete successfully by attracting quality faculty members and maintaining quality programs for students.

The methodology of determining capital needs for academic facilities varies with each institution. It is often obvious, for example, that a library is gradually becoming inadequate, but an institution must decide the point at which it becomes imperative to address the need for expansion or reconfiguration through the use of modern technology. Each institution also decides in its own manner whether science facilities or a computer center will receive capital allocations, even if both can independently justify the support. An institution's tolerance of older facilities for certain departments that are considered less capital-intensive is a case-by-case proposition. Often, these generalizations are inaccurate when one considers state-of-the-art teaching techniques in areas as diverse as education, psychology, arts and music, foreign languages, and economics. Teaching methods ranging from computer simulations to adaptations of "lab" approaches have made many traditional space configurations and lecture halls outmoded. Institutions need constant capital infusions to adapt to current teaching techniques as well as new substantive developments.

Dormitories and Residence Halls

Because of their revenue-producing character, dormitories and residence halls differ categorically from many other higher education financing purposes. In the past, many institutions have used these revenues as security for capital financings by pledging the cash flow in a revenue bond financing. Upon closer inspection, however, many of these revenue bond transactions were double-barrelled security, with an underlying general obligation pledge of the institution's tuition and fees should the revenues prove to be insufficient to pay debt service. Dormitories and residence halls have more recently been part of the general trend toward "general obligation" pledges in higher education financings. Chapter 9 provides an examination of the factors that influence the choice of a security pledge and an overview of security pledge choices.

The revenue-producing character of dormitories and residence halls is more significant than ever before for internal capital financing considerations, however. The revenues offer the potential ability to undertake the project even during periods of general fiscal restraints. If the project can be substantially or totally self-supporting, then other considerations such as competitive position for students and developing the character of the institution can become primary considerations in the decision to undertake the construction or renovation project. See the introduction of this guide for a discussion of the policy bases for capital financing.

Athletic and Recreation Facilities

An increasing number of colleges and universities no longer view their athletic and recreational facilities as optional services or items to be easily postponed at the first sign of budget difficulty. Because of increased public interest in athletic activities, such facilities have become a central element of student recruiting and retention at many institutions.

Whether athletic and recreation facilities become revenue-producing depends on the availability of student fees and outside income. Many of these factors are functions of the location and character of the institution and outside the control of business officers. However, for many institutions, the design of the facility will dictate the mix of revenue and nonrevenue based services the facility will offer. Business officers should take an active role in the planning of the facility and should inject the discipline of revenue projections into the plan of finance for the facility.

Business officers should not rely on such projections, however, without review by counsel experienced in tax-exempt finance. The federal tax code and regulations include provisions restricting the "private use" of tax-exempt bond financed facilities, and a development plan that inadvertently violates these parameters may cause the institution to forgo the large economic benefit of the spread between tax-exempt and taxable interest rates.

Infrastructure

For the purposes of this section, infrastructure is the support facilities of a college or university that are not related to the construction or renovation of a building-specific project. Examples of infrastructure include steam pipes, water and sewer lines, common area lighting, utilities such as telecommunication lines and electrical system support, and basic facility renewals and replacements such as roofing and maintenance of exterior facades.

In the past, colleges and universities funded infrastructure expenditures from internal cash sources, incorporated them into more general equipment financings, or avoided making necessary investments. However, now some institutions have separately identified and managed infrastructure programs. Princeton University has had such a program since the mid-1980s, which includes a constant revolving $150 million tax-exempt bond component using 10-year maturi-

ties. As bonds mature each year, another annual tax-exempt bond issue of 10-year maturity is implemented to return the outstanding amount to $150 million and provide new funds for infrastructure work and maintenance during that year.

Deferred Maintenance

Annual financial needs for physical plant maintenance at colleges and universities are very large. In many cases, these needs have been inadequately funded in the past, resulting in the accumulation of a category known as "deferred maintenance," which is simply those projects that should be undertaken to bring existing property, plant, and equipment to a state of good repair. Deferred maintenance is not new construction, although at some level, certain facilities are obsolete or beyond reasonable repair.

Deferring maintenance is one of the easiest budgetary traps for a college or university to fall into. Institutional pressures from academic, student, and administrative constituencies can make the decision to defer maintenance the point of least resistance. Yet the decision to do so can undermine the basis of future budget stability by accumulating costs that can be ignored for varying periods of time, but are sure to surface eventually, often in the form of a more critical and expensive problem.

Capital financing can serve as an intermediary between cash budget allocations and the total deferral of needed maintenance. It is important, however, that capital financing be amortized over the useful life of the project to prevent the deferred maintenance problem from becoming a deferred debt problem.

To learn more about the principles of deferred maintenance, consult NACUBO's *Managing the Facilities Portfolio*. This publication, developed by Coopers & Lybrand in 1991, remains the most comprehensive review of the deferred maintenance issue available, and the principles of defining, identifying, and addressing the deferred maintenance problem at individual institutions and across the higher education industry are fully applicable today. A copy of the book can be obtained from NACUBO.

Equipment

Equipment financing can be analyzed either as a component for another project, such as construction or renovation, or as a stand alone project. Institutions supporting large research activities may find that substantial capital financing needs can be traced solely to equipment needs. The financial analysis supporting capital financing of equipment needs analyzes factors that are essentially similar to longer-term projects: matching capital expenditures to the useful life of the financed project; achieving the lowest true cost of funds after taking into account opportunity costs of cash financing; and managing the timing of projects in an environment of scarce financial resources.

Land Acquisition

Capital financing for land acquisition can be important to an institution either in connection with the development of a specific project or in the context of the acquisition of land for the cosmetic appearance of the campus, future expansion, or use in a future project.

Health Care Facilities as Part of a University

Health care financing is an area mixing dramatic shifts and steady transitions, and no health care organization is immune from the forces of change. Such forces include national health care policy, but also are localized to the extent of intensive market competition in individual service areas.

Health care organizations require access to the capital markets for many reasons, including the following:

Financing Capital Investments in Plant. Hospital physical plants are capital intensive and are more vulnerable to the effects of aging. While an old building may be a positive or neutral feature in a university facility, it is always a distinct negative factor for a hospital.

Financing Capital Investment in Equipment. Advances in medical technology are costly and con-stant. Significant capital expenditures are necessary on a regular basis to obtain new equipment and to replace existing equipment.

Using Financing to Preserve Cash and Liquidity. Uncertainty in the health care community has created a disincentive to use cash on hand to fund capital projects to any significant extent. Rating agencies consider cash on hand and liquidity to be key benchmarks of fiscal stability for hospitals during this period of financial stress and change.

Using Financing as a Management Tool. Many health care organizations have an ongoing interest in health care accounts receivable financing. This area has not been easily integrated into permissible tax-exempt financing techniques, which has restricted its use. In spite of their restrictions, however, receivables programs are used by some entities.

Responding to Health Care Reform. Many health care organizations (including but not limited to hospitals and hospital systems) require capital to implement their strategic plans. These strategic plans can include merger or acquisition of other facilities or doctor practice groups and the development of more fully integrated health care delivery and payment systems.

Health care facilities at universities generally fall into two general categories. They can be integrated with the university for legal status (the same 501(c)(3) corporation) or financing pledge or both. For example, hospital bonds issued in connection with Yale University and Georgetown University are structured as unified through the mechanism of a university guarantee. The University of Virginia has issued bonds for hospital facilities using its general revenue pledge (the net revenues of the hospital are but one stream of income that supports the general revenue pledge). Health care facilities can be separated from the university by legal status or financing pledge. Stanford University Hospital, for example, maintains a bond rating separate from Stanford University.

SIX

Refinancings and Refundings

Refundings

A refunding involves the issuance of bonds, the proceeds of which are used to pay debt service (principal, interest, and if necessary, premium) on any other outstanding bonds ("old bonds"). A refunding may be "current," in which proceeds of the refunding bonds are expanded in payment of debt service or redemption price of the refunded bonds within 90 days of the issuance of the refunding bonds, or "advance," which includes all other refundings. Generally, in a current refunding, the refunded bonds are called or mature within that 90 day period. The principal distinction is made for federal tax purposes. In an advance refunding, the institution uses the proceeds of the new bonds to purchase highly rated securities (usually U.S. government securities) for placement in an escrow. These escrowed securities are used to satisfy debt service requirements on the old bonds until their call date and then to pay the remaining principal, and call premium, if any, of the old bonds.

For example, assume an institution has outstanding $10 million of 1987 bonds with an average interest rate of 8 percent that are callable on and after July 1, 1997, at a premium of 102 percent. Also assume that interest rates have fallen 2 percentage points and the institution wishes to take advantage of the resulting debt service savings. The institution would issue bonds at the lower interest rate and use the proceeds of the bonds to purchase securities to place in an escrow. The escrow would be structured so that principal and interest on the 1987 bonds would be paid through July 1, 1997, and the remaining escrowed securities would be sufficient to pay the principal of the 1987 bonds and call premium of 2 percent on July 1, 1997.

The federal tax law imposes many restrictions on tax-exempt refundings including the number of times outstanding bonds may be refunded, the yield at which escrowed securities may be invested, and the length of time refunding bonds may be outstanding.

Most frequently, institutions refund their existing securities to take advantage of lower interest rates. Such refunding is referred to as a "high-to-low" refunding (higher interest rate debt is being refunded with lower interest rate debt).

Occasionally, institutions choose to refund existing debt because restrictions or covenants are associated with the existing debt that the institution considers to be unnecessarily burdensome. By using the proceeds of the refunding bonds to "defease" the old bonds, the institution is released from the requirements incorporated in the documents underlying the old bonds. Also, the security underlying the old bonds is released upon a defeasance. For example, if an institution provided a first mortgage on one or more of its assets as security for holders of old bonds and circumstances have changed such that, in today's environment, it is now possible to issue bonds with the sole source of security for bondholders being the general, unsecured obligation of the institution, it may be advantageous to issue refunding bonds even though the institution may recognize little or no savings.

Other reasons for refunding prior bonds may be to restructure debt service. An institution may "stretch out" its debt service payments, thus lowering annual payments, as well as reallocating debt service among various years.

Refunding Bonds

There are three basic types of refunding bonds: fixed rate, variable rate, and cross-over refunding. Each type is described below.

Fixed Rate. A fixed rate refunding occurs when an institution refunds existing debt (bearing fixed or variable rate interest) with bonds bearing a fixed interest rate.

Variable Rate. A variable rate refunding occurs when an institution refunds existing debt (bearing fixed or variable rates) with bonds bearing variable interest rates.

Cross-Over Refunding. Occasionally, an institution is prohibited from defeasing or may not choose to defease existing bonds to their first call date. In such an event, an institution may issue refunding bonds and use the escrowed securities purchased with the proceeds of the refunding bonds to pay the interest on the refunding bonds until the call date of the old bonds, and, at such call date, to pay the outstanding principal and call premium, if any, on the old bonds. The refunding bonds commence principal amortization after the call date of the old bonds. In effect, the institution continues to pay the debt service on the old bonds until their call date, at which time the institution begins to pay the debt service on the new bonds.

Measuring Savings

A common method of measuring savings is by expressing savings—the difference between the aggregate debt service over the life of the old bonds and the aggregate debt service of the refunding bonds—in terms of present value. Such a calculation is derived by discounting, at a certain rate (for example, the rate on the refunding bonds), the annual savings to present day dollars. Present value savings often are stated as a percentage of outstanding principal of the refunded bonds or refunding bonds, and such a percentage is used as threshold for determining whether a refunding is necessary. For example, many issuers of tax-exempt bonds choose not to effect a high-to-low refunding unless present value savings equal at least 5 percent of the principal amount of the refunded bonds or refunding bonds. The critical assumption in a present value calculation is the choice of the discount rate to be applied.

Cash savings represent the reduction in total debt service dollars paid over the life of the refunding bond issue compared to the refunded bond issue. Most market participants recognize that the time value of money makes a cash savings analysis incorrect as the sole measure of savings. However, knowledge of the cash savings figure will make it easier for business officers to test the different effects of changes in the discounting rate assumption that is inherent in a present value savings measurement.

Advance Refundings

The advance refunding of an outstanding bond issue is a widely accepted tool of financial management for the tax-exempt issuer. This section will examine the rationale for utilizing advance refunding, provide an overview of advance refunding techniques, and describe some of the legal considerations relating to advance refunding.

Advance refunding is a financing method that provides for the retirement of an outstanding issue of tax-exempt bonds through the issuance of a new series of tax-exempt bonds. The proceeds of the new series are invested in taxable securities, usually U.S. Treasury obligations, the principal of and interest on which provide for the payment of debt service on either the outstanding bonds or the new series until the date on which the outstanding bonds are to be retired. Some common terms in all advance refundings include:

Outstanding Bonds: The bonds to be advance refunded.

Refunding Bonds: The new bonds issued to provide the funds to accomplish the advance refunding.

Escrow Fund: The fund that contains cash or securities sufficient to provide payment of the debt service on either the outstanding bonds or the refunding bonds until the outstanding bonds are retired. The net proceeds from the refunding bonds are used to purchase the investments for the escrow fund. The escrow fund is held and administered by a trustee, which almost always is the trustee for the refunded bonds.

Objectives

A college or university would choose to use the advance refunding technique for any of the following three reasons:

To Reduce Debt Service—If refunding bonds are issued at rates lower than those of the outstanding bonds, the overall debt service of the college or university may be reduced. In analyzing this reduction in debt service, it is important to realize that the timing of the savings achieved through advance refunding is a function of the structure of the refunding bond issue.

To Restructure Restrictive Outstanding Debt—A college or university may structure a refunding issue in many ways. Advanced refunding can help an institution lengthen or shorten the maturity of its indebtedness.

To Eliminate or Amend Restrictive Indenture Provisions—Through the issue of advance refunding, outstanding bonds may be *defeased.* Once the outstanding bonds are defeased, they are discharged as an obligation and the institution is no longer required to observe the security provisions contained in the trust indenture or bond resolution for the outstanding bonds. When a college or university first enters the bond market, it may be necessary to incorporate restrictive provisions and covenants in its trust indenture. Such provisions and covenants may become unnecessary as the institution gains experience and acceptance in the bond market. Advance refunding allows the institution to defease the restrictive trust indenture and adopt a more manageable class of provisions and covenants in the refunding bonds.

The terms of the original bond issue form the contractual basis for the subsequent defeasance of the bond issue. These contractual parameters, together with federal tax law requirements, make the structuring and execution of a refunding and defeasance a highly technical transaction apart from the challenge of marketing the securities to achieve the best interest rates for the institution.

Types of Advance Refunding

There are three basic categories of advance refunding: standard defeasance (net) refunding, crossover refunding, and full cash defeasance (gross) refunding. Each category is described below.

Standard Defeasance (Net) Refunding—In a standard defeasance, the proceeds of the refunding bonds are used to purchase investments for the escrow fund. Both the principal and interest from the investments in the escrow fund are used to pay debt service on the outstanding bonds. The revenue stream previously used to provide debt service on the outstanding bonds is used for debt service on the refunding bonds. Since debt service on the outstanding bonds is provided for by the escrow fund, where bond indentures and local laws permit, the outstanding bonds are defeased and no longer considered an obligation of the institution. (See Figure 6-1.)

Crossover Refunding—In a crossover refunding, the refunding bond proceeds are used to purchase investments for the escrow fund. Prior to the call date of the outstanding bonds, the interest earned on the investments in the escrow fund is used to pay interest on the refunding bonds and the institution's revenues continue to pay debt service on the outstanding bonds. On the call date of the outstanding bonds, the principal amount of the escrow fund is used to pay the principal and call premium, if any, on the outstanding bonds. After the call date, the institution's revenues pay debt service on the refunding bonds. For a crossover refunding, the initial principal required for deposit in the escrow fund, and accordingly the amount of the refunding bonds, is determined by the amount of principal and premium required to discharge the outstanding bonds on their call date. A crossover refunding requires that the interest earned on the escrow fund investments (together with the other moneys escrowed for the payment) must be at least equal to the interest payable on the refunding bonds during the escrow period. If this is not the case, the escrow fund investments will not produce sufficient interest to pay debt service on the refunding bonds. In this type of advance refunding, the institution's objective usually is not realized until the call date of the outstanding bonds. (See Figure 6-2.)

Full Cash Defeasance (Gross) Refunding—This type of advance refunding is similar in structure to a standard defeasance refunding except that only the *principal* of the investments in the escrow fund is used to pay the debt service on the out-

Figure 6-1. Standard Defeasance (Net) Refunding

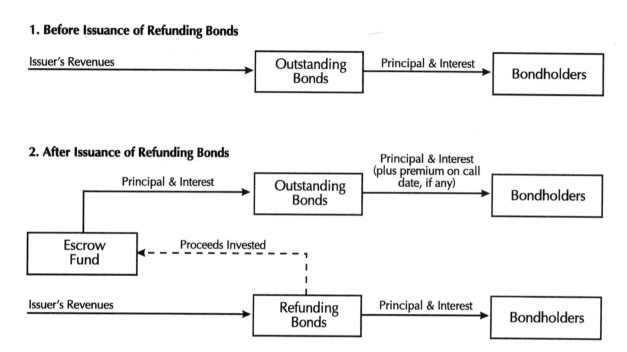

1. Before Issuance of Refunding Bonds

Issuer's Revenues → Outstanding Bonds → Principal & Interest → Bondholders

2. After Issuance of Refunding Bonds

Principal & Interest → Outstanding Bonds → Principal & Interest (plus premium on call date, if any) → Bondholders

Escrow Fund ← Proceeds Invested ←

Issuer's Revenues → Refunding Bonds → Principal & Interest → Bondholders

standing bonds. The interest earned on the escrow fund investments is used to pay a portion of the debt service on the refunding bonds. The revenues previously used to pay debt service on the outstanding bonds are used to provide the remaining portion of the debt service on the refunding bonds.

Full cash defeasance requires the issuance of a greater principal amount of refunding bonds than standard defeasance in order to produce sufficient funds to purchase the required principal amount of investments for the escrow fund. Therefore, the debt service on the refunding bonds will most likely exceed the debt service on the outstanding bonds due to the increased principal amount of the refunding bonds. However, because the interest from the escrow fund investments is not required to pay debt service on the outstanding bonds, using such interest to pay a portion of the debt service on the refunding bonds may produce a saving in the debt service that must be supported by the institution's revenues.

The Internal Revenue Service (IRS) regulations pertaining to advance refundings require, in most cases, the use of two refunding bond issues when full cash defeasance is used. One issue of refunding bonds (generally referred to as "special obligations bonds") is structured so that its debt service is paid entirely from the interest earned on the escrow fund investments, and a second refunding bond issue is supported solely by the institution's revenues. The proceeds from both refunding bond issues are used to purchase the investments for the escrow fund. Since the escrow fund generally contains U.S. Treasury obligations, the special obligation bond issue supported by the interest earned on such obligations may be sold at lower interest rates than the second refunding bond issue, which is paid from the institution's revenues. While the principal amount of the escrow fund is determined by the amount of principal, interest, and premium, if any, required to repay the outstanding bonds, the interest earned on the escrow fund investments is determined by the interest rates of both refunding bond issues. (Actual investment rates will be influenced by both market conditions and tax law limitations on allowable investments.) (See figure 6-3.)

Legal Issues

The laws of most states expressly authorize the issuance of refunding bonds and, in most cases, statutory refunding provisions have been interpreted to permit advance refunding transactions. State laws may, however, impose special requirements on the issuance of refunding bonds, such as limitations on the aggregate principal amount of the refunding bonds or requirements that minimum benefits be realized by issuers in refunding transactions. In addition, state laws may restrict the type of refunding transaction that may be employed, by requiring, for example, standard defeasance or a full cash defeasance refunding.

Most recently adopted bond resolutions contain provisions that authorize the defeasance of the resolution if moneys or obligations adequate to pay the bonds are deposited with a trustee. Some bond resolutions, including a significant number of older resolutions, either do not contain such provisions or impose more stringent requirements for defeasance. For example, some resolutions provide that defeasance may be accomplished only if the outstanding bonds are called at their earliest possible redemption date or only on a full cash basis. In some states, judicial interpretations may address some restrictions of older documentation. In other states, the refund-

Figure 6-2. Crossover Refunding

1. Before Issuance of Refunding Bonds

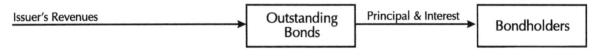

2. After Issuance of Refunding Bonds

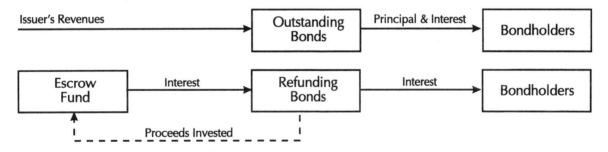

3. At the Call Date of Outstanding Bonds

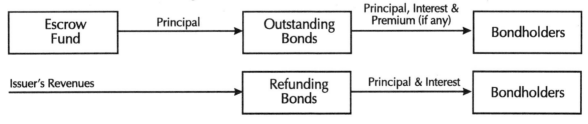

Figure 6-3. Full Cash Defeasance (Gross) Refunding

1. Before Issuance of Refunding Bonds

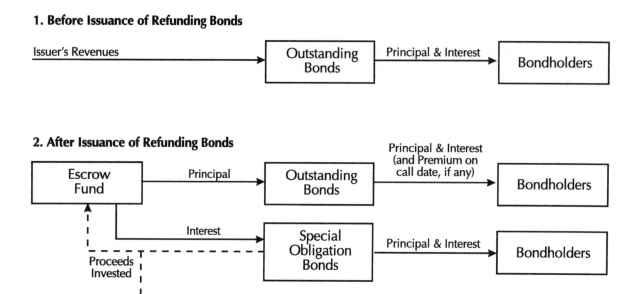

2. After Issuance of Refunding Bonds

ing transaction may be effected without defeasance by the deposit with a trustee of United States obligations adequate to pay the outstanding bonds. The refunding bonds would be secured by a lien on the revenues of the issuer that is junior to the lien of the outstanding bonds but, because the United States obligations are held as security for the outstanding bonds, the refunding bonds may be marketed as if they were secured by a senior lien.

Many bond resolutions contain provisions authorizing the issuance of refunding bonds on a parity with other bonds issued under the resolution. An issuer that determines to issue additional parity bonds under an existing bond resolution to refund outstanding bonds, issued under the resolution, must comply with these provisions. In many cases, these provisions require that in each year the debt service on the refunding bonds not exceed the debt service on the outstanding bonds being refunded. In situations where all of the institution's outstanding parity bonds are re-

funded and a defeasance is obtained, the refunding bonds may be issued under a new resolution without regard to the terms of the existing bond resolution relating to refunding bonds.

Under the Internal Revenue Code (IRC) an issue of refunding bonds will be "arbitrage bonds," the interest on which will be subject to federal income taxation if, subject to certain limited exceptions, any portion of the proceeds is invested directly or indirectly in taxable securities the yield on which exceeds the yield on the refunding bonds. As a result, the proceeds of refunding bonds sometimes must be invested in United States Treasury obligations at a yield below that otherwise available in the market. That may involve investment in U.S. Treasury obligations of the State and Local Government Series (SLGs), a special series of Treasury obligations designed to facilitate compliance by issuers with the arbitrage rules. Expenses of the transaction, including underwriters' discount, counsel fees and printing costs, may not be taken into account in computing yield, but credit enhancement fees (e.g., bond insurance premiums or letter of credit fees) can be taken into account if the present value of the fees are less than present value on the interest savings attributable to the credit enhancement. The IRS has interpreted the IRC to prohibit any form of indirect arbitrage through a prohibition against the use of an "abusive arbitrage device" that both overburdens the market for tax-exempt securities and permits the issuer to obtain a material financial advantage from the difference between the yield on tax-exempt and taxable securities. Compliance with the arbitrage restrictions entails careful analysis by counsel and extensive and complex mathematical computations that may efficiently and safely be performed only through the use of specially designed computer software.

Using Limited Tax-Exempt Advance Refunding Opportunities Wisely

The tax code (IRC) limits the number of times a tax-exempt security can be advance refunded. An advance refunding is one in which the proceeds of the refunding bond issue are used to pay debt service on the refunded bond issue more than 90 days after the issuance of the refunding bonds. The limitations are:
- new money financings issued before January 1, 1986, may be refunded twice, and all advance refundings completed prior to March 15, 1986, collectively count as only one advance refunding;
- new money financings issued on or after January 1, 1986, may be advance refunded once;

- current refundings (in which the proceeds of the refunding bond issue are used pay off the refunded bond issue within 90 days after the issuance of the refunding bonds) may be done without limitation as to number;
- for 501(c)(3) entities, both the refunded and refunding bonds are considered outstanding for purposes of the $150 million cap on outstanding tax-exempt securities until the refunded bonds are actually redeemed; and
- with respect to the $150 million cap, the first refunding of a pre-January 1, 1986 bond issue may take place without regard to the $150 million cap, although measurement of issuance capacity for all future issues will require the double counting of refunded bonds, which is described above.

Business officers should develop a refunding strategy with their investment banker, financial advisor, and financing counsel. The sequencing of refunding and new money transactions can be critical, as it was for Seton Hall University when the institution used the "pre-1986" refunding rule to exceed the $150 million cap with respect to bonds originally issued in 1985 after Seton Hall had completed all of its new money financings and brought its outstanding bond total relatively close to the $150 million limit. The relative value of paying a small premium to investors at the time of issuance to purchase a reduced call protection period of less than the standard 10 years should be considered. Changes in law in the refunding area are expected to occur regularly, and business officers should stay up to date on issues and current techniques.

❖ SEVEN ❖

Student Loan Funding

Students and administrators see student loans as simply a useful way to finance a college education. But student loans, particularly federally guaranteed student loans, have become a multi-billion dollar business. Banks originate them; states guarantee them; for-profit and not-for-profit institutions service them; the U.S. Department of Education regulates, subsidizes, and reinsures them; and public and independent financial institutions purchase them. Over the past 15 years, federally guaranteed student loans have contributed more than $142 billion to higher education financing costs. Approximately $30 billion of those loans have been financed with student loan revenue bonds.

The last section of this chapter refers to the August 1993 enactment of federal legislation, which will process federal government loans directly through colleges and universities rather than through banks. The new procedures, referred to as "direct loans," will comprise 5 percent of the loans in the 1994–1995 academic year and will increase to 60 percent of the loans by the 1998–1999 academic year, at which time Congress will review the status of the program.

The direct loan program will not replace all other methods of student loan financing. Direct loans are authorized to reach 60 percent of student loans over a five year transition period. The remaining 40 percent of the market is expected to attract fewer market participants than at present, but several industry leaders have separately projected significant growth in the volume of total student loans to partially offset the new federal direct loan program.

The direct loan program will cause changes in student loan funding. Conventional student loan revenue bonds will be affected. New initiatives such as the loan programs financed with general obligation indebtedness of individual colleges and universities are likely to expand as the loan supply seeks an equilibrium with demand and creative higher education professionals attempt to maximize their institution's assistance to prospective students. (See chapter 1 for a case study discussion of general obligation funding of student loans.) Market participants will change. The size of the student loan market will change and, almost inevitably, expand substantially when viewed as a whole. Despite the significant changes encompassed within direct loans, further legal alterations can be assumed and the potential clearly exists for further dramatic developments in the public policy and political arenas.

This chapter will provide an overview of the conventional education loan industry from the standpoint of the public and private entities that finance them prior to the implementation of the large direct loan program. It will emphasize the primary contribution of the capital markets to education loan finance up to this time: student loan revenue bonds.

The Federal Student Loan Program

Student loans, particularly federally guaranteed student loans, are often the backbone of a student's financial aid package. Financial aid administrators have become experts at navigating the maze of regulation and red tape that accompanies the lending process. But attaining this expertise has been worthwhile; a federally guaranteed loan can contribute up to $7,500 per year, at favorable rates and terms, to a student or parent.

The federal student loan program as it exists today is formally known as the Federal Family Education Loan (FFEL) Program. The FFEL program, administered by the Department of Education, is the successor to the Guaranteed Student Loan (GSL) program, which in turn was an outgrowth of the now-defunct Federally Insured Student Loan (FISL) program. FFEL loans are governed by Title IV of the Higher Education Act of 1965 (HEA), as amended. The federal program changes constantly, as financial aid administrators know only too well; the HEA has been reauthorized and amended at least once every five years since 1976, most recently in late 1992.

The HEA creates three categories of loans eligible for an indirect federal guarantee: Stafford loans for dependent students, PLUS/SLS loans for parents and independent students, and Consolidation loans for graduates. Full- or part-time students attending accredited institutions and meeting certain income limits may obtain one of these loans from an eligible lender. Eligible lenders are mostly, but not exclusively, banks.

The HEA stipulates maximum rates of interest, annual and cumulative borrowing limits, and payment terms for each kind of loan. The maximum interest rate, depending on the type of loan and when it is made, can either be a fixed rate of 7 percent to 10 percent, or else a variable rate of 3.1 percent to 3.25 percent above the yield on 3-month or 1 year Treasury bills, subject to a maximum of 9 percent to 12 percent. The maximum term can be from 10 to 15 years, subject to a minimum monthly payment.

Loans are often subsidized as well as guaranteed. In many cases, the Department of Education pays the borrower's interest while the student is in school or in qualified "grace" or "deferment" periods. Further, the Department of Education pays the lender an interest subsidy, called "special allowance," when short-term interest rates rise. (The borrower does not receive special allowance payments—these are paid directly to the lender—but the borrower does receive the benefit indirectly in the form of a lower interest rate.) Finally, under some circumstances, the borrower may receive an interest rebate from the lender when short-term interest rates decline.

Originating a Student Loan

It takes more than just a bank to create a student loan. The student's loan application initiates a process that will eventually include not just the lender and the Department of Education, but also a servicer, a guarantor, and quite possibly a secondary market purchaser.

The original *lender* can be a bank, insurance company, credit union, or designated nonprofit or public entity. Most lenders are banks; some 100 lenders originated 68.1 percent of student loans made in 1991.

Large lenders do their own servicing, but most lenders contract with a specialized servicer to handle billing, collections, and administration of the majority of student loans. As might be imagined, servicing student loans poses very different challenges than servicing, for example, home mortgages. Student loans are highly regulated; new graduates are more mobile than homeowners; and perhaps most important, a student loan has no physical collateral. (It's hard to repossess an education.) In addition, a student loan is much more costly to service than a mortgage, due not only to its complexity but also to its relatively small size.

Another party to the loan is the *guarantor*. Contrary to popular belief, guaranteed student loans are not guaranteed directly by the federal government. Rather, the guarantee is provided by a special purpose intermediary, which is in turn reinsured by the Department of Education. A guarantor is the single state agency or not-for-profit corporation designated by a state to administer the loan program in that state. There are currently 47 guarantors. (One nonprofit corporation serves several states.) Guarantors pay the lender 100 percent[4] of defaulted principal and accrued interest, out of reserves that are funded partly from "points" paid by the borrowers. The Department of Education later reimburses the guarantor for the net claims it has paid. Reimbursement on defaults exceeding certain levels can be less than 100 percent, but in practice the guarantors are generally reimbursed in full.

The Secondary Market

The five parties discussed above—borrower, lender, servicer, guarantor, and government—create the student loan. But often it takes a sixth party, the *secondary market purchaser,* to create the capital with which new loans are made.

The secondary market purchaser provides liquidity to lenders. Some of the bigger banks, notably Citibank, Chemical Bank, and Norwest Bank, are equipped to service and finance their own loan portfolios over the long-term. Most lenders, by contrast, prefer to sell their loans shortly after origination, usually while the student is still in school or recently graduated. Lenders that sell loans before borrowers begin to repay can take their profits much earlier and avoid the need to establish a sophisticated servicing and financing operation.

Secondary market purchasers are equipped to finance and service student loans for the long-term. There are three major classes of purchasers: for-profit lenders, the Student Loan Marketing Association (Sallie Mae), and the tax-exempt state secondary markets.

For-Profit Lenders and Sallie Mae

A handful of the large banks that are equipped to hold and finance loans over the long term will from time to time purchase portfolios from other, smaller banks. The biggest single purchaser and owner of student loans, however, is Sallie Mae. Sallie Mae is a private, for-profit organization that was sponsored by Congress in the 1972 amendments to the HEA.

Sallie Mae funds itself in the capital markets with a combination of stocks, bonds, notes, and debentures. While Sallie Mae is not a federal agency, its credit is perceived as similar to an agency's. As a consequence of this credit strength, Sallie Mae enjoys a very low cost of funds, compared with that of private sector borrowers. This low cost of capital, together with the operating efficiencies gained from its large loan volume, enables Sallie Mae to offer lenders a very competitive price on portfolios that meet its criteria.

However, many portfolios do not meet Sallie Mae's criteria, and many lenders have preferred for other reasons not to sell their loans to Sallie Mae. For these lenders and for these portfolios, Sallie Mae does not offer an acceptable source of liquidity.

State Secondary Market Agencies

By the late 1970s, it had become clear that not all eligible students were able to obtain the loans to which they were entitled. In some parts of the country, banks were simply not making enough loans to meet the needs of students in their communities. Elsewhere, many of the banks that were making loans became interested in obtaining an easier and cheaper source of liquidity for a wider variety of loans than was offered by Sallie Mae.

The states responded to this demand for capital by creating or designating agencies, authorities, or nonprofit corporations to purchase, sell, or in some cases originate, student loans. These entities are generically called "state secondary market agencies" even though they are seldom state agencies and may not primarily be secondary market makers. By the 1990s, 42 state secondary market makers were making and purchasing student loans in 36 states (Texas has more than one secondary market maker).

Subject to a great many qualifications, state designated secondary market makers are eligible for tax-exempt financing. Their access to this relatively inexpensive source of funds, together with their nonprofit status, enable these agencies to finance student loans even where Sallie Mae cannot. In many states, the state secondary market maker acts as the lender of last resort; in at least one instance it makes a market specifically in delinquent loans. In many states, the secondary market maker also takes on the job of marketing the federal student loan program to local lenders. The main source of financing for these designated state agencies is tax-exempt student loan revenue bonds.

Student Loan Bonds

The first bonds backed by federally guaranteed student loans were issued in the late 1970s. By 1981, the student loan bond market had grown into a small but significant portion of the overall municipal revenue bond market: 21 issues totalling $1.2 billion were sold in that year. Since that time, student loan bonds, while remaining a "niche" business for investors and investment banks, have continued to represent a substantial source of capital for issuers and a useful investment vehicle for purchasers. From 1980 to the end of 1992, student loan bond issuers sold 460 issues totalling $27.6 billion. In 1992, 89 issues for $5.1 billion represented 2 percent of the tax-exempt revenue bond market.

Student loan bonds are revenue bonds. The proceeds of a student loan bond issue are used to purchase a portfolio of student loans. The revenues produced by that portfolio—principal and interest payments by borrowers, guarantee payments, federal subsidies paid by the Department of Education, investment income on reserves and other invested funds, and the proceeds of any sale of student loans are pledged to the repayment of the bonds. Other sources of security, such as bond insurance, letters of credit, or other third-party credit enhancement, may also be used to support the bonds as well. Within this general framework, several different financing structures have evolved over the years.

Tax-Exempt Structures

The simplest type of student loan bond issue is the *fixed rate, long-term revenue bond,* wherein the issuer sells one class of bonds supported solely by pledged student loan revenues. Bonds of this type are typically structured as serial maturities, or as serial and term bonds, whose final maturity corresponds to the longest expected loan payments, about 10 to 15 years. The amount and timing of debt service corresponds to the projected receipts of revenue. Revenues received earlier than projected (because of a variation in default experience, loan size, deferment experience, or interest rate levels, among other reasons) are used either to purchase additional loans or to redeem bonds in advance of maturity. This simple structure, generally awarded an "A" rating by Moody's and Standard & Poor's, was the basic form of tax-exempt student loan finance for much of the late 1970s and early 1980s.

But long-term fixed rate issues can be too expensive a source of funds for a portfolio of student loans when interest rates are high. When rates rose in the early 1980s, issuers turned to the *short-term "takeout"* transaction structure. In a takeout transaction, the issuer sells a single two- to five-year maturity, and a third party—a commercial bank or other lender—agrees to purchase loans, at a specified price, at the issuer's option, before the maturity of the bonds. At maturity, the issuer seeks to refinance the bonds; if refinancing is unavailable, the issuer can sell the loans to the third party and use the proceeds of the sale to retire the bonds. Takeout deals were generally rated AA or even AAA, based on the credit rating of the third party takeout provider. Still, takeout transactions, while effective, were perceived to be less desirable than long-term financings because

they were not permanent sources of funds and relied on the potential sale of collateral for creditworthiness.

The takeout structure was rapidly eclipsed by a new long-term instrument—the *long-term variable rate demand obligation* (VRDO). A long-term variable rate bond issue consists of a single maturity, as much as 30 years long. Its interest rate resets every week to a "market clearing rate" (i.e., whatever rate keeps the market price of the bonds at par). This short-term rate reset mechanism gives the issuer a short-term, variable rate cost of funds.

Although an improvement over the takeout transaction, VRDOs are not without drawbacks. Like the takeout, the VRDO depends on a third party for its execution. Because the rate reset procedure is not perceived as foolproof, the market demands that VRDOs be accompanied by agreements with a third party entity, typically a bank, to provide liquidity support (a "standby purchase agreement" to be the bond purchaser of last resort). Similarly, because the return on student loans does not exactly match the cost of VRDOs, the market usually also requires credit support in the form of bond insurance or a letter of credit facility. These transactions generally obtained a rating consistent with the rating of the credit providers: Aaa/AAA or Aa/AA.

These three mechanisms—long-term, takeout, and VRDOs—were for several years the principal structures available to student loan issuers. But the market has recently come to accept two new variations: the *senior/subordinate* transaction and the fixed/floater transaction. Both are generally considered an improvement over the earlier structures.

The senior/subordinate structure is based on a concept borrowed from other kinds of asset-backed securities transactions (such as mortgage-backed securities). The structure of a senior/subordinate issue generally resembles the fixed rate long-term issues described above, except that a small portion of the total issue (perhaps 5 percent or less) is subordinated to the rest of the bonds. The bonds are just as likely to be paid as they would have been had there been only one class of bonds, but if revenues do prove insufficient to pay both senior and subordinate bonds, the seniors are paid first. The senior bonds' prior claim on assets makes them more creditworthy, and can be rated "AA" or even "AAA" without external credit enhancement. The subordinate bonds are generally rated "A." The higher rating on the majority of the issue translates into lower interest costs for the issuer.

A fixed/floater structure, as the name implies, combines under one indenture a series of fixed rate long-term bonds and a series of floating rate bonds. Under such an approach, an increase or decrease in short-term rates causes a corresponding increase or decrease in interest cost that more closely matches the unusual interest rate structure of the student loan asset. As with the senior/subordinate structure, market acceptance of this more complicated issuance structure has enhanced the issuer's ability to manage its asset/liability profile in a more favorable way.

It has also become possible to integrate both concepts into a single financing, so that the market will now accept a single *senior/sub, fixed/floating* issue containing, for example, senior lien fixed rate, senior lien variable rate, and subordinate fixed rate bonds. Because this approach uses subordination as a form of credit support, it can enable the senior lien floating rate issue to be marketed without external credit enhancement.

Taxable Structures

Not every secondary market maker can issue tax-exempt bonds, and those that can are limited in their ability to do so. To qualify to issue tax-exempt bonds, an issuer must at a minimum be a political subdivision of a state, an agency or instrumentality acting "on behalf of" a political subdivision of the state, or a unique 501(c)(3) not-for-profit corporation designated to make a secondary market in student loans in that state. The issuer must file a "plan for doing business" with the Department of Education. Tax-exempt issues must comply with the "arbitrage rules" of the IRC, which provide for limits on, among other things, investment earnings, loan yield, issue size, bond maturity, and use of proceeds. Student loan bonds are subject to state volume caps on private activity financing; each state is limited as to how many student loan, housing, and industrial development issues it can permit in a given year, and obtaining "cap allocation" can be an intensely political process. Perhaps most relevant, loans acquired with the proceeds of tax-exempt bonds must fall generally within the "nexus" of the issuer; loans must be originated by lenders within the state, made to borrowers who reside in the state or attend state institutions, or guaranteed by the state guarantor.

Several taxable sources of funds have become available in response to these limitations. Most basic is the *bank line of credit,* in which a bank simply opens a credit facility, on which a secondary market maker can draw in order to finance its purchases of loans. Lines of credit typically are collateralized by the loans that they finance and can bear a rate based either on the lender's prime rate or, less often, on a Treasury bill-based rate.

A second taxable source that is commonly used by state secondary market makers is the *taxable commercial paper facility.* Commercial paper is simply short-term debt, ranging in maturity from 30 to 270 days, that can be sold in flexible amounts on short notice. The basis of a commercial paper facility is found in two agreements: a letter of credit from a bank, and a placement agreement with a commercial paper dealer. When a secondary market maker needs funds, the dealer simply places some additional commercial paper with investors. The commercial paper is "rolled over" when it comes due—refinanced with more commercial paper—and can either be repaid when loans are sold or refinanced with a permanent funding source.

Lines of credit and commercial paper facilities are almost always short-term in nature, subject to renegotiation in two years or less. In the recent past, however, a market has begun to develop in *long-term taxable financings* comparable to the long-term tax-exempt financings described above. The financial structure of long-term taxable bonds draws liberally from both the tax-exempt world and, perhaps, more importantly, from the field of asset securitization. As of this writing, long-term taxable financings bear either a fixed rate or a LIBOR-based variable interest rate and can include a wide variety of credit features.

Finally, the market has begun to see a number of *hybrid financings,* that may combine any or all of the above techniques. For example, it is possible to have a series of taxable fixed rate bonds that are senior to a series of subordinate fixed and variable rate tax-exempt bonds, to which another series of tax-exempts are further subordinated.

Credit Issues

Regardless of whether the bonds are taxable or tax-exempt, an investor's main concern is the same for student loan bonds as for any other investment: the timely payment of principal and interest.

The evaluation of credit quality is almost always performed by one of the three major rating agencies. Ratings on student loan bonds have customarily come from Standard & Poor's and Moody's, and recently the Fitch rating has become equally accepted by the investment community. When assigning a rating to a student loan bond issue,[5] they all focus on the same major issues, among which are defaults, guarantee reimbursement, servicing, and cash flows.

Loan defaults have a different effect on bond performance than one might suppose. Because the loans are guaranteed, a default on a student loan does not necessarily trigger a default on the bonds; a borrower's failure to pay does interrupt the cash receipts, but eventually the guarantor makes good on defaulted principal and the accrued interest. Consequently, if the guarantee is creditworthy, loan defaults are simply treated as an acceleration of cash flow, not as a loss.

But this analysis depends on the quality of the *guarantee*. The guarantee on a student loan comes not from the federal government, but from a designated state-level guarantor. These guarantors are eventually reimbursed by the federal Department of Education, but for their guarantee to be creditworthy their reserves must be sufficient to meet their obligations until the federal check arrives. Most are sufficient. But if a guarantor's defaults are excessive in a given year, the federal government will not reimburse it for the full 100 percent of claims. There also are some technical circumstances, such as servicer nonperformance, in which a guarantor need not cover a loan loss.

That limitation calls attention to the *servicer*. The servicer must collect payments in a timely manner, "work" delinquent loans properly, and comply with myriad regulations; any failure to do so can disrupt cash flow or possibly even void the guarantee. The servicer must also charge an affordable fee; because servicing fees are typically paid from loan income, excessive costs can weaken the credit of the bonds.

Finally, the rating agencies analyze the cash flow structure of the bonds. An investment grade rating implies that the income from loans and investments will be sufficient to meet the debt service on the bonds even under extreme economic circumstances. A cash flow analysis uses sophisticated and highly specialized computer software to model the revenues and expenses of the transaction under various interest rate, default, reimbursement, timing, and other assumptions.

Supplemental Student Loan Programs

Although most student loans are made under federal programs, the federal programs frequently do not provide all the money that a student really needs. As administrators are all too aware, lending limits under the federal programs restrict not only how much a student can borrow, but also who can borrow.[6] Particularly at four-year independent institutions, but also at public, proprietary, and other institutions as well, the per annum limit on undergraduate borrowing is frequently inadequate to meet the costs of tuition, books, fees, and living expenses. And although some financial institutions do make student loans apart from the federal program, nonguaranteed loans simply are unavailable for most students.

State governments and other entities have attempted to fill this need by instituting *supplemental student loan programs*. While these programs vary in their details, they tend to resemble the federal loan programs in several fundamental ways, such as loan origination procedures, loan terms, and deferment and forbearance provisions. They all strive to create a source of capital—loans or loan guarantees—for students for whom the federal program is unavailable or inadequate.

The majority of these supplemental programs are funded by bonds. As one might imagine, the absence of the federal guarantee markedly changes the credit analysis of these bonds as compared to the federal program financings described above. The focus is still on defaults, guarantees, servicing, and cash flows, but in these programs the scrutiny is much greater. Moreover, those concerns are perhaps equaled in emphasis by an evaluation of the underwriting standards: who can get loans and how much they can borrow.

The Future

The student loan industry is now in a time of enormous uncertainty. Major initiatives are underway to completely revise the way in which student loans are made, financed, and repaid. Together with the sweeping changes enacted in 1992, these legislative changes are likely to produce, within five years, a student loan program that is radically different from the one that has been in place since 1965.

Among the potential changes that are affecting the student loan revenue bond market, the two most important are direct lending and a further reduction in subsidies to tax-exempt issuers.

Direct lending is a centerpiece of President Clinton's student loan reform initiative. Under this plan, loans will be originated not by the private sector but directly by the schools. The source of funds will be the federal government rather than the capital market. Students will be able to choose between a traditional loan payment schedule and an "income contingent" plan, in which the payments are a percentage of the borrower's annual income. Some borrowers may have their loans forgiven in exchange for a term of national service. Funding for the direct lending program will start at a modest level of 5 percent for the 1994–1995 academic year but is targeted to make up 60 percent of all student loan volume by the 1998–1999 academic year, at which time Congress will review the program. Banks and other private lenders would provide the remaining lending, primarily to students at institutions that are unable or unwilling to participate.

The same legislation would reduce federal interest subsidies to all lenders, and particularly to those financing with tax-exempt bonds. These reductions add to cuts made in the 1992 reauthorization of the HEA, and will further squeeze the profitability of all but the most efficient lenders.

The effect of these changes is unclear. On one hand, it seems certain that the reduction in subsidies will compel some private sector lenders to cease lending. These lenders may choose to sell their remaining loan portfolios to the public sector secondary markets, thereby increasing in the short-term the need for additional student loan revenue bonds. On the other hand, it is possible that some of the less efficient secondary markets will be precluded from issuing bonds in light of their own reduced profitability. In either event, it seems likely that these measures will cause some consolidation among secondary markets, among lenders, and among services.

Despite the potential for an industry downsizing, experienced public sector student loan professionals have been viewing these possible changes with some equanimity. The federal student loan program has passed through periods of evolution before, most notably in 1980 and 1986, to which it has not only adapted but thrived. In the view of these experts, it is likely that the federally guaranteed student loan program, and the public sector contribution to it, will continue to be a useful and vital part of the education funding process.

Notes

4. Recent federal legislation has reduced this reimbursement to 98 percent on most loans originated on or after October 1, 1993.
5. This discussion pertains only to issues not supported by a letter of credit or other external credit enhancement.
6. The 1992 amendments to the Higher Education Act changed this somewhat.

❖ EIGHT ❖

Special Situations and Planning Keys

Higher education finance is characterized by the same rapid rate of change as many other aspects of our economy and society. Neither this guide nor any similar source of information can substitute for the current expertise of business officers and higher education finance professionals. This is particularly applicable to references to laws, regulations, and policies, which are always subject to change. References to market-driven prices and practices also are only reflections of individual markets.

Effective planning will be rewarded and lack of planning will carry at least an opportunity cost if not an affirmative penalty. Financing decisions cannot be made on the basis of this guide because the information is subject to change.

Reimbursement for Prior Expenditures

As of March 2, 1992, new Treasury regulations became effective with respect to reimbursement of money spent for capital expenditures where the reimbursement is made from the proceeds of tax-exempt bonds, notes, and other securities. Modifications to the 1992 regulations became effective on July 1, 1993. The 1992 and 1993 regulations will be referred to in this section as the "reimbursement regulations."

All public and independent colleges and universities are affected by the reimbursement regulations because they apply generally to the tax-exempt bonds that can be issued for the benefit of colleges and universities.

The reimbursement regulations change the previous standards governing reimbursements and formalize the rules. Failure to follow the new formalities will prevent reimbursement of prior expenditures from tax-exempt bond proceeds. The consequences for colleges and universities could include: the inability to refinance higher interest debt or bank borrowings; the inability to reimburse interfund borrowings—even from funds like quasi-endowment, which are capital in nature; and the inability to replenish operating budgets when money may have been advanced on the assumption that it would be reimbursed in the present fiscal year. Other longer-term impacts arising from failed reimbursements will occur if financing capacity is reduced by having to pay a higher portion of a financing budget to interest than would otherwise be necessary.

These problems can be avoided by becoming aware of the types of situations where problems can arise and by systematically building "reimbursement planning" into the normal capital financing planning process of all colleges and universities.

To satisfy the reimbursement regulations and have a reimbursement allocation effective for state law purposes treated as an expenditure for federal tax purposes, the issuer must comply with the three general requirements outlined below and must not use the amounts in certain prohibited ways. In order for an allocation to even be considered under the reimbursement regulations, it first must be evidenced by an appropriate entry on the issuer's records, must identify the prior expenditure being reimbursed, and must be effective as an expenditure of the bond proceeds for purposes of state law. These requirements are summarized below.

1. The issuer must declare a reasonable official intent to reimburse the expenditure with proceeds of the borrowing (the "official intent requirement"). This declaration must be made within 60 days after the date the expenditure is paid; must be stated in a reasonable form by a person or body designated by the issuer to satisfy the declaration requirement; must contain either a general functional description of the project for which the expen-

diture is being made or identify the account (including its general functional purpose) from which the expenditure to be reimbursed is paid; and must contain a statement of the maximum principal amount of debt expected to be issued for total project costs, not just reimbursement purposes. The declaration also must be "reasonable"; blanket declarations that ultimately are not met, thereby establishing a pattern of failure, will be a factor in determining whether the declaration is reasonable.

2. The allocation of bond proceeds to reimburse an expenditure must take place generally within the later of 18 months after the expenditure was originally paid or the date 18 months after the financed facility was "placed-in-service." A global limitation of three years from the date the expenditure is paid also is applicable without regard to the "placed in service" date. Certain exceptions to these time periods can extend the period to five years or extend the 18-month periods for certain small issues. This is referred to as the "reimbursement period requirement."

3. The reimbursed expenditure must be a capital expenditure for federal tax purposes or certain extraordinary and nonrecurring working capital expenditures (the "nature of the expenditure requirement").

4. The reimbursement regulations contain "anti-abuse rules," including a general anti-abuse rule that prohibits any allocation that is an "artifice or device" to avoid, whole or in part, arbitrage yield restrictions or rebate requirements. In addition, the reimbursement regulations impose restrictions upon the use of amounts "corresponding" to reimbursement allocations to pay debt service on bonds.

Management Contract Rules

The federal tax laws place limitations on the private use of facilities financed with the proceeds of tax-exempt securities. Some limitations apply to allowable percentages of private use and private benefit. Another set of limitations applies to management or service contracts that relate to facilities financed with the proceeds of tax-exempt securities. The management contract rules

have been relatively stable since 1982, when the IRS released Revenue Procedures 82-14 and 82-15. The management contract rules were updated in 1993.

The variety of applicable rules can be illustrated in the following excerpt from a certification from the law firm of Mudge Rose Guthrie Alexander & Ferdon that would be required from a college or university in the course of completing a routine tax-exempt financing.

Management, Physician, and Other Service Contracts. Except as otherwise described in [this certificate], the Institution has not entered into, does not expect to enter into, and will not enter into any compensation arrangements (a "service contract") with any person or organization (a "nonqualified user") (other than a state or political subdivision of a state or a 501(c)(3) organization not using the Project in the organizations's unrelated trades or businesses under section 513 of the Code) which provide for such nonqualified user to provide services (such as management services for the entire facility, or for a specific department, that is part of the Project, janitorial services for any part of the facility that is part of the project or physician services to patients with respect to a facility that is part of the project), manage, operate or use any part of the Institution's facilities acquired as part of the Project (the "service provider") that do not satisfy the requirements set forth in each of the subsections below:

1. Fees. The service contract provides for no more than reasonable compensation for the services rendered and none of the compensation is based, in whole or in part, on a share of net profits (or similar amount) from the operation of the institution's facilities that are part of the Project.

    (a) Periodic Fixed Fee. At least 50 percent of the compensation for each annual period during the term of the service contract is based on a periodic fixed fee; or

    (b) Capitation Fee. All of the compensation is based on a capitation fee or a combination of a capitation fee and a periodic fixed fee. For the purpose of this section

(1)(b), a capitation fee means a fixed periodic amount for each person for whom the service provider assumes responsibility to provide all needed services for a specified period so long as the quantity and type of services actually provided to covered persons varies substantially. For example, a capitation fee includes a fixed dollar amount payable per month to a medical service provider for each member of a health maintenance organization plan for whom the service provider agrees to provide all needed medical services for a specified period; or

(c) Per-Unit Fee. All of the compensation is based on a per-unit fee or combination of a per-unit fee and a periodic fixed fee and the per-unit fee is specified in the service contract or otherwise limited by the institution or an independent third party; or

(d) Percentage of Revenue or Expense Fee. All of the compensation is based on a percentage of fees charged pursuant to a service contract (i) under which the service provider primarily provides services to third parties or (ii) involving a facility during an initial start-up period for which there have been insufficient operations to establish a reasonable estimate of the amount of the annual gross revenues and expenses.

2. Term.
   (a) In the case of a periodic fixed fee or a capitation fee described in section (1)(a) or (b) above, the term of the service contract does not exceed five years, including renewal options, and the institution may cancel the service contract on reasonable notice, without penalty or cause, at the end of the third year of the service contract;
   (b) In the case of a per-unit fee described in section (1)(c) above, the term of the service contract does not exceed three years, including renewal options, and the institution may cancel the service contract on reasonable notice, without penalty or cause, at the end of the second year of the service contract;

(c) In the case of a percentage of revenue or expense fee described in section (1)(d) above, the term of the service contract does not exceed two years, including renewal options, and the institution may cancel the service contract on reasonable notice, without penalty or cause, at the end of the first year of the service contract.

3. Increases in Fees. In the case of a service contract that provides for automatic increases in the periodic fixed fee described in section (1)(a) above, the increases in that periodic fixed fee do not exceed the percentage increases determined by the application of an objective external standard for computing such increases that are mutually agreed upon and specified in the service contract and the increases are not the subject of any incentive adjustment (e.g., based on the output or efficiency of the project).

4. Independent Entities. Except as described in [Exhibit A to the applicable certificate], (a) the service provider does not have any role or relationship with the institution that substantially limits the institution's ability to exercise its rights, including cancellation rights, under the service contract, (b) not more than 20 percent, in the aggregate, of the voting power of the governing body of the institution is vested in the service provider and its directors, officers, shareholders, and employees, (c) not more than 20 percent, in the aggregate, of the voting power of the governing body of the service provider is vested in the institution and its directors, officers, shareholders, and employees, (d) the overlapping board members do not include the chief executive officers of the service provider and the institution, or their respective governing bodies, and (e) the institution and the service provider are not members of the same controlled group, as defined in section 1.150-1(f) of the regulations, or related persons, as defined in section 144(a)(3) of the Code.

5. New Contracts. With respect to any new service contract, the institution represents that any new service contract it enters into will

satisfy each of the requirements set forth in this certification.

6. No Lease of the Project. Notwithstanding this certification, except as set forth in Exhibit A hereof, the institution has not entered into, does not expect to enter into, and will not enter into any lease agreement with a non-qualified user for the use of the Project.

Caution Needed for Gifts and Grants Relating to Financed Projects

Gifts and grants have important tax implications in higher education capital finance and they must be taken into account as early as possible in the capital planning process.

A tax principle known as "overissuance" requires that tax-exempt financing not be used for a project to the extent that other moneys are reasonably available for that project. This principle does not require the liquidation of all endowment or quasi-endowment before tax-exempt financing can be used, but it does capture gift and grant moneys received specifically for the same purpose for which the tax-exempt borrowing is being made. Some bond counsel require that such moneys be subtracted from the bond issue size as follows: first, the amount on hand at the time of issuance of the bonds is subtracted on a dollar for dollar basis, and then a reasonable estimate of the amount to be received during the construction period of the project is subtracted from the original bond size. In addition, amounts received in excess of these discounted amounts, including after the construction period ends and while the bonds are outstanding, must be segregated in a separate account that is invested at a yield not to exceed the yield on the tax-exempt securities ("yield restricted"). Federal tax law also limits the uses of these yield restricted amounts. The issue should be reviewed with the particular bond counsel handling the transaction, however, because there are other methods that are considered to satisfy the applicable tax requirements.

Business officers must integrate capital planning with the development staff's efforts to avoid soliciting gifts and grants that could otherwise be directed toward unrestricted or at least nonfinanced projects. Otherwise, the institution is imposing an artificial limitation on itself in terms of its access to the favorable interest rates of the tax-exempt market.

Using Limited Tax-Exempt Advance Refunding Opportunities Wisely

The tax code limits the number of times a tax-exempt security can be advance refunded. An advance refunding is one in which the proceeds of the refunding bond issue are used to pay debt service or redeem the refunded bond issue more than 90 days after the issuance of the refunding bonds. See chapter 6 for an examination of these limitations and some possible responses.

Part III

Structuring a Financing

❖ NINE ❖

Designing a Security Pledge

This chapter covers the issues involved in designing a security pledge, which is an important step in structuring a financing.

Choosing a Security Pledge

The process of choosing a security pledge is influenced by three factors: financing authority statute or policy, institutional legal parameters, and investor or credit enhancer demands. Each of these factors is described in more detail below.

Financing Authority Statute or Policy

The issue of statutory authority or policy influences on the design of a security pledge will be present for tax-exempt financings that rely on a conduit public entity for market access. These entities often will have statutory provisions that detail the types of security that can be offered to bondholders and even the types of documentation (loan agreement, lease agreement, resolution, indenture, etc.) to be used in the financing. Issues of statutory interpretation sometimes arise, but these usually are limited to new financing techniques.

Business officers should gain a general understanding of the nature of their statutory financing authority, because this is essentially the rulebook that will guide the tax-exempt financing market alternatives. Older statutes that have not been amended may be restrictive in odd ways, including, for example, the redemption provisions that may be employed. One area of frequent examination relates to derivative products and interest rate swaps in particular. Several states have express authority for swap transactions; most still do not. The absence of express authority is not a prohibition on the use of a swap, but the question should be posed at the planning phase before an entire financing plan is designed around a technique that ultimately may be determined to be unavailable.

The presence of interest rate ceilings was a problem in several states during the late 1970s and early 1980s, but has since been remedied in most situations. These issues may still arise in the context of default rates under letter of credit reimbursement agreements.

Institutional Legal Parameters

Independent colleges and universities legally are organized under the not-for-profit law of the state or commonwealth in which they are located. As corporations, independent institutions are subject to the provisions of the not-for-profit corporation law, which can be expected to contain restrictions. For example, the power to mortgage real property may be totally restricted or may require special procedures such as approvals from the state attorney general or a court. College counsel should be familiar with the applicable not-for-profit laws and able to advise the business officer of the ability to carry out the proposed financing technique.

Investor or Credit Enhancer Demands

Investors or credit enhancers may demand or prefer a particular financing structure and the institution's investment banker will be responsible for determining this information. Investors and credit enhancers traditionally have frequently wanted mortgages, but the evolution of environmental liability statutes as assigning financial responsibility to the owner of property have called into question the cost/benefit of having a mortgage. In response, parties requesting mortgages now accompany that request with a demand for an environmental review.

Investors normally will choose to purchase securities based on what is offered to them, except in the case of major institutional investors who are considering buying a substantial portion of an issue of revenue bonds. In that case, the investment banker often will solicit input from the investor as part of the negotiation process with respect to the interest rate. The security feature of tax-backed or general obligation bonds normally is not subject to negotiation.

Overview of the Security Pledge Choices

General Obligation

A general obligation pledge is a full faith and credit security of the independent college or university or of the taxing power of the sponsoring governmental issuer for the public college. The general obligation pledge in a revenue bond context makes the bondholders general creditors of the institution or the government, placing them behind senior lien holders and specific liens such as a revenue bond pledge.

General obligation bondholders protect their position with covenants having the cumulative effect of maintaining the credit strength of the obligor. The covenants often will include a negative pledge of real property, thereby assuring that this asset is not overleveraged. Debt service ratios to net income also are utilized to cause the obligor to maintain sound operating practices. The general obligation pledge in a tax revenue bond context is backed by the taxing capacity of the issuer.

Revenue

Revenue pledges can be as varied as a college or university's available revenues. Tuition, room and board fees, student activity fees, parking fees, and the proceeds of dedicated special purpose taxes for public institutions are examples of revenue pledges.

Revenue pledges for independent colleges and universities often are backed up by a secondary level general obligation pledge from the institution. Therefore, if revenues are not sufficient to pay debt service, the institution still will be obligated to pay from legally available moneys. Such a combination pledge is beneficial for the bondholder because the investor can establish a superior lien with respect to revenues from the facility while maintaining its participation in the

security derived from the general operations of the institution.

Covenants

Covenants are among the most important elements of structuring a higher education financing. Covenants represent the ongoing operating promises of the institution that will form parameters within which the institution must be managed. See the introduction of this guide for a discussion of covenants in the context of post-closing responsibilities. Violations of covenants are events of default under financing documentation, triggering remedies that can rise to the level of eventual acceleration of the debt to make it payable immediately in full.

Covenants are a flexible feature of the financing structure if the institution recognizes that there may be a rating price to be paid or rating benefit to be realized depending on the strength of the covenants. Covenants should not be given or abandoned lightly; some institutions have found it necessary or desirable to refinance outstanding debt to remove certain covenants (sometimes even in situations in which the refunding results in additional costs rather than financial savings). (See figure 9-1.)

The significance of higher education covenants generally can be categorized as follows:

Traditional, Good Credit, without Credit Enhancement. These transactions can be implemented without restrictive covenants. Higher education has been treated in a radically different manner from health-care with respect to covenants for more than 10 years. All health care transactions include rate covenants, additional bonds tests based on net revenues and other restrictive covenants that vary in degree but always are present. This has not been the case with higher education in the past, but more sophisticated higher education investors, bond insurers, and purchasers of private placements have been insisting upon health care-type covenants for several years. The trend toward more covenants should continue except for the strongest credits.

Credit-Enhanced Financings. Both letter of credit and bond insurance providers have been emphasizing covenants in higher education financings

Figure 9-1

Covenant Topics Typically Addressed by Business Officers	
Payment of principal and interest	Routine
Enforcement of duties and obligations of the institution	Routine
Accounts and audits (informational)	Negotiated
Corporate existence; acquisitions; consolidations; mergers	Negotiated
Tax covenants	Routine
Maintenance of auditing standards	Routine
Maintenance of properties	Routine
Sale, lease, or disposition of assets	Negotiated
Insurance and self-insurance	Routine/Negotiated
Restrictions as to creation of mortgages	Negotiated
Additional debt limitations	Negotiated
Contingent liabilities and guarantees	Negotiated

for several years, although the development of higher education covenants has still lagged the comparative use of covenants in other market segments, including health care specifically. Credit enhancers are more demanding than general market investors, however, and the enhancers have developed more refined covenant requirements, including net revenue coverage tests.

Weaker or Less Stable Credits. These institutions should expect to offer significant restrictive covenants with respect to debt service coverage ratios, the incurrence of additional debt (including short-term borrowing), the maintenance and disposition of assets, and the agreement to engage an outside consultant to recommend changes should established ratio requirements not be met.

Business officers should view covenants as potentially affecting the daily operations as well as the capital financing flexibility of the institution. Covenants should be negotiated carefully during the document drafting process with particular care given to covenants that involve measurements derived from audited financial statements. Calculations based on proposed covenants should be performed during the negotiations to ensure that adequate management discretion is maintained.

Changes in covenants after the closing can be more or less problematical depending on the type of covenant involved and the flexibility of the

original financing documents. Certain of the most fundamental covenants may be alterable only with bondholder consent. However, many credit-enhanced transactions delegate the right to consent for all bondholders to the provider of the credit enhancement, thereby affording a single party with whom the institution must negotiate. From a pragmatic perspective, obtaining bondholder consent is very difficult, even for a noncontroversial change. This is because bondholders either will seek a compensation for any modification, and particularly for a substantive change, or it will be difficult to engage bondholders' attention enough to obtain a response.

Mortgages

Mortgages have become both less expected and less common in higher education financings. Investors currently focus predominantly on the general credit strength of the institution, even in a revenue bond structure. Institutions and their higher education financing authorities have taken advantage of this trend to remove discretionary mortgages from revenue bond financing structures. In connection with strictly general obligation pledges, the financing structure itself supports the omission of a mortgage. In addition, as discussed below, environmental liability has decreased the attractiveness of mortgages to lenders.

Reliance on a general obligation security puts a premium on the preservation of assets, however.

Therefore, the "negative mortgage" covenant has become more common. This covenant provides that the institution will not give a mortgage to any other party without providing a parity lien to the bondholders. This approach allows the bondholders to retain their position where no other party can be in a superior position in the event that the real property assets of the institution need to be used to repay creditors.

Some higher education financing authorities have statutory requirements for a mortgage pledge relating to the financed facility. Some investors, particularly institutional investors in lower-rated financings, and some credit enhancers, remain committed to receiving a mortgage. Reasons for including the mortgage range from the objective value of the mortgaged property to the subjective value of having a pressure point against the institution should credit problems develop.

Environmental liability has become an important consideration in mortgage financing. Environmental laws have developed with the concept that the owner of the property is responsible for the cleanup of all environmental problems that are discovered on the property, regardless of fault or when the problem is discovered. Therefore, becoming the owner of a property upon foreclosure can be problematical. The unpredictability of lender liability concepts present another risk to creditors, particularly those who will be viewed as "deep pocket" targets in an environmental litigation setting. Investors and credit enhancers have moved in the direction of environmental investigations before taking a mortgage and insisting upon strong environmental covenants during the term of the financing.

Collateral

Collateralized transactions were quite common in higher education financing prior to the enactment of the Tax Reform Act of 1986. Colleges and universities were able to use one of their assets, namely their endowment or quasi-endowment, to structure a stronger credit package than would be presented by the general obligation credit of the institution alone.

The 1986 tax law changes extended the concept of an "invested sinking fund" to all amounts pledged to the repayment of a bond issue or reasonably expected to be used to pay debt service on the securities. The consequence of the invested sinking fund designation is to restrict the allowable investment return on those amounts to a yield not higher than the yield on the underlying tax-exempt securities. Given the relationship of tax-exempt rates to the other endowment investment opportunities for colleges and universities, yield restriction is detrimental to the institutions. For this reason, these tax law changes have virtually eliminated the use of collateralized tax-exempt bond issues.

Colleges and universities can enter into financing covenants based on calculations measuring endowment or other assets of the institution without causing those assets to become yield restricted as an invested sinking fund. Such covenants must be drafted very carefully in consultation with bond counsel, however, to be sure the yield restriction rules are not triggered accidentally.

Public Higher Education Security Matrix

Figure 9-2 relates the prevailing public higher education security types to the rating and cost of capital implications of each debt financing method.

As a state general obligation pledge evolves down through the matrix to a project revenue pledge, the security weakens, the revenues available for debt service narrow, ratings decline, and the cost to the issuer increases. Seven general types of debt financing methods are described in the matrix. These are general examples only and do not exhaustively cover all variations. In practice, the lines between the types of debt can be blurred. Bond titles often are not a guide to classification. In the "Examples" column of the matrix, some states are listed twice because they use more than one type of structure. California, for example, could be listed in each category. The list of examples is not comprehensive.

The cost implications of moving to a different level on the matrix are effective for a particular market only and this presentation illustrates general relative costs as contrasted to absolute costs. The quality spreads reflected in this matrix (i.e., the extra interest cost to the issuer for an "A" as opposed to "AAA" rating) are significantly compressed when compared to most time periods in the last decade. Further, the cost differences do not take into account the tiering of institutions within a state. Standard & Poor's explicitly names a "flagship" institution in each state and gives it a higher rating than similar obligations of four other tiers of institutions. To the extent that the market recognizes these tiers, institutions may experience lesser or greater effects of classification in a given category. Market conditions, such as scarcity, may allow a security to trade beyond the indicated limits for the general obligation issues of the state. Finally, the spreads do not reflect priority of lien, that is, they do not indicate whether the specific pledge is a parity lien or subordinated to prior liens.

The "Public Higher Education Debt Financing Methods" listed in the chart are defined below.

General Obligation of the State: Pledge of the full faith and credit of the state for the benefit of the higher education institutions. In some states, this includes reimbursable bonds representing arrangements whereby the state receives university revenues sufficient to provide for debt service although the investor has a full faith and credit pledge.

Higher Education Purpose State Appropriation Revenue Bonds: Pledge of state appropriations specifically for debt service on the bonds, yet

Figure 9-2. Public Higher Education Security Matrix

Public Higher Education Debt Financing Methods	Rating	Examples	Cost of Capital
General Obligation of the State	same as state general obligation	WA, FL, MA, OR, WI, VA	same as state
General Obligation of the University	same as state general obligation to half step below	MN, PA	10 basis points higher than state general obligation
Higher Education Purpose State Appropriation Revenue Bonds	one step below state general obligation	NY, CA	10-20 basis points higher than state general obligation
Multi-campus, Multi-project System Revenue Bonds	one step below state general obligation	MI, MD, TX	15-20 basis points higher than state general obligation
Combined Fee System Revenue Bonds	half to full step below state general obligation	IL, IN, AL, NY, NV	15-20 basis points higher than state general obligation
System Revenue Bonds	half to one and a half steps below state general obligation	CA	20-30 basis points higher than state general obligation
Auxiliary Revenue Bonds (Housing, Dining Facilities, etc.)	half to one and a half steps below state general obligation	CO, WA, FL, NC	20-30 basis points higher than state general obligation

Developed by Patrick J. Hennigan, J.P. Morgan Securities Inc.

subject to appropriation risk. Generally tuition fees and auxiliary revenues are not pledged. This pledge may include an "intercept" of state appropriated operating moneys of the institution.

General Obligation of the University: Pledge of the full faith and credit of the institution but not the state. The investor has access to all unrestricted funds of the university that may include unrestricted state appropriations.

Multi-campus, Multi-project System Revenue Bonds: Pledge of a broad stream of revenues, typically including auxiliaries, indirect cost recovery, and all other unrestricted revenues, which are aggregated from all campuses of the system. The limits on access to certain fund types differentiate this security from the general obligation of the university. For example, state appropriations are not available for payment. In some cases, only a portion of tuition or a special fee is included.

Combined Fee System Revenue Bonds: Pledge typically is a specifically defined stream of revenues selected from among housing, dining, parking, health care, and athletic services. Combined fee system revenue bonds usually do not include a pledge of tuition, all other unrestricted revenue, or state appropriations. The difference between this and the multi-campus, multi-project system revenue bond is the lack of investor access to all unrestricted revenues, such as tuition and state appropriations.

System Revenue Bonds: These issues come in many varieties, two common examples of which are a pledge of revenues from one specific auxiliary service such as housing or dining, or parking, for all campuses of a system.

Auxiliary Revenue Bonds: Narrowest type of pledge in that it is limited to a single auxiliary such as dormitories, dining halls, and student centers on one campus. These issues are differentiated from system revenue bonds because the revenue pledge is usually limited to a single revenue-generating facility.

Variable Rate Debt Liquidity and Credit Support

Outside Providers

Credit enhancement (the subject of chapter 12) is optional in most financing situations, but in the variable rate market there is a general market demand that the variable rate bonds be rated in the highest rating categories, thereby mandating credit enhancement in most cases. This situation is a result of two factors. First, investors in variable rate securities are dominated by tax-exempt money market funds that have requirements dictating their investment in highly rated securities. Second, liquidity providers are involved in financings to provide liquidity support for bond tenders and are not being compensated to take credit risk. Liquidity providers do not want to risk a failure on reimbursement and credit enhancement provides them with more assurances.

Liquidity providers are usually banks that provide letters of credit or lines of credit that can be drawn upon in the event variable rate bondholders exercise their right to tender the securities for repurchase. Such repurchases nearly always are funded from the proceeds of the resale of the securities to other investors. In the highly unlikely event that new purchasers cannot be located by the remarketing agent, the liquidity provider is committed to purchase the securities.

Business officers should discuss the ramifications of variable rate financing in detail with the financing team before proceeding in this direction because choosing the variable rate mode will have security structure ramifications.

Self-Funded Liquidity Support and Lines of Credit

Certain higher education institutions in the highest rating categories have been able to structure their financings to provide internal liquidity support. This is possible because of the deep reserves of such institutions both in terms of total endowment and liquid assets. In choosing to use an institution's liquid assets to provide liquidity support, the total asset management strategy must be taken into account, as well as the restrictive covenants that the rating agencies and the market will require.

❖ TEN ❖

Choosing a Financing Vehicle

There are several financing vehicles to choose from when structuring a financing, each with its own advantages and disadvantages. This chapter provides an overview of available options.

Tax-Exempt Securities

Tax-exempt securities—which include tax-exempt bonds, tax exempt notes, and certificates of participation—are commonly used by colleges and universities undergoing capital financing projects. The different types of tax-exempt securities are described below.

Tax-Exempt Bonds

The viability of tax-exempt bonds as a vehicle for addressing an institution's capital financing needs depends first upon the availability, pursuant to state law, of a mechanism through which an institution may access the tax-exempt bond market.

The type of mechanism available will be influenced by the characterization of the institution as either public or independent (see chapter 1).

An independent institution that qualifies under IRC Section 501(c)(3) as a nonprofit charitable or educational organization may be able to access the capital markets through state or local issuing authorities (see chapter 19 for a listing of state issuing authorities).

A public institution characterized as a state institution may, in some jurisdictions, be able to structure its financing as a general obligation of the state or, in other jurisdictions, as a general obligation of the institution itself. In the alternative, public institutions often may access the capital markets through the same state or local issuing authorities that serve the capital financing needs of private institutions.

Whether the institution is public or private, tax-exempt bonds issued by a state or local issuing authority are neither an obligation of the state nor any political subdivision thereof, other than the issuing authority. Such financings may be structured in either of two ways. First, under the terms of a lease agreement between the issuing authority and the institution, the issuing authority retains title to the project to be financed with the tax-exempt bonds for the time during which the bonds remain outstanding and will pay the principal of and interest on the tax-exempt bonds from the rental payments paid by the institution in exchange for use of the project. In the second option, the institution retains title to the project to be financed with the tax-exempt bonds under the terms of a loan agreement between the issuing authority and the institution. The issuing authority will pay the principal of and interest on the tax-exempt bonds from payments made by the institution pursuant to the loan agreement, in which payments are further secured by a mortgage on real property of the institution in favor of the issuing authority.

Once an institution determines that a legally sanctioned mechanism exists that will provide access to the tax-exempt bond market, it must evaluate the nature of the project to be financed to ensure that tax-exempt bonds are the appropriate vehicle.

The term of tax-exempt bonds usually is determined in relation to the useful life of the period during which the bonds will remain outstanding. Tax-exempt bonds are typically five, 10, 20, or 30 year obligations. Thus, tax-exempt bonds are intended to address long-term capital financing needs such as an academic building, a dormitory or an athletic facility. Subject to tax and statutory restrictions, tax-exempt financing also can be used for short-term purposes like equipment financing.

Tax-Exempt Notes

An institution may issue tax-exempt notes by the same mechanisms described above for tax-exempt bonds. However, notes differ from bonds in that they are short-term obligations of a duration of less than one year. There are two types of notes which, under certain circumstances, are likely to be appropriate financing vehicles for higher education institutions—bond anticipation notes and revenue anticipation notes.

Bond anticipation notes are an appropriate vehicle when the public or independent institution intends to issue bonds in the manner set forth above, but is either reluctant to make long-term financing commitments due to market conditions such as high interest rates or is unable to specify the exact amount of bonds to be issued due to such factors as undetermined construction expenses. The issuance of bond anticipation notes allows the institution to address its immediate capital financing needs while providing it with time to allow interest rates to improve or to finalize the details of its long-term financing needs. Once issued, bond anticipation notes may be repaid from the proceeds of subsequent bond anticipation notes and ultimately from the proceeds of the long-term bonds.

There is one circumstance in which bond anticipation notes are impractical as a financing vehicle. In a period of low interest rates, the incentive is to issue long-term debt at fixed interest rates as soon as possible, before market conditions have an opportunity to deteriorate. Reliance on bond anticipation notes during a period of low interest rates creates the risk of losing the most favorable market conditions for the issuance of long-term debt.

Revenue anticipation notes are an appropriate vehicle for public institutions that receive a substantial amount of revenues each fiscal year from government appropriations, but that require working capital prior to the date of receipt of such appropriated funds. In this scenario, the public institution can issue revenue anticipation notes to be repaid by the appropriated funds when received. This financing vehicle is intended to be an interim measure. It is not undertaken in anticipation of long-term financing needs.

Certificates of Participation

Certificates of Participation (COPs) are a particular type of lease financing that have become an increasingly significant part of the municipal market in recent years. Public sector higher education institutions also may be able to use this technique depending on their individual legal authorizations.

In general, a lease financing is an alternative to the issuance of traditional long-term debt that is available to state and local governments. In a lease financing, under the terms of a lease-purchase agreement, a government entity makes regular rental payments in exchange for the right to enjoy current use of the leased real property or equipment. Over a period of time, these rental payments in the aggregate will constitute the purchase price plus interest of the real property or equipment, at which point title is transferred to the government entity.

The key difference between a lease financing and traditional long-term debt is that lease financings are not subject to constitutional debt limitations and do not require voter approval. Additionally, unlike debt service on traditional long-term debt, lease payments are subject to annual appropriation by the government entity. This need for annual appropriation presents a significant risk for the lessor. However, the risk of nonappropriation is minimized to the extent that the real property or equipment being financed through the lease is essential to the government's operation—the so-called "essentiality" argument. Nonappropriation is also discouraged because it creates the risk of a decrease in credit rating.

In a certificate of participation lease financing, certificates, which evidence an interest in the lease payments being made by a governmental entity are sold to the public. COPs are used to finance both short to medium term lease obligations (such as those relating to equipment) and larger lease transactions involving real property.

COPs are a capital financing alternative that presents many advantages for public higher education. For example, a county may issue COPs to finance the lease-purchase of real property for the local college. By choosing this alternative, the cost of the real property is spread out over several years at interest rates lower than those for a bank loan, yet, unlike traditional long-term debt obligations, the need for voter approval is eliminated and the financing is not subject to constitutional debt limitations. The disadvantage is that COPs are increasingly controversial due to the risk of non-appropriation. Despite the essentiality of the leased property and the certainty of rating downgrades, there have been recent, highly publicized instances of failure of public entities to appropriate annual lease payments as well as grass-roots efforts intended to prevent appropriation. In addition, legal challenges to debt and voter approval exemptions have increased. In response to such developments, the capital finance market is cautious with respect to COPs.

Federally Taxable Bonds

The Tax Reform Act of 1986 implemented changes in federal tax law that have had an important impact on the ability of independent higher education institutions to access capital markets through the issuance of tax-exempt bonds. First, the act limits to $150 million the aggregate principal amount of bonds that an independent institution may have outstanding at any given time. Second, the law limits the ability of an independent institution to advance refund outstanding bonds.

If an independent institution seeks to exceed the $150 million limit or advance refund a series of bonds that may not be advance refunded on a tax-exempt basis, interest on such bonds, while potentially exempt from state and local taxation if the bonds can be issued through a governmental authority, will not be excluded from gross income for federal income tax purposes.

Federally taxable bonds clearly are generally not the most desirable vehicle for addressing an institution's capital financing needs. Nevertheless, if an institution must exceed its $150 million limit or face interest rates that are substantially lower than those applicable to a previously advance refunded series of bonds, federally taxable bonds are an option to be considered.

Bank Loans

Bank loans present major advantages as well as significant disadvantages when compared with tax-exempt securities and federally taxable bonds as a vehicle for addressing an institution's capital financing needs.

The advantage of bank loans is that the institution need not bear the burden of compliance with federal and state securities laws and tax laws. For example, the institution avoids the burdens of complying with public disclosure requirements and of working with the large number of capital finance market participants, which includes bond counsel, the issuing authority and underwriters (see chapter 2). Consequently, an institution usually is able to arrange a bank loan more quickly and easily than the issuance of a note or bond.

The disadvantage of bank loans is that interest rates generally are higher than interest rates payable on tax-exempt notes and bonds and often higher than federally taxable bonds. Thus, servicing bank loan debt is almost always more expensive than servicing securities debt. This disadvantage becomes more significant as the size of the financing becomes larger.

If the institution needs to move quickly to address a relatively small financing need, a bank loan may be more appropriate. If, however, the institution has the luxury of time and must address a large financing need, tax-exempt notes, bonds, certificates of participation, or federally taxable bonds may be a more attractive alternatives.

Vendor Leasing

Vendor leasing is a form of tax-exempt leasing available to public sector higher education institutions that involves all of the basic elements applicable to lease financing as discussed generally in the section dealing with certificates of participation.

Specifically, however, with vendor leasing, the vendor acts as lessor to the institution, although as an alternative the vendor may choose to assign its interest in the tax-exempt lease to an investor. Equipment leases are typically short-term, with a duration of five years or less.

Vendor leasing provides the higher education institution with the advantage of immediate use of the equipment while spreading the purchase price over a period of several years. This mechanism also has the advantage of being simpler to employ than the issuance of bonds, notes, or certificates of participation. The tax-exempt nature of the lease also results in lower interest rates than the rates available with a bank loan.

Repurchase Agreement

For institutions with a large amount of fixed income investments, a repurchase (repo) agreement may offer an inexpensive and flexible means of raising taxable capital. Technically, a repurchase agreement is a contract to sell and repurchase financial securities, typically U.S. treasury obligations. The repurchase price is set to reflect prevailing interest rates. A repurchase agreement is a form of collateralized debt with the lender taking possession of the securities. The transaction is treated as debt by the IRS. In most cases the securities remain with the institution's custodian.

The advantages of using a repurchase agreement are that the issuance costs are minimal and interest rates are very low.

There are two disadvantages. First, the borrower loses the ability to lend the securities and the related securities lending income. Second, the borrower must be careful that "selling" the securities does not interfere with portfolio management.

It cannot be overemphasized that repurchase agreements must be implemented with attention to the process in order to protect the borrower from bankruptcy of the other party to the transaction and other risks. The rating agencies have useful informational guides to repurchase agreements that can provide background information. Counsel to the institution should review any repurchase agreement prior to its use.

The Internal Fund Borrowing Option and Internal Cash Financing

Some colleges and universities prefer to pay for capital improvements with cash—either reserve funds that they hold or funds donated by benefactors. This approach can have financial and policy merit, but cash financing may be an inefficient use of funds for colleges and universities with access to the tax-exempt markets and good credit ratings, because the cost of borrowing

in the tax-exempt market may be lower than the investment return that these funds could otherwise earn. Moreover, the investments and the debt can be structured in a complementary fashion to reduce risk. It is critical, however, to consult with tax counsel familiar with tax-exempt financing well in advance of planned internal financing in order to structure the relationship among institutional reserve funds, outside donations, and tax-exempt financing proceeds within the tax rules applicable to tax-exempt bonds. An institution may not, for example, raise funds for the construction of a building and then issue tax-exempt debt for the same purpose.

Even if cash is the preferred mode of financing, many higher education institutions will not have sufficient cash available. Consequently, institutions must plan if it seems likely that they will need cash to finance capital projects in the future. One planning method is to develop a realistic depreciation schedule and fund it.

Another type of cash funding is interfund borrowings. If the plant fund borrows from the endowment fund at the same rate it would pay if it went to market, the endowment fund can earn a market rate of return with no third party credit risk. In addition, the plant fund will save the costs of issuance. It is more complicated to use these techniques when raising funds for research facilities. If a facility ultimately will be supported by payments on grants and contracts, the institution may want to issue the debt because imputed interest on interfund borrowings may not be an "allowable" cost for purposes of determining overhead.

It is important to maintain an arm's length transaction. For example, if the loan allows for prepayment, there should either be a prepayment penalty agreement set in advance of the borrowing or the interest rate should be adjusted for this option. Furthermore, the institution should avoid locking in a major portion of its fixed income portfolio with internal loans. One way to avoid problems is to use an investment committee as a clearing mechanism for all internal loans. The committee's mandate to protect the endowment should be clearly reiterated as it carries out the internal loan approval process.

Other issues to consider in connection with internal borrowing and financing include liquidity, endowment management and investment policies, fiduciary responsibility of those in the endowment management role, and the enforceability of budget discipline if an internal borrower does not meet its obligations. In sum, however, internal borrowing and financing is always a customized decision of the particular college or university.

❖ E L E V E N ❖

Financing Options

This chapter describes three types of financings typically used by higher education institutions—fixed rate, variable rate, and derivative products—and the advantages and disadvantages of each.

Traditional Fixed Rate

In a fixed rate financing, the institution establishes interest rates on a given date that are fixed for the life of the outstanding debt. Typically, each maturity is assigned a certain rate. While it is possible to issue bonds with a maturity of any length (e.g., one year, five years, 20 years, etc.) subject to statutory and tax law restrictions, most institutions choose to issue long-term debt with a final maturity no longer than 30 years. Some issuing authorities are subject to statutory limits on the maximum terms of any bonds. In addition, federal tax law constraints, particularly in the case of financings for independent institutions, generally limit the weighted average life of a bond issue to 120 percent of the weighted average useful life of the assets financed or refinanced by the bond issue. Over the last several years, the tax-exempt bond market has experienced a normal yield curve, which means that shorter maturities bear lower interest rates than longer maturities. Frequently, in order to take advantage of the positively sloped yield curve, leveling off after approximately 10 to 15 years, institutions will issue serial bonds (bonds with annual maturities) for one to 12 years and term bonds (bonds with one maturity) with a maturity of 20 to 30 years. While term bonds do not have annual maturities, they do require annual sinking fund payments, which operate in the same manner as serial bonds. Institutions can structure the amount of serial bonds and sinking fund payments to produce level debt service over the life of the outstanding bonds.

When issuing long-term, fixed rate bonds, institutions are usually required to provide the purchasers of the bonds with call protection. For example, if an institution issues 30-year, fixed rate bonds, the market may require that the bonds not be callable for 10 years at which time the institution will be required to pay a premium (e.g., 2 percent of the bonds that are being called). These terms are negotiated at the time the bonds are initially sold to the public.

Fixed rate bonds allow institutions to lock in long-term interest rates and eliminate the risk of increasing rates in the future. Often, rating agencies such as Moody's and Standard & Poor's require that an institution limit the amount of its floating rate debt so that, even though variable rates are lower than fixed rates, the institution is encouraged to issue fixed rate debt because it already has a substantial amount of variable rate debt outstanding.

The main advantage of fixed rate debt is that it enables an institution to lock in current market rates. This may also be a disadvantage if interest rates decline after the issuance of the fixed rate debt. Since it is relatively expensive to "refund" fixed rate debt (i.e., presence of transactional costs) interest rates must decline substantially before it is economically feasible to effect a refunding. Also, federal tax law limits the number of times bonds can be advance refunded.

It is possible to issue fixed rate debt and enjoy some of the benefits of variable rate debt by entering into an interest rate swap with a financial institution.

Traditional Variable Rate

A variable rate financing differs from a fixed rate financing in that interest rates for the life of the bond issue are not set on the date of sale. Rather, the institution sets interest rates only for a discrete period of time, at the end of which it resets interest rates either for the same period of time or for a different period of time. For example, on the date of sale, the institution may determine that interest rates lasting seven days are most advantageous. It would then, through a rate-setting agent, obtain an interest rate for those seven days. At the end of the seven-day period, the institution again has the ability to enter the "seven-day market" or, assuming certain conditions are met, set rates for a longer period of time. Because the structuring of a variable rate financing is generally more complex than a fixed rate financing, variable rate bonds are usually initially sold on a negotiated basis.

Historically, variable rates have been substantially lower than fixed rates and, like fixed rates, have followed a downward trend over the last several years. Accordingly, the issuer of variable rate debt has realized a much lower cost of capital than the issuer of fixed rate debt over the last several years. By not fixing interest rates, however, the risk exists that interest rates will increase and the institution will ultimately pay a much higher cost of capital than if it had locked in long-term fixed rates.

The most prevalent variable rate instrument available to higher education institutions are "multi-mode, variable rate demand bonds." Such bonds are characterized by an institution's ability to switch the time period for which interest rates are set. For instance, an institution that has initially issued its bonds in a "seven day" mode may later determine that it would be beneficial (perhaps because of the existing interest rate environment) to convert to a longer-term mode (for instance six months, one year or three years). The multi-mode feature allows institutions to effect such a change. The institution may even convert to a 30-year fixed rate if it so desires. In a tax-exempt financing, such conversions require the opinion of bond counsel that the bonds will remain tax-exempt.

The demand feature in multi-mode, variable rate demand bonds requires that if the bondholder is dissatisfied with the rate that has been set on the bonds, the bondholder can demand that the institution take back the bond at a price of par plus accrued interest, if any, to the tender date. Since most institutions are ill-equipped to

manage such a process, the institution will contract with a remarketing agent (usually a major underwriter of municipal bonds) to handle the purchasing and reselling of bonds in the variable rate market. Because the remarketing agent is usually also the rate setting agent, the lowest rate at which bondholders will hold on to their bonds should be easily derived. The remarketing agent usually charges an annual fee on the amount of bonds outstanding.

Also, because it is impractical for most institutions to make available liquid assets (cash) sufficient to repurchase bonds that are not remarketed by the remarketing agent, most variable rate demand bonds are secured by a letter of credit and/or line of credit. Often, the financial markets will require that some sort of credit facility be used.

For the most part, the same financing team participants are involved in a variable financing as in a fixed rate financing. The institution can count on more input from the rating agencies on matters concerning the structuring of credit facility and other legal documents because of the possibility of the bonds being "put" back to the institution requiring the institution to provide for their repayment. Also, the institution must contract with a remarketing agent (to remarket bonds that have been put back to the institution), a rate setting agent (to set rates), and a tender agent (usually a commercial bank to handle the actual tender of the bonds by the bondholder and their repayment).

Derivative Products

Derivative products represent a new range of financing alternatives for business officers. The credit markets have systematically created a new line of financing products by isolating individual elements of a security and allowing parties to engage in transactions affecting only that element. In addition, combinations of such elemental transactions can be created in a large variety of configurations. Derivative products also have been used to implement traditional financing objectives in a synthetic manner (e.g., creating fixed rate payment obligations or variable rate payment obligations with an interest rate swap).

Additional dimensions of derivatives must be considered, such as the tax treatment of the derivative in terms of its effect on the yield of the institutions's tax-exempt securities and the accounting treatment of the derivative in terms of its effect on the balance sheet.

Discussions of derivative products often are characterized in terms of "hedging" and "speculation." This is accurate in theory if each transaction is taken in isolation. For example, in a situation in which an institution has a variable rate payment obligation and enters into a swap agreement resulting in a net fixed rate payment obligation, the variable rate risk has been hedged. On the other hand, if an institution entered into an isolated swap that produced a net variable rate payment obligation, that could theoretically be categorized as a speculation on future variable rates. These analyses can be misleading, however, unless the transaction is viewed in the context of an institution's overall financial plan or a particular financing's complete plan of finance. The decision to issue variable rate debt might be prudent and correct for a college or university as part of an overall plan; attaching the label of speculation to this decision would cloud the analysis. In fact, creating a variable rate payment obligation could be viewed as a hedge against declining rates of return on a portfolio of endowment securities that were invested in short-term maturing investments pursuant to the endowment management policy of an institution. Given the volume of writing and commentary on the subject of derivative products, it is important to understand the essence of derivative product transactions and not to attach generic labels to transactions or categories of transactions.

As business officers analyze derivative products and reach their own conclusions based on the needs of their institution, it should be remembered that the municipal derivatives market has matured in the past several years to the point that either standardized or highly customized transactions can be structured. *The Bond Buyer* reported on February 16, 1994, that in 1993 $9.6 billion of municipal derivatives were sold on 328 issues, up 39 percent from $6.8 billion on 110 issues in 1992. Further, a layer of secondary market derivative transactions has developed in response to investor demand (from institutional investors in municipal securities, including mutual funds). This secondary market expanded 72 percent from

1992 to 1993. Moody's rated 292 of such issues (representing $4.69 billion) in 1993 as compared to 108 issues (representing $2.7) billion in 1992. Standard & Poor's rated $4.0 billion of secondary market derivatives in 1993 as compared to $2.0 billion in 1992.

Participants Involved

The derivatives market introduces new participants into the financing process. The participants will vary depending on the derivative product used, but the following parties will become familiar over time:

Counterparty. This term is encountered most often in the realm of interest rate swaps and interest rate cap agreements. The counterparty is the entity on the other side of an interest rate swap agreement (an exchange of a fixed rate payment obligation for variable rate payment obligation or the reverse) or an interest rate cap agreement (whereby the institution initially pays a fixed sum in exchange for a payout by the cap provider if the interest rate on the underlying security exceeds a specified level).

Auction Agent, Broker Dealer, and Market Agent. These parties are participants in a structure involving inverse floating rate securities. Inverse floating structures can involve several variations, including the use of an interest rate swap.

Index Agent and Market Agent. There is an entire product line of "indexed" products in which the interest rate payable is determined in whole or in part by reference to an index. These indices typically include J.J. Kenney, the PSA Index, or LIBOR. The index agent officially determines the interest rate from time to time based on the specified index.

Underlying Bondholders and Municipal Call Rights Owners. These designations relate to the owners of a bond and a municipal call right when the call right on a bond is detached and sold to a party who may or may not be the bondholder.

Securities Depositories and CUSIP Bureau. Most derivative products either require or encourage the use of book-entry-only securities depository (the most common being The Depository Trust Company in New York). The CUSIP numbers assigned to securities often must be changed to coincide with the terms of securities that have been transformed as a result of implementing a feature of a derivative product. Each derivative product is different in this respect. (CUSIP numbers are a seven-digit combination of numbers and letters that is unique to each maturity of each bond registered with the CUSIP bureau. CUSIP numbers facilitate electronic pricing, trading, and recordkeeping.)

Advantages

Derivative products offer tremendous potential advantages. Interest rate swaps can create any possible variation and sequence of variable and fixed rate payment obligations. Inverse floating rate and other structured coupon securities can meet specialized investor needs, which can be traded for an interest rate concession by the investor. Municipal call rights can lower the yield on a traditional noncallable bond by allowing investors to purchase the call right alone, thereby increasing investor competition for the securities as a whole and forcing an interest rate concession by the investor. Interest rate caps enable the issuer to create variable rate securities with a customized maximum interest rate exposure. Interest rate collars allow both the maximum and minimum interest rates for variable rate securities to be negotiated. The flexibility in derivative product contracts provides a useful manner of controlling risks for colleges and universities.

Disadvantages

Derivative products are a relatively new entry in the municipal securities market and are new products for most colleges and universities. As such, derivatives suffer from the same growing pains as earlier new products. Many people do not understand derivatives and fear the unknown. Still others partially understand the products and jump to incorrect conclusions. Business officers probably will encounter individuals in each of these categories in the course of using a derivative product financing technique. Therefore, it is critical to invest the necessary time at the initiation of the derivative product financing process. Lack of a complete understanding by the business

officer will confirm the negative suspicions of other parties.

Using a derivative product often will result in a market risk of some type, but as described above, this risk should be examined on its own merits. The risk usually related to the derivative product is a performance risk of some type. For example, in an interest rate swap, the other party to the swap agreement must perform, thereby creating counterparty risk.

Business officers should examine risks in the context of the offsetting response to the risk. For example, counterparty risk in a swap transaction usually is addressed by dealing with a highly rated counterparty, obtaining "swap insurance" from a municipal bond insurer, or negotiating collateralization provisions. Performance risk in some municipal call rights structures is substantially offset by requiring the advance posting of cash equal to the exercise price of the municipal call right. Various contingencies in inverse floating rate or similar security transactions are addressed in ways that assign the consequences between different classes of bondholders to the exclusion of the issuer.

Derivative products involve considerations that have not become routine in the municipal market. Therefore, business officers will be limited in accessing derivative products if their financing team is not experienced in this segment of the capital markets.

Finally, derivative products are a rapidly evolving field for regulators as well. Government regulators and professional organizations, particularly in the auditing field, are constantly reviewing the proper regulation and reporting of derivative product transactions. Therefore, there is some risk that the treatment of certain derivative transactions could change after closing.

Process Recommendations Concerning Derivative Products

Business officers should be aware of the special educational needs of senior management and the board of trustees before they can approve a derivative product transaction. Other members of the college's financing team, such as financing counsel or investment bankers, may be helpful in making presentations or providing educational materials, but the business officer must reach a level of comfort and understanding of the transaction before a derivative strategy is recommended as institutional policy.

It is important to distinguish between real risks and perceived risks of derivative products. Some of the risks of derivatives are not created by the derivative or synthetic technique, but rather are a feature of the institutional business objective that the derivative achieves. For example, an interest rate swap from a fixed to a variable rate does not create variable rate risk for the institution. The variable rate risk is the real issue, and the swap is only the technique by which the variable rate payment obligation is created.

Legal considerations should be an early topic of review. State law issues may need to be resolved before a particular derivative product can be used. Existing financing documents probably do not contemplate all derivative products explicitly, and matters of interpretation will have to be passed through appropriate channels.

The best process for business officers center on gaining a thorough working understanding of the proposed derivative product. Ask a lot of questions and insist on understandable explanations. Use the diagrams that most investment bankers offer as companion pieces to the legal documents, but do not rely on the diagrams as a substitute for reviewing the legal papers. Expand your range of questions and inquiry to a broader understanding of the market in which the product operates (e.g., the swap market generally and the LIBOR rate in the case of a LIBOR-based swap). Obtain a fair negotiating position by learning the economics of the products in terms of how the providers of the products and the counterparties earn their fees.

The investment of time and resources in choosing a financing team that has derivatives capability or in developing that expertise within the financing team will benefit both the business officers and their institutions. The costs of researching and implementing derivative products are one-time fees, but the benefits in the form of savings in the otherwise prevailing interest rate will be an annual benefit to the institution over the life of the issue. The present value of the savings, projected over the term of the derivative product, often will be a substantial net benefit, but can be captured only if the institution has the expertise to act prudently in the derivatives market.

❖ T W E L V E ❖

Credit Enhancement

Credit enhancement can be either an enhancement or a requirement for one of many reasons. The following are examples of the context in which a credit enhancement decision might arise:

Legal or Government Policy Requirement. Many states have minimum credit rating requirements. In New York, for example, the state-level Public Authorities Control Board, which has approval powers for bond issues of state-level issuing agencies, has a longstanding policy that securities issues must have specified minimum credit ratings in order to proceed without credit enhancement.

Legal Requirement. In some instances, an existing bond indenture or other credit document such as a reimbursement agreement with a letter of credit bank may require that additional bonds also have credit enhancement or achieve a specific rating. In the alternative, the existing credit enhancer may have approval powers with respect to additional debt and require credit enhancement on subsequent issues (which may be with the same provider or another provider).

Economic Imperative. There may be situations where the credit enhanced interest rate is essential to the success of a financing plan. For example, a refunding transaction might be economical with credit enhanced rates and noneconomical without credit enhanced rates depending on the spread between the unenhanced (lower rated) interest rates and the credit enhanced (higher rated and often Aaa/AAA) interest rates.

Market Access. A particular financing structure might demand credit enhancement to be marketable. For example, a variable rate transaction usually requires an external liquidity provider in case of a tender by the bondholders, and the liquidity provider, in turn, may mandate the participation of a credit enhancer to protect its liquidity role. Also, certain asset-backed securities require credit enhancement as a structural feature.

The growth of credit enhanced transactions has been attributed to many factors combining initiative by the insurers with favorable market circumstances. The introduction of bond insurance in the early 1980s coincided with the trend throughout the 1980s and the early 1990s toward increasing individual investor participation in the municipal securities market. At the same time, deficits and budget crises affected all levels of government in the United States, the Washington Public Power Supply System suffered its default in 1983, and several certificates of participation financings suffered nonpayments or near-nonpayments that investors characterized as defaults notwithstanding the legal structures of the COPs (under which a nonpayment is not necessarily a default). Bond insurers were able to expand their business in reaction to investor uncertainty, and the insurers also mounted wide-ranging advertising programs that reached out directly to the individual investor in mainstream publications and on television. The insurers did suffer some losses when insured bond issues defaulted, but for the most part, these losses were statistically minor from the rating agencies' points of view and the bond insurer market continues to be dominated by a group of triple-A rated firms. The federal government even got involved in the credit enhancement trend by facilitating the creation of the College Construction Loan Insurance Association (Connie Lee), the higher education insurer that concentrates on the lower rated end of the higher education and teaching hospital sector (although Connie Lee is continuing efforts to expand its range of authorized transactions).

The letter of credit portion of the credit enhancement market has received less attention in recent years for a number of reasons. First, the providers of letters of credit have been reluctant to extend their commitments beyond the five, seven, or 10 (maximum) year terms, thereby making their enhancements noncompetitive with bond insurance that extends for the full term of the bonds (e.g., up to 30 years). Second, the ratings of many banks that have provided letters of credit have been reduced below the triple-A ratings that prevail in the bond insurance sector, thereby limiting the interest rate differential between nonenhanced and enhanced structures. Third, a sustained period of low interest rates has reduced issuer demand for variable rate bonds, thereby eliminating a natural market for the letter of credit providers. Fourth, as the bond insurers made great progress in standardizing their commitments and emphasizing user-friendly approaches to dealing with issuers, underwriters, and counsel, many letter of credit banks have retained their traditional one-sided and unpredictable negotiating styles, which has not encouraged solicitation of letter of credit alternatives to bond insurance. (See figures 12-1 and 12-2 below.)

Figure 12-1. Credit Enhancement Data 1982–1992

Year	LOC* Higher Education Volume (millions)	Total Higher Education Bonds Annual Volume	LOC-Backed as Percentage of Total Higher Education Bonds	Insured Higher Education Volume (millions)	Insured as Percentage of Total Higher Education Bonds	Combined Credit-Enhanced as Percentage of Total Higher Education Bonds
1993	87.2	$13,123.8	0.66 %	4,863.90	37.06 %	37.73 %
1992	86.8	9,892.7	0.88	4,058.70	41.03	41.90
1991	42.0	7,265.9	0.58	2,984.60	41.08	41.65
1990	69.8	7,677.4	1.26	2,716.70	35.39	36.65
1989	122.0	6,260.3	1.95	1,497.90	23.93	25.88
1988	127.7	5,536.3	2.31	1,189.50	21.49	23.79
1987	85.1	3,873.4	2.20	767.60	19.82	22.01
1986	111.4	6,722.6	1.66	966.80	14.38	16.04
1985	280.1	9,737.8	2.88	2,447.90	25.14	28.01
1984	211.4	3,140.2	6.73	956.50	30.46	37.19
1983	39.7	2,175.1	1.83	375.80	17.28	19.10

*LOC volumes listed are from domestic banks only.

Source: J.P. Morgan Securities Inc.

Figure 12-2

Year	Japan	Europe	North America	Total
1993	$ 2,552.7	$4,435.6	$116.6	$ 7,104.9
1992	2,211.1	3,005.4	104.2	5,320.7
1991	3,044.8	3,891.2	143.8	7,079.8
1990	5,263.4	3,484.3	101.1	8,848.8

Letter of Credit Providers
(Market share of top 25 letter of credit
providers on long-term issue; in millions of dollars.)

Source: J.P. Morgan Securities Inc.

Bond Insurance

Bond insurance is an irrevocable, noncancellable credit enhancement that is applicable for the life of the securities insured. The insurer agrees that if the issuer fails to make scheduled principal or interest payments when due, the insurer immediately will pay such amounts and seek reimbursement from the issuer. Therefore, the insurance company is positioning itself as an intermediary and assuming the credit risk of the issuer. If the bond insurer fails to perform its obligation to make debt service payments, the bondholders still have recourse against the issuer.

In exchange for a one-time up-front fee paid out of bond proceeds, institutions are able to issue debt that carries the ratings (typically "Aaa/AAA") of the bond insurer. Bond insurance can be applied to all or a portion of an issue. On some large issues, insurers will divide the financing into different portions secured by different insurers. Because the interest rate required to sell insured, higher rated bonds can be substantially below that of bonds issued under an institution's own credit rating, borrowers may enjoy substantial savings on debt service by obtaining insurance.

Pricing

Bond insurance premiums typically are paid upon issuance of the bonds and are based on total principal and interest paid over the life of the bonds. Such fees historically have had large ranges, and each transaction will require its own cost-benefit analysis. The pricing factors vary for each credit and should be reviewed in connection with each transaction.

Bond insurance premium fees are based on a number of factors and are presented as a percentage applied to aggregate debt service. The insurance companies must allocate capital to each transaction, and the cost of capital as well as targeted return on equity for the insurer is one pricing factor that cannot be determined by the higher education institution. In addition, the insurance company will compare the spread between the interest rates available to the college or university on insured and uninsured bases. The insurance companies recognize that if the cost of the premium is excessive when compared to the benefit of the rating upgrade, there will be no economic incentive to purchase the insurance. Competition from other insurers will be another pricing influence.

Availability

In today's market, "AAA" rated bond insurance is available from any of seven major insurance companies. The availability of insurance is directly related to the creditworthiness of the borrower, and institutions whose stand alone credit rating is at least "A" can usually obtain an insurance bid from one or more of the major bond insurance companies.

The municipal bond insurance industry has both expanded and contracted in terms of which companies are offering the insurance. This evolution has occurred as new companies have been formed, firms have been acquired by others, and firms have expanded their business from reinsurance to primary market activity and shifted their emphasis to include specific areas of the municipal market. Each of the municipal bond insurance firms can be generally characterized by their view of higher education credits, but this will change from time to time. Business officers should review the status of the various insurers with their investment banker and financial advisor.

Advantages and Disadvantages

The choice between issuing bonds with the institution's own credit rating and issuing bonds with credit enhancement will depend on the availability of bond insurance, the business covenant requirements of the commercial insurer, and prevailing market conditions. Availability of and business covenants for insurance will be directly related to the borrower's credit. Business covenants imposed by the insurer typically are more restrictive than those required under standard noncredit enhanced indentures. However, in most cases, the requirements are not overly burdensome. Therefore, in most cases, bond insurance considerations will be part of the planning process, and a cost-benefit analysis of the all-in borrowing costs will be required to determine the desirability of insurance. The final decision to purchase insurance can be completed shortly before the pricing of the bonds.

Letters of Credit

In exchange for the payment of an annual fee, higher education institutions can purchase a letter of credit that guarantees the immediate repayment of bond principal plus a specified number of days of interest (generally an interest rate period plus additional time to allow claims for payment). Letters of credit are issued by a large number of banks and thus carry a range of credit ratings. Under April 1993 market conditions, for example, letters of credit are issued with a maximum maturity of five to seven years, (i.e., the maturity of the credit facility does not match the maturity of the securities as it does with bond insurance). Given this relatively short maturity,

such credit enhancement generally supports short-term obligations or debt with a mandatory redemption if the letter of credit terminates without renewal or substitution of a comparable credit facility.

Pricing

Letters of credit guarantee only the repayment of principal plus a specified number of days of interest and pricing is based on the dollar amount covered from time to time. Therefore, the annual fee for a letter of credit would decline as the principal amount (and the interest attributable to that principal amount) decreased over time. Letter of credit fees are established at closing but are paid on an annual basis. Under April 1993 market conditions, for example, "A" rated higher education issues could obtain a letter of credit at a cost of between 65 and 90 basis points per year. Modest commitment and closing fees are one-time expenses. Alternative pricing arrangements can be negotiated as the terms of the letter of credit are altered.

Availability

Though the number of letter of credit providers has declined significantly from 1990 to 1993, the number of active municipal market participants is well over 50, compared to the seven providers in the bond insurance industry. Moreover, letters of credit are available to institutions whose credit rating is "A-" and in some cases "BBB+." In addition, higher education institutions often have local banking relationships that can assist in securing a letter of credit. A letter of credit from some local banks may be strong enough to assist in market access, or a nationally recognized credit enhancer may be willing to "wrap" a transaction that has a local bank letter of credit as part of its structure. In this case, the credit enhancer would book the transaction as one relating to the bank risk rather than the institution's risk.

Advantages and Disadvantages

Letters of credit are issued for a period of five to seven years. Consequently, one of the major risks letter of credit purchasers face is "credit rollover risk" or "renewal risk" (i.e, the possibility that credit enhancement will not be available upon maturity of the letter of credit). In addition, unlike the insurance industry that has faced limited credit deterioration in the past two decades, the letter of credit community has experienced serious credit deterioration. This has been the case for both domestic and foreign bank providers. Many transactions that were initially completed with letters of credit have faced severe rollover and renewal problems in complying with the substitution requirements of their loan documents. For the college and university issuer, this credit erosion translates into higher capital costs, assuming the financing relying on the letter of credit can even be kept in place. On the positive side, however, a letter of credit is more flexible than bond insurance due to the variety of banks that participate in the market for different reasons, ranging from simply receiving a rate of return to supporting a customer relationship with the college or university. This availability and the flexibility in the business terms offered by the bank make letters of credit a realistic alternative for a financing structure.

Other Enhancements

While bond insurance and letters of credit are the most common forms of credit enhancement, other techniques are either available or in the developmental stages.

Higher education institutions with endowment or liquid assets have the option of collateralizing their bond issues. This is not a favored financing technique, however, because federal tax law captures collateral in a concept known as "replacement proceeds." Replacement proceeds are amounts that have a sufficient tie to a bond issue or the governmental purpose of the bond issue to conclude that the amounts would have been used for that purpose if the other bond proceeds were not so used. Examples of replacement proceeds include amounts pledged to a bond issue under circumstances in which bondholders have reasonable assurance that the funds will be available to them even if the issuer encounters financial difficulty ("pledged funds"). A pledge of collateral sufficiently strong to constitute credit enhancement will almost certainly cause the collateral to be treated as a pledged fund and subject to arbitrage restrictions.

Prior to the imposition of rebate requirements by the Tax Reform Act of 1986, applicable Treasury regulations permitted, in many instances, a pledge of endowment funds to be treated as a reasonably required reserve fund. Thus, even though such funds were replacement proceeds, such characterization had little effect since moneys in a reasonably required reserve fund could be invested without regard to arbitrage yield restriction and without adversely affecting the tax-exempt status of the bonds. The imposition of rebate requirements by the 1986 act, however, subjected these moneys to arbitrage rebate requirements. Although the endowment funds could, pursuant to the reasonably required service fund exception, continue to be invested without regard to yield restriction and without adversely affecting the bonds, any arbitrage earned on the investments would have to be periodically rebated to the federal government. As a result of imposition of the rebate requirement, collateralized transactions have become rare.

Another alternative for credit enhancement is a guaranty from another party. The availability of this approach depends on the corporate structure of the college or university in relation to other entities such as a hospital. Guarantees have been used from universities for the benefit of university hospitals. Guarantees enable the credit strength of the guarantor to be applied to the overall credit rating of the underlying securities.

Certain public higher education institutions may benefit from a "moral obligation" on the part of a state or local government. A moral obligation usually is structured as a separate reserve fund from which the bond trustee can draw if the institution's funds are insufficient. While the funding of the reserve is "subject to appropriation" by the governmental entity, the credit markets evaluate the structure as evidencing the intention (hence, the "moral obligation") of the government to make any necessary periodic appropriations to cover shortfalls in debt service. Moral obligations are not legally enforceable and for that reason carry a slightly lower credit rating benefit than a guaranty.

Government pension funds are an emerging area of potential credit enhancement. At least one transaction has been completed in Oregon, and other states have been actively researching the issue. These funds involve public policy issues as well as relatively complex legal issues that need to be addressed on a case by case basis. An institution should not plan to utilize a governmental pension fund credit enhancement without a thorough investigation into the realistic availability of the credit enhancement on the time schedule applicable to the transaction.

❖ THIRTEEN ❖

Rating Agencies and Tax Considerations

The role of rating agencies and ratings has been introduced earlier in this book. The discussion of ratings in this chapter will focus on the rating process, followed by a detailed presentation of the Standard & Poor's, Moody's, and Fitch rating definitions.

The rating process will vary slightly among the three principal nationally recognized agencies listed above, but the most important factor is the degree of prior familiarity of the rating agency with the college or university seeking the rating. The process outlined below assumes that no prior relationship or familiarity exists.

Step 1 is the request for a rating, which will be communicated on behalf of the institution by the higher educational facilities authority or another member of the financing team (e.g., the investment banker or financial advisor).

Step 2 is the process of meeting the rating agency's requests for information. Basic information such as financial and enrollment data always is requested. Specialized requests may arise in response to the individual characteristics of the particular college or university.

The manner of presentation of the information provided is significant. Information concerning the college or university eventually to be included in the official statement for disclosure purposes should be included in this credit package. Assembling such information is a time-consuming task and adequate lead time for an experienced member of the finance team (usually college financing counsel or underwriter's counsel) to coordinate the preparation of this description should be added to the financing process. See figure 4-2 in chapter 4 for a sample table of contents for a disclosure section describing an independent college.

Step 3 is the rating agency's analytical period, during which the data is reviewed according to various criteria, many of which are statistical.

These statistical measurements form the context for additional and more subjective evaluations.

Step 4 is an interactive period of questions and answers between the rating agency and the financing team. The college or university may have direct or indirect contact with the rating agency during this period depending on the nature of the questions.

Step 5 consists of either an issuer traveling to a rating agency's office to make a presentation to agency personnel or a visit by the rating agency to the college or university for a presentation on-site. Such presentations are a critical part of the rating process and require extensive preparation, particularly if the institution's management does not have experience with this process.

Step 6 is the post-presentation analysis and follow-up by the rating agency staff. The staff will develop a credit profile of the institution in the form of a written report. The report will be reviewed in advance by the rating agency credit committee.

Step 7 is the presentation by the rating agency staff to the agency's credit committee. The committee then will assign a rating to the issue. It should be emphasized once again that ratings are assigned to individual issues; the rating is not a rating of the institution. Different security pledges and financing structures, as well as the utilization of credit enhancement, can cause different rating outcomes for issues of the same institution.

Step 8 is the communication of the rating result to the institution. An appeal process is available, but this is generally only effective if there is additional significant information that can be brought to the process.

Step 9 is formal notification of the rating by letter of the rating agency. The rating and often an accompanying brief rating report then are released into the rating agency's public database for reference by anyone who chooses to access the information.

Ratings are maintained through a surveillance process that involves the periodic receipt of information by the rating agencies. Ratings change over time through upgrades and downgrades to reflect changed circumstances.

There are variations on the process for institutions that have worked with the rating agency in the past and with respect to institutions that seek preliminary ratings or private rating opinions. Such preliminary or private rating opinions are not always available from all of the rating agencies, but when offered, they allow the institution to get a general sense of the rating evaluation without the public publication of a rating and without incurring the time and expense of a full rating process. Preliminary and private rating opinions can be upgraded to published ratings at the request of the institution provided the comprehensive rating process is completed.

The Role of Federal and State Tax Considerations

Federal tax considerations play a critical role in higher education capital finance because public colleges and universities have unlimited access to the tax-exempt market and independent colleges and universities have access up to $150 million (with some narrow technical exceptions) of outstanding tax-exempt debt at any one time. Business officers must, therefore, be familiar with at least some basic tax concepts in order to engage in realistic capital planning. A capital plan prepared in the absence of a sophisticated tax review lacks credibility and probably has omitted a benefit otherwise available to the institution. Further, such plans frame expectations within the institution and setting internal expectations without a tax review creates a credibility risk.

At the same time, business officers cannot maintain up-to-date knowledge in this area because the rules are constantly changing. Tax advice is one of most critical contributions that the investment banker, financial advisor, and financing counsel can make to the institution in the capital planning phase.

The following two sections provide a list of issues that business officers can discuss with their financing counsel to expand their knowledge and sensitivity in the area of federal tax implications. It is not possible to refer to each of these issues in depth in this publication. In addition, the area of tax regulations is particularly subject to change.

Representative Sample of Bond-Related Tax Provisions for Tax-Exempt Financing of an Independent 501(c)(3) College or University

1. Distinction between new money bonds and refunding bonds is significant for tax purposes.
2. No early issuance (bona fide financial reasons).
3. Two percent costs of issuance limit.
4. Transferred proceeds and transferred proceeds penalty (unexpended proceeds of the refunded bonds that have not been expended as of the date the refunded bonds are issued become transferred proceeds of refunding).
5. Investment earnings usage/no overissuance.
6. No hedge bonds (spending timetable and limited investment term of investable proceeds of the bonds).
7. Aggregation of bonds in a single "issue" for tax purposes.
8. Loan yield limitations (limit issuer's fees and administrative costs).
9. Rebate and yield restriction.
10. Bona fide debt service funds / 13 months / exemption from yield restriction.
11. Replacement proceeds (the shift away from collateralized financings and pledges of endowment funds) (the DASNY springing collateral fund concept response).
12. Debt service reserve fund funding limitations (10 percent of the proceeds of the bonds).
13. Rebate calculations and payment.
14. Rebate exceptions.
    (A) Six month expenditure exception (debt service reserve fund deposits are outside the expenditure requirement).

    Consequences of selecting of six month exception and not complying: normal rebate from the date of issuance
    (B) Eighteen month expenditure exception where the following spend down schedule of proceeds is followed: 15 percent (six months), 60 percent (12 months), and

100 percent (18 months) except that a reasonable retainage of up to 5 percent of proceeds can be held until the 30 month date. The reasonable retainage cannot exceed 5 percent and there must be an affirmative factual justification for the retainage.

Consequences of selecting 18 month exception and not complying: normal rebate from the date of issuance.

A failure to satisfy the spending requirement is disregarded if the issuer exercises due diligence to complete the project and the amount of the failure does not exceed the lesser of 3 percent of the issue price of the bonds or $250,000.

(C) Two year exception for construction financing where (i) 75 percent of the available construction proceeds of a new money issue are used for construction expenditures and (ii) the following spend down schedule of available construction proceeds is followed: 10 percent (6 months), 45 percent (12 months), 75 percent (18 months), and 100 percent (24 months) except that a reasonable retainage of up to 5 percent of available construction proceeds can be held until the 36 month date. The reasonable retainage cannot exceed 5 percent, and there must be an affirmative factual justification for the retainage.

Consequences of selecting of 2 year exception and not complying: (i) if a predetermined penalty election is made at time of issuance of the bonds: certain recurring 1.5 percent penalties applied to unspent proceeds with a 3 percent onetime penalty; or (ii) if the predetermined penalty election is not made: retroactive normal rebate on the whole amount

The relief for a de-minimis failure to satisfy the spending requirements described above also applies to the two year exception.

15. Allocation rules for multipurpose financings.
16. Investment contract regulations.
17. No federal guaranty.
18. Private use limits.
 • Maximum of 5 percent to private or unrelated trade or business use (but costs of issuance apply toward the 5 percent so 3 percent is the more practical outcome),
 • Up to 2 1/2 percent incidental use flexibility, and
 • $5 million private loan limit.
19. Management contract limitations.
20. Private activity bond compliance:
 • 120 percent weighted average maturity test,
 • TEFRA procedure,
 • 25 percent limit for use of proceeds to acquire land,
 • acquisition of used property must include additional rehabilitation cost within two years of acquisition of property, and
 • certain prohibited uses.
21. 8038 reporting requirement.

Representative Sample of 501(c)(3) College or University Institutional Tax Issues

1. 501(c)(3) standing and exemption notification.
2. Does the project have any "unrelated trade or business use" implications?
3. Private use limited to 5 percent (but note that costs of issuance apply against the 5 percent).
4. Contracts with related persons.
5. Management or service contracts.
6. Use of excess revenues by the institution and use of assets upon dissolution.
7. Transactions with directors, staff, employees, or board.
8. Use of gift or grant funds to pay a portion of the cost of the project.
9. Affiliation agreements and private benefit implications.
10. Operation of the institution:
 • Governing board derived from cross section of the community,
 • Admissions are nondiscriminatory,
 • Research usage limitations,
 • Shops, housing, and parking, etc. for benefit of institution-related persons only, and
 • Federal grant use limitations.
11. Purchase and sale of assets at fair market value.
12. $150 million limitation.

13. Expenditure of proceeds schedule.
14. No purchase of bonds by institution.
15. Single bond issue within 14 days.
16. Economic life of project compared to average maturity of the bonds.
17. Arbitrage bonds issues.
18. Prohibited facilities.
19. No other funds securing or reasonably expected to be used to pay the bonds.
20. Costs of issuance limited to 2 percent (does not include recoverable insurance premium).
21. Compliance with tax certificate.

Figure 13-1 identifies places where tax issues and rating agency issues are discussed in order to help business officers recognize the manner in which tax and credit considerations influence many higher education institution financing decisions.

Standard & Poor's Corporate Ratings Definitions

Long-term debt

A Standard & Poor's corporate or municipal debt rating is a current assessment of the creditworthiness of an obligor with respect to a specific obligation. This assessment may take into consideration obligors such as guarantors, insurers, or lessees.

The debt rating is not a recommendation to purchase, sell, or hold a security, inasmuch as it does not comment on market price or suitability for a particular investor.

The ratings are based on current information furnished by the issuer or obtained by S&P from other sources it considers reliable. S&P does not perform an audit in connection with any rating and may, on occasion, rely on unaudited financial information. The ratings may be changed, suspended, or withdrawn as a result of changes in, or unavailability of, such information, or based on other circumstances.

The ratings are based, in varying degrees, on the following considerations:

1. Likelihood of default—capacity and willingness of the obligor as to the timely payment of interest and repayment of principal in accordance with the terms of the obligation
2. Nature of and provisions of the obligation
3. Protection afforded by, and relative position of, the obligation in the event of bankruptcy, reorganization, or other arrangement under the laws of bankruptcy and other laws affecting creditors' rights

Investment grade

AAA   Debt rated 'AAA' has the highest rating assigned by Standard & Poor's. Capacity to pay interest and repay principal is extremely strong.

AA   Debt rated 'AA' has a very strong capacity to pay interest and repay principal and differs from the highest rated issues only in small degree.

A   Debt rated 'A' has a strong capacity to pay interest and repay principal although it is somewhat more susceptible to the adverse effects of changes in circumstances and economic conditions than debt in higher rated categories.

BBB   Debt rated 'BBB' is regarded as having an adequate capacity to pay interest and repay principal. Whereas it normally exhibits adequate protection parameters, adverse economic conditions or changing circumstances are more likely to lead to a weakened capacity to pay interest and repay principal for debt in this category than in higher rated categories.

Speculative grade

Debt rated 'BB', 'B', 'CCC', 'CC', and 'C' is regarded as having predominantly speculative characteristics with respect to capacity to pay interest and repay principal. 'BB' indicates the least degree of speculation and 'C' the highest. While such debt will likely have some quality and protective characteristics, these are outweighed by large uncertainties or major exposures to adverse conditions.

BB   Debt rated 'BB' has less near-term vulnerability to default than other speculative issues. However, it faces major ongoing uncertainties or exposure to adverse business, financial, or economic conditions

Figure 13-1. Cross Reference Chart for Ratings and Tax Considerations

Cross References Chapter (CH) then page number (P)	Tax Topics
CH 2 P 38-39	Bond counsel tax opinions
CH 2 P 40	Role of verification agent
CH 4 P 45	Federal tax role in examination audits
CH 8 P 75-76	Reimbursement regulations (1992)
CH 8 P 76-78	Management contract rules (1992)
CH 8 P 78	Gifts and grants
CH 8 P 78	Refunding limitations and strategies

Cross Reference Chapter (CH) then page number (P)	Rating Agency Topics
CH 2 P 36	Credit quality: rating agency groups; nonrated institutions
CH 13 P 105-106	Rating process
CH 13 P 108-117	Rating criteria for Standard & Poor's Corporation, Moody's Investors Service, and Fitch Investors Service
CH 17 P 142-158	Charts of ratings distributions for private colleges and public colleges

that could lead to inadequate capacity to meet timely interest and principal payments. The 'BB' rating category is also used for debt subordinated to senior debt that is assigned an actual or implied 'BBB–' rating.

B   Debt rated 'B' has a greater vulnerability to default but currently has the capacity to meet interest payments and principal repayments. Adverse business, financial, or economic conditions will likely impair capacity or willingness to pay interest and repay principal.

The 'B' rating category is also used for debt subordinated to senior debt that is assigned an actual or implied 'BB' or 'BB–' rating.

CCC   Debt rated 'CCC' has a currently identifi-

able vulnerability to default, and is dependent upon favorable business, financial, and economic conditions to meet timely payment of interest and repayment of principal. In the event of adverse business, financial, or economic conditions, it is not likely to have the capacity to pay interest and repay principal.

The 'CCC' rating category is also used for debt subordinated to senior debt that is assigned an actual or implied 'CCC' debt rating.

CC   The rating 'CC' typically is applied to debt subordinated to senior debt that is assigned an actual or implied 'CCC' debt rating..

C   The rating 'C' typically is applied to debt subordinated to senior debt that is assigned an actual or implied 'CCC–' debt rating. The 'C' rating may be used to cover a situation where a bankruptcy petition has been filed, but debt service payments are continued.

CI   The rating 'CI' is reserved for income bonds on which no interest is being paid.

D   Debt rated 'D' is in payment default. The 'D' rating category is used when interest payments or principal payments are not made on the date due even if the applicable grace period has not expired, unless S&P believes that such payments will be made during such grace period. The 'D' rating also will be used upon the filing of a bankruptcy petition if debt service payments are jeopardized.

Plus (+) or Minus (–): The ratings from 'AA' to 'CCC' may be modified by the addition of a plus or minus sign to show relative standing within the major rating categories.

c   The letter 'c' indicates that the holder's option to tender the security for purchase may be canceled under certain prestated conditions enumerated in the tender options documents.

Provisional Ratings: The letter 'p' indicates that the rating is provisional. A provisional rating assumes the successful completion of the project being financed by the debt being rated and indicates that payment of debt service requirements is largely or entirely dependent upon the successful and timely completion of the project. This rating, however while addressing credit quality subsequent to completion of the project, makes no comment ont he likelihood of, or the risk of default upon failure of, such completion. The investor should exercise judgment with respect to such likelihood and risk.

L   The letter 'L' indicates that the rating pertains to the principal amount of those bonds to the extent that the underlying deposit collateral is federally insured and interest is adequately collateralized. In the case of certificates of deposit the letter 'L' indicates that the deposit, combined with other depositions being held in the same right and capacity, will be honored for principal and accrued pre-default interest up to the federal insurance limits within 30 days after closing of the insured institution or, in the event that the deposit is assumed by a successor insured institution, upon maturity.

Continuance of the rating is contingent upon S&P's receipt of an executed copy of the escrow agreement or closing documentation confirming investments and cash flows.

NR   Indicates no rating has been requested, that there is insufficient information on which to base a rating, or that S&P does not rate a particular type of obligation as a matter of policy.

Debt Obligations of Issuers outside the United States and its territories are rated on the same basis as domestic corporate and municipal issues. The ratings measure the credit worthiness of the obligor but do not take into account currency exchange and related uncertainties.

Bond Investment Quality Standards: Under present commercial bank regulations issued by the Comptroller of the Currency, bonds rated in the top four categories ('AAA', 'AA', 'A', 'BBB', commonly known as "investment grade" ratings) generally are regarded as eligible for bank investment. In addition, the laws of various states governing legal investments impose certain rating or other standards for obligations eligible for investment by savings banks, trust companies, insurance companies, and fiduciaries generally.

Rating Outlooks: An S&P rating outlook assesses the potential direction of an issuer's long-term debt rating over the intermediate to longer term. In determining a rating outlook, consideration is given to any changes in the economic and/or fundamental business conditions. An outlook is not necessarily a precursor of a rating change or future CreditWatch action.

- Positive indicates that a rating may be raised.
- Negative means a rating may be lowered.
- Stable indicates that ratings are not likely to change.
- Developing means ratings may be raised or lowered.
- N.M. means not meaningful.

Municipal Notes

An S&P note rating reflects the liquidity factors and market access risks unique to notes. Notes due in 3 years or less will likely receive a note rating. Notes maturing beyond 3 years will most likely receive a long-term debt rating. The following criteria will be used in making that assessment.

- Amortization schedule (the larger the final maturity relative to other maturities the more likely it will be treated as a note).
- Source of payment (the more dependent the issue is on the market for its refinancing, the more likely it will be treated as a note).

Note rate symbols are as follows:

SP-1   Very strong or strong capacity to pay principal and interest. Those issues determined to possess overwhelming safety characteristics will be given a plus (+) designation.

SP-2   Satisfactory capacity to pay principal and interest, with some vulnerability to adverse financial and economic changes over the term of the note.

SP-3   Speculative capacity to pay principal and interest.

A note rating is not a recommendation to purchase, sell, or hold a security inasmuch as it does not comment as to market price or suitability for a particular investor. The ratings are based on current information furnished to S&P by the issuer or obtained by S&P from other sources it considers reliable. S&P does not perform an audit in connection with any rating and may, on occasion, rely on unaudited financial information. The ratings may be changed, suspended, or withdrawn as a result of changes in or unavailability of such information or based on other circumstances.

Commercial Paper

A Standard & Poor's commercial paper rating is a current assessment of the likelihood of timely payment of debt having an original maturity of no more than 365 days.

Ratings are graded into several categories, ranging from 'A-1' for the highest quality obligations to 'D' for the lowest. These categories are as follows:

A-1   This highest category indicates that the degree of safety regarding timely payment is strong. Those issues determined to possess extremely strong safety characteristics are denoted with a plus sign (+) designation.

A-2   Capacity for timely payment on issues with this designation is satisfactory. However, the relative degree of safety is not as high as for issues designated 'A-1'.

A-3   Issues carrying this designation have adequate capacity for timely payment. They are, however, more vulnerable to the adverse effects of changes in circumstances than obligations carrying in the higher designations.

B   Issues rated 'B' are regarded as having only speculative capacity for timely payment.

C   This rating is assigned to short-term debt obligations with a doubtful capacity for payment.

D   Debt rated 'D' is in payment default. The 'D' rating category is used when interest payments or principal payments are not made on the date due, even if the applicable grace period has not expired, unless S&P believes that such payments will be made during such grace period.

A commercial paper rating is not a recommendation to purchase, sell, or hold a security inasmuch as it does not comment as to market price or suitability for a particular investor. The ratings are based on current information furnished to S&P by the issuer or obtained by S&P from other sources it considers reliable. S&P does not perform an audit in connection with any rating and may, on occasion, rely on unaudited financial information. The ratings may be changed, suspended, or withdrawn as a result of changes in or unavailability of such information or based on other circumstances.

Dual Ratings

Standard & Poor's assigns "dual" ratings to all debt issues that have a put option or demand feature as part of their structure.

The first rating addresses the likelihood of repayment of principal and interest as due, and the second rating addresses only the demand feature. The long-term debt rating symbols are used for bonds to denote the long-term maturity and the commercial paper rating symbols for the put option (for example, 'AAA/A-1+'). With short-term demand debt, S&P's note rating symbols are used with the commercial paper rating symbols (for example, 'SP-1+/A-1+').

Source: Copyright 1993. *Standard & Poor's Municipal Finance Criteria.* New York: Standard & Poor's Corporation.

Moody's Investors Service Municipal Bond Ratings

Purpose

The system of rating securities was originated by John Moody in 1909. The purpose of Moody's Ratings is to provide investors with a simple system of gradation by which the relative investment qualities of bonds may be noted.

Rating Symbols

Gradations of investment quality are indicated by rating symbols, each symbol representing a group in that the quality characteristics are broadly the same. There are nine symbols as shown below, from that used to designate least investment risk (i.e., highest investment quality) to that denoting greatest investment risk (i.e., lowest investment quality):

Aaa Aa A   Baa Ba B   Caa Ca C

Absence of Rating

Where no rating has been assigned or where a rating has been suspended or withdrawn, it may be for reasons unrelated to the quality of the issue.

Should no rating be assigned, the reason may be one of the following:

1. An application for rating was not received or accepted.
2. The issue or issuer belongs to a group of securities or companies that are not rated as a matter of policy.
3. There is a lack of essential data pertaining to the issue or issuer.

4. The issue was privately placed, in which case the rating is not published in Moody's publications.

Suspension or withdrawal may occur if new and material circumstances arise, the effects of which preclude satisfactory analysis; if there is no longer available reasonable up-to-date data to permit a judgment to be formed; if a bond is called for redemption; or for other reasons.

Changes in Rating

The quality of most bonds is not fixed and steady over a period of time, but tends to undergo change. For this reason changes in ratings occur so as to reflect the quality of the bond as now seen. While because of their very nature, changes are to be expected more frequently among bonds of lower ratings than among bonds of higher ratings, nevertheless the user of bond ratings should keep close and constant check on all ratings—both high and low ratings—thereby to be able to note promptly any signs of change in investment status that may occur.

Limitations to Uses of Ratings

Bonds carrying the same rating are not claimed to be of absolutely equal quality. In a broad sense they are alike in position, but since there are a limited number of rating classes used in grading thousands of bonds, the symbols cannot reflect the fine shadings of risks that actually exist. Therefore, it should be evident to the user of ratings that two bonds identically rated are unlikely to be precisely the same in investment quality.

As ratings are designed exclusively for the purpose of grading bonds according to their investment qualities, they should not be used alone as a basis for investment operations. For example, they have no value in forecasting the direction of future trends of market price. Market price movements in bonds are influenced not only by the quality of individual issues but also by changes in money rates and general economic trends, as well as by the length of a maturity, etc. During its life even the best quality bond may have wide price movements, while its high investment status remains unchanged.

The matter of market price has no bearing

whatsoever on the determination of ratings, which are not to be construed as recommendations with respect to "attractiveness." The attractiveness of a given bond may depend on its yield, its maturity date, or other factors for which the investor may search, as well as on its investment quality, the only characteristic to which the rating refers.

Since ratings involve judgments about the future, on the one hand, and since they are used by investors as a means of protection, on the other, the effort is made when assigning ratings to look at "worst" potentialities in the "visible" future, rather than solely at the past record and the status of the present. Therefore, investors using the ratings should not expect to find in them a reflection of statistical factors alone, since they are an appraisal of long-term risks, including the recognition of many nonstatistical factors.

Though ratings may be used by the banking authorities to classify bonds in their bank examination procedure, Moody's Ratings are not made with these bank regulations in view. Moody's Investors Service's own judgment as to desirability or nondesirability of a bond for bank investment purposes is not indicated by Moody's Ratings.

Moody's Ratings represent the mature opinion of Moody's Investors Service, Inc. as to the relative investment classification of bonds. As such they should be used in conjunction with the description and statistics appearing in Moody's Manuals. Reference should be made to these statements for information regarding the issuer. Moody's Ratings are not commercial credit ratings. In no case is default or receivership to be imputed unless expressly so stated in the Manual.

Key to Moody's Investor Service Municipal Bond Ratings

Aaa Bonds that are rated Aaa are judged to be of the best quality. They carry the smallest degree of investment risk and are generally referred to as "gilt edge." Interest payments are protected by a large or by an exceptionally stable margin and principal is secure. While the various protective elements are likely to change, such changes as can be visualized are most unlikely to impair the fundamentally strong position of such issues.

AA Bonds which are rated Aa are judged to be of high quality by all standards. Together with the Aaa group they comprise what are generally known as high grade bonds. They are rated lower than the best bonds because margins of protection may not be as large as in Aaa securities or fluctuation of protective elements may be of greater amplitude or there may be other elements present which make the long-term risks appear somewhat larger than in Aaa securities.

A Bonds which are rated A possess many favorable investment attributes and are to be considered as upper medium grade obligations. Factors giving security to principal and interest are considered adequate but elements may be present which suggest a susceptibility to impairment sometime in the future.

Baa Bonds which are rated Baa are considered as medium grade obligations, i.e., they are neither highly protected nor poorly secured. Interest payment and principal security appear adequate for the present but certain protective elements may be lacking or may be characteristically unreliable over any great length of time. Such bonds lack outstanding investment characteristics and in fact have speculative characteristics as well.

Ba Bonds which are rated Ba are judged to have speculative elements; their future cannot be considered as well assured. Often the protection of interest and principal payments may be very moderate and thereby not well safeguarded during both good and bad times over the future. Uncertainty of position characterizes bonds in this class.

B Bonds which are rated B generally lack characteristics of the desirable investment. Assurance of interest and principal payments or of maintenance of other terms of the contract over any long period of time may be small.

Caa Bonds which are rated Caa are of poor standing. Such issues may be in default or there may be present elements of danger with respect to principal or interest.

Ca   Bonds which are rated Ca represent obligations which are speculative in a high degree. Such issues are often in default or have other marked shortcomings.

C   Bonds which are rated C are the lowest rated class of bonds and issues so rated can be regarded as having extremely poor prospects of ever attaining any real investment standing.

Those bonds in the Aa, A, Baa, Ba, and B groups, which Moody's believes possess the strongest investment attributes, are designated by the symbols Aa1, A1, Baa1, Ba1, and B1.

Moody's bond ratings, where specified, are applied to senior bank obligations and insurance company senior policyholders and claims obligations with an original maturity in excess of one year. Obligations relying upon support mechanisms such as letters-of-credit and bonds of indemnity are excluded unless explicitly rated. Obligations of a branch of a bank are considered to be domiciled in country in which the branch is located. Unless noted as an exception. Moody's rating on a bank's ability to repay senior obligations extends only to branches located in countries which carry a Moody's Sovereign Rating for Bank Deposits. Such branch obligations are rated at the lower of the bank's rating or Moody's Sovereign Rating for the Bank Depositions for the country in which the branch is located. When the currency in which the obligation is denominated is not the same as the currency of the country in which the obligation is domiciled, Moody's ratings do not incorporate an opinion as to whether payment of the obligation will be affected by the actions of the government controlling the currency of denomination. In addition, risk associated with bilateral conflicts between an investor's home country and either the issuer's home country or the country where an issuer branch is located are not incorporated into Moody's ratings. Moody's makes no representation that rated bank obligations or insurance company obligations are exempted from registration under the U.S. Securities Act of 1933 or issued in conformity with any other applicable law or regulation. Nor does Moody's represent any specific bank or insurance company obligation is legally enforceable or a valid senior obligation of a rated issuer.

Fitch Investors Service Bond Ratings

Investment Grade Bond Ratings

Fitch investment grade bond ratings provide a guide to investors in determining the credit risk associated with a particular security. The ratings represent Fitch's assessment of the issuer's ability to meet the obligations of a specific debt issue or class of debt in a timely manner.

The rating takes into consideration special features of the issue, its relationship to other obligations of the issuer, the current and prospective financial condition and operating performance of the issuer and any guarantor, as well as the economic and political environment that might affect the issuer's future financial strength and credit quality.

Fitch ratings do not reflect any credit enhancement that may be provided by insurance policies or financial guaranties unless otherwise indicated.

Bonds that have the same rating are of similar but not necessarily identical credit quality since the rating categories do not fully reflect small differences in the degrees of credit risk.

Fitch ratings are not recommendations to buy, sell, or hold any security. Ratings do not comment on the adequacy of market price, the suitability of any security for a particular investor, or the tax-exempt nature or taxability of payments made in respect of any security.

Fitch ratings are based on information obtained from issuers, other obligors, underwriters, their experts, and other sources Fitch believes to be reliable. Fitch does not audit or verify the truth or accuracy of such information. Ratings may be changed, suspended, or withdrawn as a result of changes in, or the unavailability of, information or for other reasons.

AAA   Bonds considered to be investment grade and of the highest credit quality. The obligor has an exceptionally strong ability to pay interest and repay principal, which is unlikely to be affected by reasonably foreseeable events.

AA   Bonds considered to be investment grade and of very high credit quality. The obligor's ability to pay interest and repay principal is very strong, although not quite as strong as bonds rated 'AAA.' Because bonds rated in the 'AAA' and 'AA' categories are not significantly vulnerable to foreseeable future developments, short-term debt of these issuers is generally rated 'F-1+.'

A   Bonds considered to be investment grade and of high credit quality. The obligor's ability to pay interest and repay principal is considered to be strong, but may be more vulnerable to adverse changes in economic conditions and circumstances than bonds with higher ratings.

BBB   Bonds considered to be investment grade and of satisfactory credit quality. The obligor's ability to pay interest and repay principal is considered to be adequate. Adverse changes in economic conditions and circumstances, however, are more likely to have adverse impact on these bonds, and therefore impair timely payment. The likelihood that the ratings of these bonds will fall below investment grade is higher than for bonds with higher ratings.

Plus(+)Minus(−): Plus and minus signs are used with a rating symbol to indicate the relative position of a credit within the rating category. Plus and minus signs, however, are not used in the 'AAA' category.

NR: Indicates that Fitch does not rate the specific issue.

Conditional: A conditional rating is premised on the successful completion of a project or the occurrence of a specific event.

Suspended: A rating is suspended when Fitch deems the amount of information available from the issuer to be inadequate for rating purposes.

Withdrawn: A rating will be withdrawn when an issue matures or is called or refinanced, and, at Fitch's discretion, when an issuer fails to furnish proper and timely information.

FitchAlert: Ratings are placed on FitchAlert to notify investors of an occurrence that is likely to result in a rating change and the likely direction of such change. These are designated as "Positive," indicating a potential upgrade, "Negative," for potential downgrade, or "Evolving," where ratings may be raised or lowered. FitchAlert is relatively short-term, and should be resolved within 12 months.

Credit Trend: Credit trend indicators show whether credit fundamentals are improving, stable, declining, or uncertain, as follows:

Improving	⇧
Stable	⇔
Declining	⇩
Uncertain	⇕

Credit trend indicators are not predictions that any rating change will occur, and have a longer-term time frame than issues placed on Fitch Alert.

Speculative Grade Bond Ratings

Fitch speculative grade bond ratings provide a guide to investors in determining the credit risk associated with a particular security. The ratings ('BB' to 'C') represent Fitch's assessment of the likelihood of timely payment of principal and interest in accordance with the terms of obligation for bond issues not in default. For defaulted bonds, the rating ('DDD' to 'D') is an assessment of the ultimate recovery value through reorganization or liquidation.

The rating takes into consideration special features of the issue, its relationship to other obligations of the issuer, the current and prospective financial condition and operating performance of the issuer and any guarantor, as well as the economic and political environment that might affect the issuer's future financial strength.

Bonds that have the same rating are of similar but not necessarily identical credit quality since rating categories cannot fully reflect the differences in degrees of credit risk.

BB   Bonds are considered speculative. The obligor's ability to pay interest and repay principal may be affected over time by adverse economic changes. However, business and financial alternatives can be identified which could assist the obligor in satisfying its debt service requirements.

B   Bonds are considered highly speculative. While bonds in this class are currently meeting debt service requirements, the probability of continued timely payment of principal and interest reflects the obligor's limited margin of safety and the need for reasonable business and economic activity throughout the life of the issue.

CCC   Bonds have certain identifiable characteristics which, if not remedied, may lead to default. The ability to meet obligations requires an advantageous business and economic environment.

CC   Bonds are minimally protected. Default in payment of interest and/or principal seems probable over time.

C   Bonds are in imminent default in payment of interest or principal.

DDD, Bonds are in default on interest and/or
DD,   principal payments. Such bonds are ex-
and   tremely speculative and should be valued
D   on the basis of their ultimate recovery value in liquidation or reorganization of the obligor. 'DDD' represents the highest potential for recovery on these bonds, and 'D' represents the lowest potential for recovery.

Plus(+)Minus(–): Plus and minus signs are used with a rating symbol to indicate the relative position of a credit within the rating category. Plus and minus signs, however, are not used in the 'DDD', 'DD', or 'D' categories.

Short-Term Ratings

Fitch's short-term ratings apply to debt obligations that are payable on demand or have original maturities of generally up to three years, including commercial paper, certificates of deposit, medium-term notes, and municipal and investment notes.

The short-term rating places greater emphasis than a long-term rating on the existence of liquidity necessary to meet the issuer's obligations in a timely manner.

F-1+   Exceptionally Strong Credit Quality. Issues assigned this rating are regarded as having the strongest degree of assurance for timely payment.

F-1   Very Strong Credit Quality. Issues assigned this rating reflect an assurance of timely payment only slightly less in degree than issues rated 'F-1+'.

F-2   Good Credit Quality. Issues assigned this rating have a satisfactory degree of assurance for timely payment, but the margin of safety is not as great as for issues assigned 'F-1+' and 'F-1' ratings.

F-3   Fair Credit Quality. Issues assigned this rating have characteristics suggesting that the degree of assurance for timely payment is adequate, however, near-term adverse changes could cause these securities to be rated below investment grade.

F-5   Weak Credit Quality. Issues assigned this rating have characteristics suggesting a minimal degree of assurance for timely payment and are vulnerable to near-term adverse changes in financial and economic conditions.

D   Default. Issues assigned this rating are in actual or imminent payment default.

LOC   The symbol LOC indicates that the rating is based on a letter of credit issued by a commercial bank.

Claims-Paying Ability Ratings

Fitch claims-paying ability ratings provide an assessment of an insurance company's financial strength and, therefore, its ability to pay policy and contract claims under the terms indicated. The rating does not apply to nonpolicy obligations of the insurer, such as debt obligations (which are addressed under Fitch's bond ratings), nor does it apply to the suitability or terms of any individual policy or contract.

AAA   The ability to pay claims is extremely strong for insurance companies with this highest rating. Foreseeable business and economic risk factors should not have any material adverse impact on the ability of these insurers to pay claims. Profitability, overall balance sheet strength, capitalization, and liquidity are all at very secure levels and are unlikely to be affected by potential adverse underwriting, investment, or cyclical events.

AA   Insurance companies with this rating are

very strong and only slightly more susceptible to exhibiting any weakening of financial strength due to adverse business and
economic developments. Any foreseeable
deterioration in financial strength would
still leave carriers in this category with a
strong claims-paying ability.

A Insurers in this category are strong companies with no immediate expectations
for encountering events significant
enough to weaken their claims-paying
ability. However, major business or cyclical pressures are more likely to have an
adverse impact on profitability, liquidity,
and capitalization and, therefore, on the
ability to pay claims.

BBB Companies in this category have adequate
financial strength and claims-paying capability. For insurers with this rating,
longer-term obligations would be more
susceptible to claims-paying concerns under adverse circumstances than for higher
rated companies.

BB For insurers rated in this category, the
ability to pay claims is vulnerable to com-
pany-specific adverse financial events or
stressful cyclical downturns. It will be
more difficult for carriers with this rating
to maintain adequate claims-paying ability under severe business and economic
circumstances.

B There is significant risk that companies in
this category will not be able to pay claims
when due. Liquidity and capital adequacy
are likely to be impaired under even moderately negative business and economic
developments.

CCC,
CC,
and
C
Insurance companies with one of these
ratings are considered very weak with respect to their ability to pay claims. The
carrier may be under the supervision of a
state insurance department and already
may not be making all policy claims payments in a timely fashion.

D Insurance carriers have been placed in
liquidation by state insurance departments and policy claims payments are being controlled, delayed, or reduced.

Plus(+)Minus(−): Plus and minus signs are
used with a rating symbol to indicate the relative
position of a credit within the rating category.
Plus and minus signs, however, are not used in the
'AAA' and 'D' categories.

Servicer Ratings

Servicers are key to maintaining the credit
quality of a pool of nonperforming commercial
mortgages and real estate owned assets. In assessing and analyzing a servicer's capabilities, Fitch
reviews several key factors, including the servicer's management team, organizational structure, track record, and workout and asset
disposition experience and strategies.

Superior: Servicer considered to be of the highest
quality. A servicer in this category possesses a
strong, seasoned management team, extensive
workout and disposition experience, and, typically, significant financial resources.

Above Average: Servicer considered to be of very
high quality. A servicer in this category possesses
a strong management team, with good workout
and disposition experience, and may have significant financial resources.

Average: Servicer considered to be of high quality. A servicer in this category possesses adequate
workout and disposition experience but may lack
significant financial resources.

Below Average: Servicer considered to be of acceptable, but sub-par, quality. Senior management is relatively unseasoned, workout
experience is minimal, and typically lacks significant financial resources.

Unacceptable: Servicer unacceptable to Fitch.
Use of such a servicer probably would preclude
Fitch's rating the transaction's debt securities of
'BBB' or higher levels.

Source: Copyright 1994. *Fitch Ratings Book* (January 1994). New York: Fitch Investors Service, Inc.

PART IV

Implementation

❖ FOURTEEN ❖

Financing Documentation

There are rarely two higher education financing transactions that have the same documentation unless they are two issues for the same institution or multiple issues which are assembled at the same time. Figure 14-1 provides a hypothetical closing index as a case study to show one type of transaction. The financing is assumed to be a refunding in order to raise more issues.

Figure 14-1. Case Study: Tax-Exempt Independent College Financing Closing Index

Document Reference Number	Document Description	Comments
	BASIC DOCUMENTS	
1	Closing Index	Sets forth the list of all the documents to be delivered at the closing
2	The _____ University Revenue Bond Resolution, adopted by the Authority on _____, 1994	Authority action to authorize the bonds generally
3	The _____ University Series Resolution Authorizing up to $_____ Bonds, adopted by the Authority on _____, 1994	Authority action to authorize the bonds more specifically
4	Bond Series Certificate Relating to the Series 1993B Bonds, dated as of _____, 1994	Part of the delegation process of setting the final terms of the bonds
5	Loan Agreement, dated as of _____, 1994, by and between the Authority and the University	Sets forth the terms of the agreement between the authority, as issuer, and the university as beneficiary
6	Copy of the Bond Purchase Contract by and between the University and the Underwriter, dated _____, 1994	Contract for the initial side of the bonds, which is contingent upon satisfying the closing conditions
7	Copy of the Letter of Representation of the Authority, dated _____, 1994, addressed to the University and the Underwriter	Certain representations are made as of the date of sale of the bonds

Document Reference Number	Document Description	Comments
8	Copy of the Letter of Representation of the University, dated _____, 1994, addressed to the Authority and the Underwriter	Certain representations are made by the university to the issuer and the underwriter as of the date of sale of the bonds
9	Preliminary Official Statement, dated _____, 1994	See chapter 4
10	Official Statement, dated _____, 1994	See chapter 4
11	U.C.C. Financing Statements	Filings, to perfect a pledge
12	Bond Insurance Side Agreement, dated as of _____, 1994, by and among the Bank, the Authority and the Insurer	Optional supplement to terms in the Indenture and resolutions
	THE UNIVERSITY	
13	Certificate of the Education Department of the State of _____, dated as of a recent date, as to the incorporation of the University and its continued existence and good standing	Evidence of corporate good standing
14	Omnibus Certificate of an Authorized Officer of the University with respect to various authorization, litigation, and disclosure matters	Functional closing document
15	Order Directing Trustee to Authenticate and Deliver the University Bonds and as to Deposit of Proceeds	Functional closing document
16	Certificate as to Delivery and Payment	Functional closing document
17	Certificate Required by Section ____ of the Trust Indenture	Functional closing document meeting a particular individual requirement of the referenced financing document
18	Certificate of the University pursuant to Section _____ of the Bond Purchase Contract	Functional closing document meeting a particular individual requirement of the referenced financing document

Document Reference Number	Document Description	Comments
	THE BOND TRUSTEE	
19	Omnibus Certificate of the Authority with respect to various authorization, litigation, and disclosure matters	Functional closing document
20	Order Directing Trustee to Authenticate and Deliver the Bonds	Functional closing document
	THE UNDERWRITER	
21	Preliminary Blue Sky Survey, dated _____, 1994	Relates to state securities laws; see chapter 4; in some cases, a legal investment survey also is prepared
22	Final Blue Sky Survey, dated _____, 1994	Relates to state securities laws; see chapter 4
	LEGAL OPINIONS	
23	Opinion of Counsel to the University, required by Paragraph _____ of the Bond Purchase Contract	See chapter 4
24	Opinion of Counsel to the University, required by Section ____ of the Indenture	See chapter 4
25	Opinion of Bond Counsel to the Authority, required by Section _____ of the Bond Purchase Contract	See chapter 4
26	Opinion of Counsel to the Underwriter	See chapter 4
27	Opinion of Counsel to the Trustee and Escrow Agent	See chapter 4
	APPROVALS AND CONSENTS	
28	Certified Resolution of the _____ State _____ Board authorizing the issuance of the Bonds	Not every state will have such a review board at the state level
29	Evidence of Public Hearing and Approval of the Governor of the State of _____, relating to the financing by the Authority of the Project, required by the federal tax law	This process satisfies a federal tax requirement and is known as a "TEFRA" hearing

Document Reference Number	Document Description	Comments
	MISCELLANEOUS	
30	Cross Receipt and Evidence of Payment	Functional closing document
31	Rating Agency Letters	See chapter 13
32	(1) SAS35 or SAS72 Report and (2) Consent Letters of Auditors required by Section _____ of the Bond Purchase Agreement	See chapter 2
33	Verification Report	See chapter 2
34	Closing Memorandum	Sets forth the critical procedures, including flows of funds, recordings, and filings to be accomplished in connection with the closing
	POST CLOSING FILINGS	
35	Municipal Securities Rulemaking Board Rule G-36 filing of the Official Statement and any Refunding Documents	See chapter 4
36	Securities Exchange Act of 1934 Rule 15c2-12 filing of the Official Statement with a repository	See chapter 4
37	Actual filing of Form 8038	This is an informational filing which is required to be made with the IRS within a specified number of days after the closing

Competitive and Negotiated Bond Sales and Procedures

The debate between proponents of competitive and negotiated sales is long-running and can be expected to continue indefinitely. The arguments are too varied to discuss at length in this chapter and few experienced market participants would agree even on the priority of the various factors once a list was made. Instead, this chapter will touch upon only some sample considerations which illustrate the type of questions that business officers should be concerned with when approaching this topic.

Competitive Bond Sales

Competitive sales (also know as public sales) involve the publication of a notice of sale setting out a uniform description of securities to be offered to the underwriter who offers to purchase the securities at the lowest cost to the issuer, as calculated by the formula standard set forth in the notice of sale. The date, time, and place of the bid opening is set in advance, often by a time period set by statute. The right to reject all bids is reserved in a notice of sale.

Competitive sales are favored by those who believe that a particular securities issue can be prestructured, sometimes with assistance from a financial advisor, to the degree where price is the only variable among competing investment banking firms. In most cases the choice to use a competitive sale is a business judgment decision. However, some statutes require competitive sales without discretion, but these statutes are most often applicable to direct governmental bonds rather than conduit issues for higher education and health care. Most authority and agency statutes allow a choice of public sales or negotiated (private) sales.

The higher education capital markets are becoming more and more investor-driven. The most powerful forces in the market are the mutual funds which serve as the investment vehicles for many billions of dollars of securities. See chapter 2 for a discussion of the investors who make up the purchasers of higher education securities. Business officers should carefully consider their ability, acting with or without a financial advisor, to correctly predict what the market will react to most favorably on a specified sale date a week or more in advance. The ability to make such projections will vary on a case by case basis. Even the allocation of serial bonds and term bonds or the decision to test the market for a shorter call protection period is not available as an option in a competitive bid situation because the bidding terms must be absolutely uniform for all bidders, but sometimes that may not be significant.

The addition of any significant degree of complexity to the transaction, whether it be a refunding use of proceeds or the addition of a derivative product, often renders a competitive sale inappropriate even in the view of most proponents of competitive sales. There are exceptions to every generality, however, and business officers should consult with their financing team before making a final decision.

Competitive Bond Sale Procedures

Competitive sale procedures can be characterized generally as follows:

1. Publication of the notice of sale and concurrent distribution of the draft official statement.
2. Receipt of bids at the specified time and place, bid opening, verification of the calculation of the winning bid, and return of good-faith checks of the unsuccessful bidders.

3. Closing of the issue, generally two weeks after the bid opening. The underwriter often will not attend the closing if the purchase price is payable by wire transfer and the securities are delivered to a securities depository such as The Depository Trust Company.

The type of sale does not otherwise affect the financing process except to the extent that when a underwriter is involved in a negotiated sale, the terms of the bond documentation may be completed after the bond sale depending on the changes in the bond structure that are made during the pricing of the bonds.

Negotiated Bond Sales

Negotiated sales (also known as private sales) involve the negotiation of a purchase price with the institution's investment banker, which may be acting alone or as the representative of a group of underwriters. The price of this negotiation is reflected in the bond purchase agreement.

Negotiated sales are favored by those who believe that a particular securities issue should be structured with customized input from the investor community. Implicit in this analysis is the belief that an investment banker brings "value added" structuring to the transaction and that interest rates can be lowered for issuers by premarketing efforts and other customized sales techniques. Proponents of negotiated sales believe that they can assure that their investment banker gives them a proper price for the bonds by examining other new bond issues which go to market at the same time as their bond issue as well as the secondary market activity of any number of other comparative issues. In addition, business officers or representatives of the governmental issuing authority often are in attendance on the trading floor as the book of securities is constructed, thereby allowing the institution to be represented in the decisions that are driven by reactions to daily market conditions. Despite the merit in this view, the competitive sale approach has its own independent merits which are more significant in certain situations, as described earlier in this chapter.

Specific examples of situations where negoti-

ated sales are generally agreed to be preferable include large issues relative to the market and/or market sector; issues offered by a weak credit or offered into a weak market demand; issues offered in volatile market conditions; financings using or considering derivative products; and refundings.

Negotiated Bond Sale Procedures

Negotiated sales are implemented through the execution of a bond purchase agreement. The sequence of events leading up to the execution of the agreement can be characterized generally as follows:

1. Market updates through the course of the financing preparation process; integration of changing market conditions into the financing plan.
2. Prepricing conference, usually held on the day before pricing, during which market conditions are reviewed in detail, including a report on the targeted investor segments.
3. Pricing, which involves the offering of the securities in the market. Pricing involves the solicitation of orders and sometimes a resetting of the pricing terms (repricing) of the securities if sufficient investor demand can be generated to create competition on the buy side.
4. In the case of a refunding, there will be a one-day interval for verification of the escrow structuring and confirmation of compliance with the requirements of the tax code. In some cases, verification is done overnight after the pricing.
5. Execution of the bond purchase agreement.

Sample Negotiated Financing Schedule

The sample schedule exhibited in figure 15-1 focuses on the events commencing after the underwriter has been selected. This sequence would be similar for a competitively bid offering, but the responsibility column would differ significantly in terms of both giving substantive direction to the parties and coordinating multiple concurrent processes. The investment banker often functions as the central coordinator of negotiated issues.

Figure 15-1

Week No.	Event	Responsibility
	Obtain institutional policy direction to begin to structure a financing	Varies with each institution
	Identify internal financing team members and team leader	Business officer
	Review choice of issuer of the securities as internal matter; decide whether to engage the issuer or the underwriter first	Varies with each state
	Select underwriting team	Authority or state
	Select legal counsel and any required consultants	Authority or state, underwriter
	Distribute time schedule and outline process	Underwriter
	Working group meeting to discuss credit structure, new disclosure requirements, and financing plan	Finance team
	Design rating agencies and/or credit enhancement strategies and presentations	Authority or state, underwriter, bond counsel, financial advisor
	Examine the effects of tax law and regulations on the bond structure	Bond counsel, underwriter
	Distribute first draft of trust indenture, authorization resolution, bond purchase agreement, and other documents	Bond counsel, underwriter's counsel, college counsel
	Obtain final college authorization for the financing, usually involving delegation to senior staff or the executive committee	College staff and college counsel
	Select trustee, issuing and paying agent	Authority or state, college counsel
	Distribute first draft of preliminary official statement	Underwriter's counsel, college counsel
	Receive comments on first draft of documents	Finance team
	Send background information to credit enhancers	Authority or state, underwriter, financial advisor
	Solicit bids from credit enhancers	Underwriter
	Distribute revised drafts of documents	Finance team
	Working group meeting on revised documents	Finance team
	Rating agency presentations	Authority or state, underwriter, financial advisor

Week No.	Event	Responsibility
	Distribute final drafts of documents	Bond counsel, underwriter's counsel
	Receive credit enhancement commitment or ratings as appropriate	Authority or state, underwriter
	Mail preliminary official statement	Finance team
	Investor presentations including group and one-on-one market development meetings	Underwriter
	Conference call with all underwriters to discuss market conditions and pricing levels	Authority or state, underwriter
	Pricing	Underwriter
	Signing of bond purchase agreement	Underwriter, authority
	Prepare final official statement	Finance team
	Prepare closing documents	Finance team
	Preclosing	Finance team
	Closing and delivery of bonds and proceeds	Finance team

❖ SIXTEEN ❖

Issues of Cost and Cost Containment

Rarely do two higher education financing transactions have the same costs unless they are two issues for the same institution or multiple issues that are assembled at the same time. This chapter provides several different types of cost worksheet approaches as a starting point. The financing is assumed to be a refunding in order to raise a more complete a list of cost line items.

Worksheet for Cost Estimate for a Tax-Exempt Sample Bond Issue

Sample Higher Education Finance Authority 1993 Independent College Refinancing Preliminary Sizing With Bond Insurance (Assuming advance refunding of a 1988 Bond Issue of $35 million issue with a call date of 1998)

Sources and Uses Report

Sources

Bond Proceeds	$41,000,000
1988 Bonds Service Reserve Fund Requirement	3,200,000
Available Surplus in 1988 Bonds DSRF	25,000
College Equity	0
	$44,225,000

Uses

1988 Bonds Par + Premium	$36,750,000
Repay Bank Loan (Principal)	1,000,000
Other Project Costs (Excluding Costs of Issuance)	to come
Insurance Premium (% of Debt Service)	1,763,933
Debt Service Reserve Fund Deposit	3,500,000
Underwriters' Discount (1.0% of 1993 Bonds)	400,000
Costs of Issuance (less than 1.0% of 1993 Bonds)	270,000
Unallocated Contingency	to come
	$44,225,000

Figure 16-1

DETAIL OF USES OF FUNDS

PROJECT COSTS FROM 1993 BONDS and 1989 TRANSFERS			COLLEGE EQUITY EXPENSE
Project Costs Reimbursed To College at Closing	Project Costs Paid by College at Closing or Thereafter	Costs of Issuance Limited to 2%	
College Counsel (Project) 25,000 Survey 3,000	1989 Bonds Escrow 36,750,000 Repay Bank Loan (P) 1,000,000 1993 Improvements Project ? Bond Insurance (Fee) ? IRC Transferred Proceeds Penalty ? DSRF (maximum annul DS) 3,500,000 Title Search/Title Insurance 95,000 Authority Fee 35,000 Contingency 25,000 Reimbursements 28,000	Rating Agencies 20,000 Und. Discount (1%) 400,000 Auditor 25,000 College Counsel (Finance) 30,000 Bond Counsel 75,000 Underwriter's Counsel 50,000 Printing 20,000 Trustee 5,000 Trustee Counsel 5,000 Escrow Asset 5,000 Verification Report 5,000 Auditor Costs 5,000 Environmental 10,000 Miscellaneous 15,000	
	39,200,000 + [Max Avail. 98% + 1988 Funds: 42,425,000] [Unspent from COI 2%: 130,000] [Total Avail. 42,555,000]	670,000 [Max Avail. 2%: 800,000]	
Total:	32,000 + 43,654,754 + 778,000 = 44,464,754 [Preliminary Unallocated: _____]		Total: 0

Transferred Proceeds Penalty Note: This can be paid (and bonded) or paid through a yield restricted sinking fund. In this example, it will be paid over time through the yield restricted sinking fund.

Debt Service Reserve Fund Note: 1993 DSRF (3,500,000) minus 1988 DSRF (3,200,000) equals net DSRF increase of 300,000

Data Costs Sample: New Jersey Educational Facilities Authority 1990 to 1992

The following list is representative of typical and various issuance costs for certain obligations sold during the period 1990–1992 by the New Jersey Educational Facilities Authority. This chart is intended for use as a guide only; actual costs will vary for specific borrowings. It is important to note that certain costs are based on the complexity of the structure and may be negotiable depending on the level of services rendered.

Issue Profile	Tax Exempt; Fixed Rate Level Debt Service 3–5 Year Term Credit Rating: Investment Grade Construction Project Note Issue	Tax Exempt; Fixed Rate Level Debt Service 20–30 Year Term Credit Rating: Investment Grade Construction Project Bond Issue	Tax Exempt; Fixed Rate Level Debt Service 20–30 Year Term Credit Rating: Investment Grade Refunding Only Bond Issue	Tax Exempt; Fixed Rate Level Debt Service 20–30 Year Term Credit Rating: Investment Grade Construction Project & Refunding Bond Issue
Size Range of Issue	$3–5.7 Million	$7.4–15.4 Million	$7.3–10.6 Million	$10–31.7 Million
Number in Sample	2	4	3	4
Components of Issuance Costs				
Bond Counsel	$35,000	$46,100	$69,200	$72,300
Financial Advisor	10,000	12,500	10,500	12,500
Trustee	3,500	8,100	5,000	12,800
Trustee Counsel	2,750	2,875	4,200	4,250
Printing	6,500	7,400	10,000	10,000
Rating Agencies	16,000	20,800	23,900	24,500
Publication of Notice of Sale	5,500	8,600	8,600	8,600
College Auditor	3,000	5,000	7,500	7,000
Accountant Verification	—	—	7,300	6,500
Bond Insurance Premium ($ Range) -		74,704–159,000	50,500– 84,100	85,000–131,164
Purchaser's Discount (% Range)	1.15–1.19%	1.09–1.50%	1.38–1.58%	1.18–1.50%
Purchaser's Discount ($ Range)	35,700– 65,953	104,378–230,141	101,041–173,422	241,574–437,225
Total Range of Costs	$117,950–148,203	$290,457–500,516	$297,741–403,722	$485,024–726,839

Description of Components

- Bond Counsel: develops the legal documents and renders an opinion on the security, tax-exempt status, and issuance authority of an obligation.
- Financial Advisor: generally a bank or investment banking firm, who will advise the issuer on the financial matters of a proposed issue.
- Trustee: designated as the custodian of the note/bond funds and the official representative of the bondholders.
- Rating Agency: the fees are the cost of analysis and the assignment of a rating from Moody's and Standard & Poor's.
- Publication: the expenses cover the publishing of the notice of sale of the proposed issue and includes certain details such as bidding requirements, date and time of the sale, and a description of the issue. This is a cost associated with competitively sold issues only.
- College Auditor Fees: the costs associated with providing a consent or comfort letter to parties involved in the financing.
- Verification: one of the components of a refunding issue; the verification agent certifies that the initial deposit to the escrow fund, investments purchased and interest income earned are sufficient to meet all debt service as due on the refunded bond issue.

- Bond Insurance: guarantees the payment of principal and interest and provides a higher credit rating and lower borrowing cost; the premium is based on the total debt service.
- Discount: represents amount allowed to the bond purchaser as an inducement to buy the bonds; the cost is added to the total dollar cost of interest.

Part V

Interest Rates and Market Statistics

❖ SEVENTEEN ❖

Market Statistics and Interest Rates

Selected Long-Term Interest Rates

Bond Buyer 20-Bond Index and Revenue Bond Index Rates

The 20-Bond Index was compiled once a year from 1900 through 1914. The 20-Bond Index was compiled on Jan. 1, April 1, July 1, and Sept. 1 in 1915 and 1916, the first day of each month from 1915 through 1945, and once a week since 1946. The 20-Bond Index is based on a set of general obligation bonds maturing in 20 years and with Moody's Investors Services ratings ranging from Baa to Aaa. Its rating is approximately equivalent to A1.

20-Bond Index Rates

Year	Average	High	Low
1993	5.59	6.19	5.20
1992	6.44	6.79	5.89
1991	6.92	7.19	6.64
1990	7.27	7.56	7.03
1989	7.23	7.72	6.86
1988	7.68	7.97	7.33
1987	7.66	9.17	6.54
1986	7.33	8.33	6.74
1985	9.11	9.87	8.36
1984	10.10	11.07	9.51
1983	9.51	10.04	8.78

The Revenue Bond Index has been compiled weekly since it commenced on September 20, 1979. The Revenue Bond Index uses 25 bonds maturing in 30 years and with Moody's ratings ranging from Baa1 to Aaa.

Revenue Bond Index Rates

Year	Average	High	Low
1993	5.82	6.44	5.41
1992	6.59	6.87	6.12
1991	7.11	7.42	6.86
1990	7.53	7.83	7.28
1989	7.51	7.95	7.19
1988	8.03	8.34	7.64
1987	8.04	9.59	6.92
1986	7.76	8.72	7.15
1985	9.56	10.31	8.85
1984	10.52	11.44	9.86
1983	10.04	10.56	9.21

Thirty-Year Treasury Bond Rates

The 30-year Treasury bond rate has become the most widely followed benchmark of long-term interest rates, and is an effective gauge of the volatility of the market. The 30 year Treasury bond was first issued by the federal government in 1977 and reached its lowest rate ever recorded in 1993.

Thirty-Year Treasury Bond Rates

Year	Average	High	Low
1993	6.59	7.43	5.87
1992	7.67	8.06	7.25
1991	8.14	8.50	7.52
1990	8.60	9.09	8.03
1989	8.45	9.27	7.84
1988	8.95	9.42	8.37
1987	8.56	10.10	7.32
1986	7.81	9.49	7.16
1985	10.80	11.85	9.30
1984	12.40	13.86	11.43
1983	11.18	12.06	10.31

Source: CS First Boston

Ten Year Chart of Historical Interest Rate Perspectives

Figure 17-1 below illustrates the fluctuation of the 30-year Treasury bond as compared to *The Bond Buyer Revenue Bond Index* from 1983 to 1993.

Figure 17-1

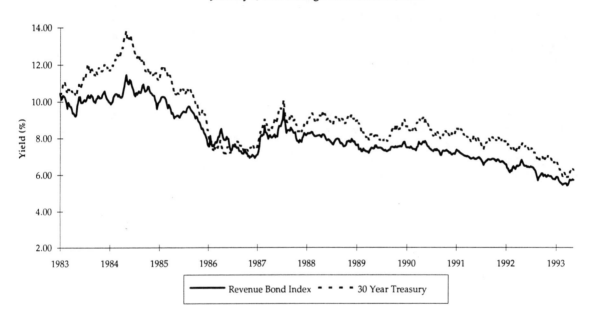

Bond Buyer Revenue Bond Index vs. 30 Year Treasury Bond
January 1, 1983 through November 30, 1993

Source: CS First Boston Fixed Income Research

Explanation of Various Short-Term Rate Indices

Figure 17-2 shows the short-term indices tracked by *The Bond Buyer*. In addition, the *J.J. Kenney Short-Term High Grade Index* is used in public finance transactions.

Figure 17-2

Name	Description
Bankers Trust TENR Rate	Bankers Trust Co.'s tax-exempt note rate for weekly floating-rate bonds with one-day or seven-day put options; set Wednesday, effective Thursday.
Chemical Securities Index (CSI)	Chemical Securities Inc.'s Chemical Securities Index for weekly floating-rate notes with seven-day put option, set Tuesday, effective Wednesday.
Lehman Brothers Money Market Index	Lehman Brothers' Money Market Municipal Index, based on money market municipal issues maturing in 25 to 36 days; set Tuesday, effective Wednesday.
Smith Barney Base Rate	Smith Barney, Harris Upham & Co.'s Base Rate, based on a selection of tax-exempt and taxable securities with maturities as long as six months and the prime rate; set Tuesday, effective Wednesday.
Bond Buyer Commercial Paper Rate	*The Bond Buyer*'s Commercial Paper Rate; the average of 30-day commercial paper rates provided daily by various securities firms.
Pander & Co.'s VariFact Index	Ponder & Co.'s VariFact index for weekly floating-rate bonds with one-day or seven-day put options; set Thursday, effective Thursday.
Bond Buyer One-Year Note Index	*The Bond Buyer*'s One-Year Note Index; the average of 12-month note rates for 10 state and local governments rated MIG-1 or MIG-2 by Moody's Investors Service and SP-1 plus or SP-1 by Standard & Poor's Corp.; set Wednesday.
PSA Municipal Swap Index	The PSA Municipal Swap Index (produced by Municipal Market Data), a weekly high-grade market index of seven-day tax-exempt variable-rate demand notes; set Wednesday, effective Thursday.

Source: The Bond Buyer 1993 Yearbook. Ed., Matthew Kreps. Copyright 1993 American Banker, Inc.

Short-Term J.J. Kenney Index Rate Chart from 1983 to 1993

Chart 17-3 below illustrates the fluctuation of the Bond Buyer Revenue Bond Index (30 years) as compared to the J.J. Kenney Short-Term High Grade Index.

Figure 17-3

Bond Buyer Revenue Bond Index vs. Kenny Short-Term High Grade Index
January 1, 1983 through November 30, 1993

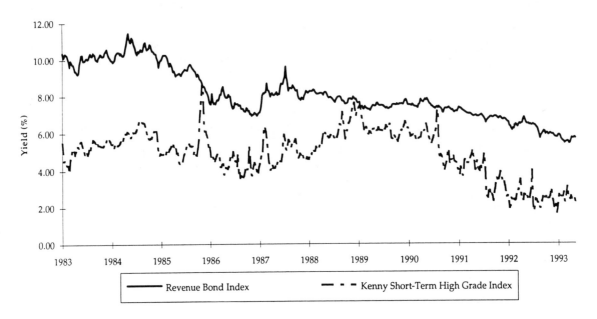

Source: CS First Boston Fixed Income Research

Yield Curves

The yield curve is a chart that illustrates the relationships between interest rates and various maturity terms of debt obligations. Interest rates reflect investors' relationships among the various risks that investors assume. A steep yield curve (figure 17-4 below) reflects a market in which investors perceive a time risk and insist on higher interest rates as the term of their investment lengthens. An inverted yield curve (figure 17-5 below) reflects a market in which investors per-ceive a relatively high degree or risk in the shorter maturities and therefore insist on higher short-term rates as compensation for purchasing those securities. A flat yield curve (figure 17-6 below) reflects a market in which the relationships of time risk and short-term market fluctuations push the short end of the yield curve up and the long end of the yield curve down. The yield curve examples below are three isolated examples; there are daily variations on these examples which can be found in many of the principal daily newspapers as well as the financial press.

Figure 17-4

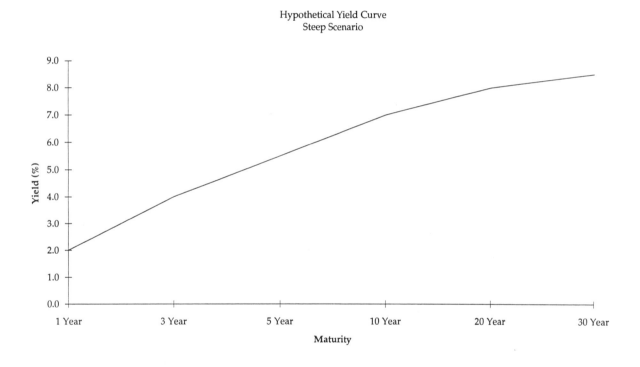

Hypothetical Yield Curve
Steep Scenario

Figure 17-5

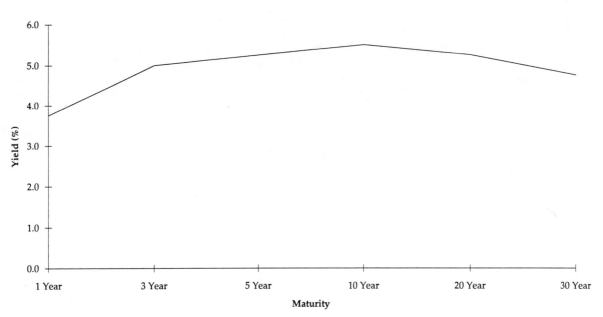

Hypothetical Yield Curve
Inverted Scenario

Figure 17-6

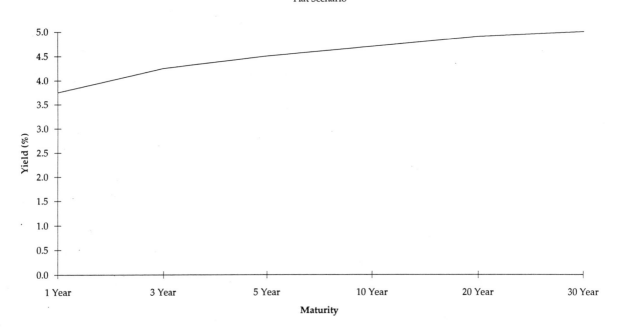

Hypothetical Yield Curve
Flat Scenario

Tax Exempt Higher Education Financing Volume 1983–1993

Figure 17-7

Higher Education New Money and Refunding Volume

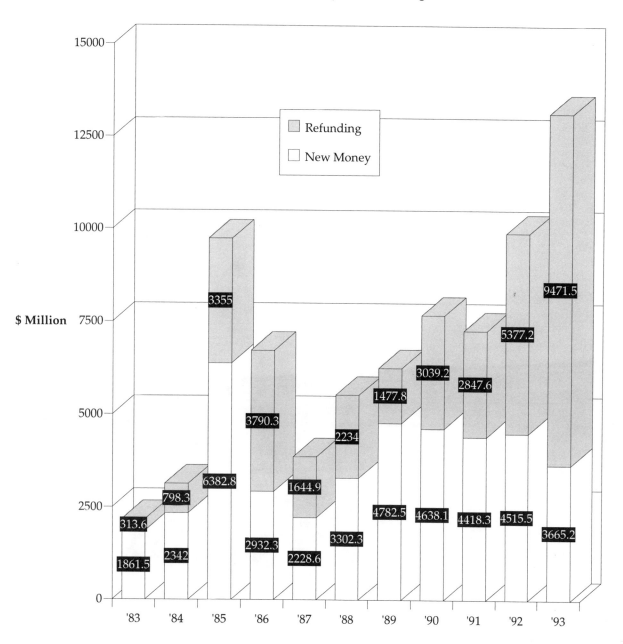

Source: J.P. Morgan Securities Inc.

College and University Rating Distributions

Figures 17-8 and 17-9 below show rating distributions for public and independent institutions, respectively.

Public Universities Rating Distribution

Standard and Poor's 1993

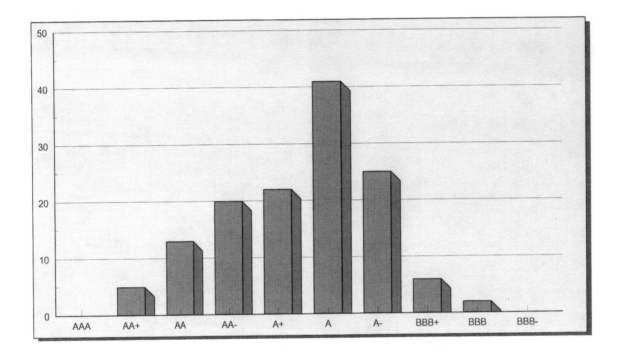

Private Colleges Rating Distribution

Standard and Poor's 1993

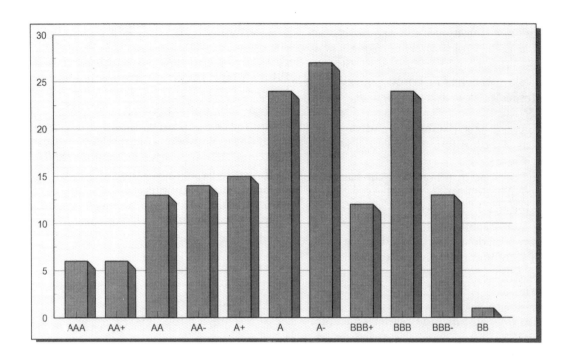

List of Colleges and Universities with Outstanding Publicly Held Indebtedness

Figure 17-10 lists higher education institutions with S&P-rated debt issues outstanding as of July 9, 1993. In many cases, the actual issuer of the debt is a higher education authority, issuing on behalf of a college or university. Connecticut Health and Educational Facilities Authority, for example, issues on behalf of Trinity College. The list includes institutions that have issued:

- unenhanced debt (issues sold and rated on the basis of the institution's own creditworthiness);
- insured debt (sold and rated on the basis of a municipal bond insurance policy);
- bank letter of credit-backed debt (rating based on bank enhancement); and
- collateralized debt (rating based on the institution's creditworthiness and enhancement in the form of collateral—generally investments).

The list does not include higher education debt rated "AAA" based on escrow structures (re-funded bonds) or community college ratings. In addition, a school with only bank-backed debt rated and outstanding may not appear on the list, as these issues are analyzed by S&P's bank group and not the higher education group.

In many cases, a college or university will have several different types of debt and ratings outstanding. For example, Loyola University of Chicago, which issues through the Illinois Educational Facilities Authority, has unenhanced, insured and bank or letter of credit-backed debt outstanding. Nearly 500 different institutions are represented, with an almost even breakdown between independent institutions (242) and state-supported institutions (230). The states with the highest concentration of rated independent institutions are Massachusetts (26), New York (46) and Pennsylvania (34). California (22) and Texas (20) have the greatest number of rated public institutions.

U = unenhanced
I = insured
C = collateralized
B = bank or letter of credit-backed

**Figure 17-10. List of Colleges and Universities
with Outstanding Publicly Held Indebtedness**

Alabama	
Rated Institution and Rating Type	Rated Institution and Rating Type
Alabama A&M University (I) Alabama State University (I) Auburn University (U,I) Jacksonville State University (I) Troy State University (I)	University of Alabama-Birmingham (U) University of Alabama-Huntsville (U,I) University of Alabama-Tuscaloosa (U,I) University of South Alabama (U,I)

Alaska	
Rated Institution and Rating Type	Rated Institution and Rating Type
University of Alaska (I)	

Arizona	
Rated Institution and Rating Type	Rated Institution and Rating Type
Arizona State University (U,I) Embry-Riddle Aeronautical University (I)	Northern Arizona University (U,I) University of Arizona (U,I)

Arkansas	
Rated Institution and Rating Type	Rated Institution and Rating Type

University of Arkansas-Medical Science
   Campus (I)
 University of Arkansas-Law/
   Medical Schools (B)
	University of Arkansas-Fayetteville (U,I)

California	
Rated Institution and Rating Type	Rated Institution and Rating Type
California Institute of Technology (U)	California State University-Stanislaus (U)
California State Polytechnic University/	Loyola Marymount University (I)
Pomona (U)	Pepperdine University (I)
California State University System (U,I)	Pomona College (U)
California State University-Bakersfield (I)	San Francisco Conservatory of Music (C)
California State University-Dominguez	Stanford University (U)
Hills (U)	University of California System (U,I)
California State University-Fresno (U)	University of California-Berkeley (U)
California State University-Fullerton (U,I)	University of California-Davis (U)
California State University-Hayward (U)	University of California-Irvine (U,I)
California State University-Los Angeles (U)	University of California-Los Angeles (U)
California State University-Northridge (U,I)	University of California-San Diego (U,I)
California State University-Sacramento (U)	University of San Diego (U,I)
California State University-San Bernadino (U,I)	University of San Francisco (U,I)
California State University-San Diego (U)	University of Southern California (U,I)
California State University-San Francisco (U)	University of the Pacific (U)
California State University-San Jose (U,I)	
California State University-Sonoma (U)	

Colorado	
Rated Institution and Rating Type	Rated Institution and Rating Type
Auraria Higher Education Center (I)	University of Colorado System (U,I)
Colorado College (I)	University of Colorado - Boulder (I)
Colorado School of Mines (I)	University of Denver (U,I)
Colorado State University (U,I)	University of Northern Colorado (I)
Fort Lewis College (I)	University of Southern Colorado (I)
Regis University (I)	Western State College (I)

Connecticut	
Rated Institution and Rating Type	Rated Institution and Rating Type
Connecticut College (I)	University of Hartford (U)
Fairfield University (U)	University of New Haven (U)
Quinnipiac College (U)	Wesleyan University (U)
Trinity College (U,I)	Yale University (U)

Delaware	
Rated Institution and Rating Type	Rated Institution and Rating Type
Delaware State College (I)	University of Delaware (U)

District of Columbia	
Rated Institution and Rating Type	Rated Institution and Rating Type
Catholic University of America (I) Georgetown University (U,I)	Howard University (U,I)

Florida	
Rated Institution and Rating Type	Rated Institution and Rating Type
Embry-Riddle Aeronautical University (I) Florida A&M University (I) Florida Institute of Technology (U) Florida International University (I) Florida State Brd. of Regents Univ. System (U) Florida State University (I)	Nova Southeastern University (U) Stetson University (I) University of Central Florida (I) University of Florida (I) University of Miami (I) University of West Florida (U)

Georgia	
Rated Institution and Rating Type	Rated Institution and Rating Type
Agnes Scott College (U) Emory University (U)	Mercer University (I) Spelman College (I)

Hawaii	
Rated Institution and Rating Type	Rated Institution and Rating Type
University of Hawaii (I)	

Idaho	
Rated Institution and Rating Type	Rated Institution and Rating Type
Boise State University (U,I)	University of Idaho (I,B)

Illinois	
Rated Institution and Rating Type	Rated Institution and Rating Type
Chicago State University (U) Columbia College (U,I) DePaul University (U) Eastern Illinois University (U,I) Illinois College of Podiatric Medicine (U) Illinois Institute of Technology (I) Illinois State University (U,I) Knox College (U) Lake Forest College (I) Loyola University of Chicago (U,I,B)	MacMurray College (I) Milliken University (I) Northern Illinois University (I) Northwestern University (U) Sangamon State University (I) Southern Illinois University (U,I) University of Chicago (U) University of Illinois (U,I) Western Illinois University (U)

Indiana	
Rated Institution and Rating Type	Rated Institution and Rating Type
Anderson University (U) Ball State University (U,I) Butler University (I) Earlham College (I) Indiana State University (U,I) Indiana University (U,I) Indiana Vocational Technical College (I) Manchester College (U)	Purdue University (U,I) St. Mary's College (U,I) Taylor University (I) University of Evansville (U) University of Southern Indiana (U,I) Valparaiso University (I) Vincennes University (U,I)

Iowa	
Rated Institution and Rating Type	Rated Institution and Rating Type
Iowa State University of Science & Technology (U,B) University of Iowa (U)	University of Northern Iowa (U)

Kansas	
Rated Institution and Rating Type	Rated Institution and Rating Type
Kansas State University (I) University of Kansas (U)	Wichita State University (U)

Kentucky	
Rated Institution and Rating Type	Rated Institution and Rating Type
Eastern Kentucky University (U,I)	Transylvania University (I)
Kentucky State University (I)	University of Kentucky (U,I)
Morehead State University (U,I)	University of Louisville (U,I)
Murray State University (U,I)	Western Kentucky University (U,I)
Northern Kentucky University (U,I)	

Louisiana	
Rated Institution and Rating Type	Rated Institution and Rating Type
Louisiana State University (U)	Southeastern Louisiana University (U)
Loyola University (U,I)	Louisiana Tech University (U)
McNeese State University (U)	Tulane University (U,I)
Nicholls State University (U)	University of New Orleans (U)
Northeast Louisiana University (U)	University of Southwestern Louisiana (U)

Maine	
Rated Institution and Rating Type	Rated Institution and Rating Type
Bates College (I)	University of Maine (I)
Colby College (I)	

Maryland	
Rated Institution and Rating Type	Rated Institution and Rating Type
Loyola College (U)	Mount St. Mary's College (I)
Johns Hopkins University (U)	St. Mary's College of Maryland (U)
Maryland State University (I)	University of Maryland (U)
Morgan State University (I)	

Massachusetts	
Rated Institution and Rating Type	Rated Institution and Rating Type
Amherst College (U,C)	Nichols College (U)
Babson College (U,I)	Northeastern University (I)
Bentley College (U,I)	Simmons College (U)
Berklee College of Music (U,I)	Smith College (U,C)
Boston College (U,I)	University of Stonehill College (I)
Boston University (U,I)	Suffolk University (I)
Clark University (U)	Tufts University (U,I)
Harvard University (U)	University of Massachusetts (U,I)
Holy Cross College (U)	Wellesley College (U)
Lesley College (U)	Wentworth Institute of Technology (I)
Massachusetts Institute of Technology (U,C)	Wheaton College (U,I)
Merrimack College (U)	Williams College (U,C)
Mount Holyoke (U,I)	Worcester Polytechnic Institute (U,I)
New England School of Law (U)	

Michigan	
Rated Institution and Rating Type	Rated Institution and Rating Type
Central Michigan University (U,I)	Michigan State University (U,I)
Eastern Michigan University (U,I)	Northern Michigan University (U,I)
Ferris State College (I)	Saginaw Valley College (I)
Grand Valley State College (U,I)	University of Michigan (U,I)
Kalamazoo College (I)	Wayne State University (U,I)
Lake Superior State University (U,I)	Western Michigan University (U,I)

Minnesota	
Rated Institution and Rating Type	Rated Institution and Rating Type
Augsburg College (I)	St. John's University (U)
College of St. Catherine (I)	St. Mary's College (U)
College of St. Thomas (I)	St. Olaf College (I)
Concordia College (I)	St. Thomas College (I)
Gustavus Adolphus College (U)	University of Minnesota (U,I)
Macalester College (U,I)	

Mississippi	
Rated Institution and Rating Type	Rated Institution and Rating Type
University of Southern Mississippi (I)	

Missouri	
Rated Institution and Rating Type	Rated Institution and Rating Type
Central Missouri State University (I) Southern Missouri State College (U) Western Missouri State College (U,I) Northwest Missouri State University (I) Southeast Missouri University (U,I) Southwest Missouri State University (I) St. Louis University (U,I)	University of Missouri-Columbia (U) University of Missouri-Kansas City (U) University of Missouri-Rolla (I) University of Missouri-St. Louis (U) Washington University (U) Webster University (I)

Montana	
Rated Institution and Rating Type	Rated Institution and Rating Type
Eastern Montana University (I) Montana College of Mineral Science & Technology (I)	Montana State University (I) University of Montana (I)

Nebraska	
Rated Institution and Rating Type	Rated Institution and Rating Type
Creighton University (I) Kearney State College (I)	University of Nebraska (U) Wayne State College (I)

Nevada	
Rated Institution and Rating Type	Rated Institution and Rating Type
University of Nevada (U,I)	

New Hampshire	
Rated Institution and Rating Type	Rated Institution and Rating Type
Dartmouth College (U) University of New Hampshire (I)	Rivier College (U)

New Jersey	
Rated Institution and Rating Type	Rated Institution and Rating Type
Drew University (U)	Rider College (U,I)
Fairleigh Dickinson University (U)	Rowan College of New Jersey (formerly Glassboro
Georgian Court College (U)	State College (U,I)
Institute for Advanced Study (U)	Rutgers University (U,I)
Jersey City State College (U,I)	Seton Hall University (U,I)
Kean College of New Jersey (U,I)	St. Peter's College (U)
Monmouth College (U)	Stevens Institute of Technology (U)
Montclair State College (U,I)	Trenton State College (U,I)
New Jersey Institute of Technology (U,I)	Union County College (U,I)
Princeton Theological Seminary (U)	William Paterson College (U,I)
Princeton University (U)	University of Medicine and Dentistry of
Ramapo College of New Jersey (U)	New Jersey (U,I)
Richard Stockton College of New Jersey (U,I)	

New Mexico	
Rated Institution and Rating Type	Rated Institution and Rating Type
Eastern New Mexico University (I)	New Mexico Military Institute (I)
New Mexico Highlands University (I)	New Mexico State University (U,I)
New Mexico Institute of Mining	University of New Mexico (U,I)
& Technology (I)	

New York	
Rated Institution and Rating Type	Rated Institution and Rating Type
Adelphi University (U,I)	Marist College (I)
Albany Law School (I)	Mount Sinai School of Medicine (I)
Brooklyn Law School (I)	New School For Social Research (U)
City University of New York (CUNY) (U,I)	New York Law School (I)
Clarkson College (C)	New York University (U,I,C)
Colgate University (U,I,C)	Pace University (U,I)
College of New Rochelle (U)	Rensselaer Polytechnic Institute (U,I)
College of St. Rose (I)	Rochester Institute of Technology (U,I,C)
Columbia University (U,C)	Rockefeller University (U)
Cooper Union (I)	Russell Sage College (U)
Cornell University (U,I)	Sage College (I)
Culinary Institute of America (I)	Siena College (U,I)
Dowling University (U)	Skidmore College (I)
Fashion Institute of Technology (U)	St. Bonaventure University (U)
Fordham University (I)	St. John Fisher College (I)
Hamilton College (I)	St. John's University (U,I)
Hartwick University (U,I)	St. Lawrence University (U)
Hofstra University (U,I)	State University of New York (SUNY) (U,I)
Houghton College (U)	Syracuse University (U)
Iona College (U,I)	Teacher's College (I)
Ithaca Cóllege (U,I)	Union College (I)
Lemoyne College (I)	University of Rochester (U,I)
Manhattan College (I)	Vassar College (U)
Manhattanville College (I)	Wagner College (U)

North Carolina	
Rated Institution and Rating Type	Rated Institution and Rating Type
Appalachian State University (I)	North Carolina State University at Raleigh (U)
Davidson University (U)	University of North Carolina-Chapel Hill (U,B)
Duke University (U)	University of North Carolina-Charlotte (U)
East Carolina University (I)	University of North Carolina-Greensboro (U,I)
Elizabeth City State University (I)	University of North Carolina-Wilmington (U,I)
Elon College (I)	Western Carolina University (U)
North Carolina Agriculture and Tech State University (I)	Winston-Salem State University (I)

North Dakota	
Rated Institution and Rating Type	Rated Institution and Rating Type
University of North Dakota (I)	

Ohio	
Rated Institution and Rating Type	Rated Institution and Rating Type
Ashland College (U)	Ohio University (U,I)
Bowling Green State University (U)	Shawnee State University (I)
Case Western Reserve University (U,C)	University of Akron (U)
Cleveland State University (U,I)	University of Cincinnati (U,I)
Kent State University (U,I)	University of Dayton (I)
Kenyon College (U,B)	University of Toledo (U,I)
Miami University (U)	Wittenburg University (I)
Oberlin College (U,I)	Wright State University (U,I)
Ohio State University (U)	Youngstown State University (I)
Ohio Wesleyan University (I)	

Oklahoma	
Rated Institution and Rating Type	Rated Institution and Rating Type
Oklahoma Baptist University (I)	University of Oklahoma (U,I)
Oklahoma State University (U)	

Oregon	
Rated Institution and Rating Type	Rated Institution and Rating Type
Lewis and Clark University (I)	Reed College (U)

Pennsylvania	
Rated Institution and Rating Type	Rated Institution and Rating Type
Albright College (I)	Muhlenberg College (I)
Allentown College of St. Francis de Sales (I)	Pennsylvania State University (U)
Bryn Mawr College (I)	Pennsylvania State System of Higher
Bucknell University (I)	Education (U,I)
Carnegie-Mellon University (U)	Philadelphia College of Textiles
Dickinson College (U,I)	& Science (U,I)
Drexel University (U,I)	Philadelphia College of Pharmacy
Duquesne University (I)	& Science (I)
Elizabethtown College (U,I)	Robert Morris College (I)
Franklin and Marshall College (I)	Seton Hill College (U)
Gannon University (U,I)	Spring Garden College (I)
Gettysburg College (U)	St. Joseph's University (I)
Haverford College (I)	Susquehanna University (U,I)
Lafayette College (I)	Swarthmore College (U)
LaSalle University (I)	Temple University (U,I)
Lebanon Valley College (U)	University of Pennsylvania (U)
Lehigh University (U,I)	University of Pittsburgh (U,I)
Lycoming College (U)	University of Scranton (U,I)
Mercyhurst College (U)	Villanova University (U,I)
Messiah College (I)	Widener University (I)
Morvavian College (U,I)	

Puerto Rico	
Rated Institution and Rating Type	Rated Institution and Rating Type
Pontifical Catholic University of Puerto Rico (U)	University of Puerto Rico (U)

Rhode Island	
Rated Institution and Rating Type	Rated Institution and Rating Type
Brown University (U)	Rhode Island School of Design (I)
Bryant College (U,I)	Roger Williams College (I)
Johnson and Wales University (I)	Salve Regina College (I)
Providence College (U,I)	University of Rhode Island (U)

South Carolina	
Rated Institution and Rating Type	Rated Institution and Rating Type
Citadel Military College of South Carolina (U)	College of Charleston (U,I)
Clemson University (U,I)	Francis Marion College (U)

South Dakota	
Rated Institution and Rating Type	Rated Institution and Rating Type
Black Hills State University (I)	South Dakota State University (I)

Tennessee	
Rated Institution and Rating Type	Rated Institution and Rating Type
Rhodes College (U) Tennessee State School Bond Authority (U)	University of the South (U) Vanderbilt University (U)

Texas	
Rated Institution and Rating Type	Rated Institution and Rating Type
Abilene Christian University (U,I) Angelo State University (U,I) Corpus Christi University (U,I) East Texas State University (U) Incarnate Word College (U) Lamar University (I) Midwestern State University (U) Pan American University (I) Prairie View A&M University (I) Sam Houston State University (U,I) Southern Methodist University (I) Southwest Texas State University (U,I) St. Mary's University (U,I)	Stephen F. Austin State University (I) Tarleton State University (U) Texas A&I University (U,I) Texas A&M University (U,I,B) Texas Southern University (I) Texas Tech University (U,I) Texas Women's University (U,I) University of Houston (I) University of North Texas (U,I) University of St. Thomas (U) University of Texas (U,I) West Texas State University (I)

Utah	
Rated Institution and Rating Type	Rated Institution and Rating Type
University of Utah (U,I) Utah State University (U,I)	Utah Tech College (I) Weber State University (I)

Vermont	
Rated Institution and Rating Type	Rated Institution and Rating Type
Middlebury College (U) University of Vermont (U)	St. Michael's College (U) Vermont State College (U)

Virginia	
Rated Institution and Rating Type	Rated Institution and Rating Type
Emory and Henry College (U) Hampden-Sydney College (U) Hampton Roads Medical College (U) Hampton University (U) Marymount University (U) Randolph-Macon College (U) Randolph-Macon Woman's College (U)	Roanoke College (U) Sweet Briar College (U) University of Richmond (U) University of Virginia (U) Virginia Polytechnic Institute (I) Washington and Lee University (U)

Washington	
Rated Institution and Rating Type	Rated Institution and Rating Type
Central Washington University (U) Eastern Washington University (I) Evergreen State College (I) Seattle University (U,I)	University of Puget Sound (I) University of Washington (U,I) Washington State University (U) Western Washington University (I)

West Virginia	
Rated Institution and Rating Type	Rated Institution and Rating Type
Marshall University (U) Shepherd College (U) West Liberty State College (U)	West Virginia State College (U,I,B) West Virginia University (I)

Wisconsin	
Rated Institution and Rating Type	Rated Institution and Rating Type
Carroll College (U) Lawrence University (I)	Marquette University (I) Medical College of Wisconsin (U)

Wyoming	
Rated Institution and Rating Type	Rated Institution and Rating Type
University of Wyoming (I)	

APPENDIX A

NACUBO and NACUBO Higher Education Financing Committee

Names of Committee Members

National Association of College and University Business Officers (NACUBO)
Robin E. Jenkins
Director, Center for Institutional Accounting,
Finance, and Management
NACUBO
One Dupont Circle, Suite 500
Washington, DC 20036-1178
(202) 861-2535
Fax: (202) 861-2583

Anna Marie Cirino
Associate Director, Center for Institutional
Accounting, Finance, and Management
NACUBO
One Dupont Circle, Suite 500
Washington, DC 20036-1178
(202) 861-2535
Fax: (202) 861-2583

Representatives from Public Institutions
Alice W. Handy [Committee Chair]
Treasurer
University of Virginia
P.O. Box 9014
1709 University Avenue
Charlottesville, Virginia 22906-9014
(804) 924-4245
Fax (804) 924-0938

Dr. Farris W. Womack
Chief Financial Officer
University of Michigan
3014 Fleming Administration Building
503 Thompson Street
Ann Arbor, Michigan 48109-1340
(313) 764-7272
Fax: (313) 936-8730

Representatives from Large Independent Institutions
Richard E. Anderson
Vice Chancellor for Administration and Finance
Washington University
Campus Box 1080
229 North Brookings Drive
St. Louis, Missouri 63130-4899
(314) 935-5153
Fax: (314) 935-5188

Joseph P. Mullinix
Vice President for Finance and Administration
Yale University
20 Ashmun Street
P.O. Box 208304
New Haven, Connecticut 06520
(203) 432-1094
Fax: (203) 432-0130

Representatives from Small Independent Institutions
Louis R. Morrell
Vice President for Business & Finance and
Treasurer
Rollins College
1000 Holt Avenue (2717)
Winter Park, Florida 32789-4499
(407) 646-2117
Fax: (407) 646-2600

Michael O. Stewart
Vice President for Business and Finance
and Treasurer
Marian College of Fond du Lac
Fond du Lac, Wisconsin 54935
(414) 932-7610

Representative from the National Association of Higher Educational Facilities Authorities (NAHEFA)
Joan A. Panacek
Deputy Executive Director
New Jersey Educational Facilities Authority
133 Franklin Corner Road
Lawrenceville, New Jersey 08648-2531
(609) 530-4377
Fax: (609) 530-4587

Representative of Combined Higher Education Finance and Law
George A. King
Vice President
CS First Boston
Park Avenue Plaza
55 East 52nd Street, 37th floor
New York, New York 10055
(212) 909-2000
Fax: (212) 318-1221

Representative from an Investment Banking/Financial Institution
David M. Cyganowski
Director and Manager, Higher Education
CS First Boston
Park Avenue Plaza
55 East 52nd Street, 37th Floor
New York, New York 10055
(212) 909-2806
Fax: (212) 318-1221

Representative from an Institutional Counsel/Financing Counsel
Stanford G. Ladner
Mudge Rose Guthrie Alexander & Ferdon
180 Maiden Lane
New York, New York 10038
(212) 510-7275
Fax: (212) 248-2655

Higher Education Consultant Representative
Dr. Edward J. Bambach
17 Scullin Drive
Yardville, New Jersey 08620
(609) 585-4726

APPENDIX B

National Association of Higher Educational Facilities Authorities

The National Association of Higher Educational Facilities Authorities (NAHEFA) promotes the common interests of organizations that have the authority to provide capital financing for the development of higher education and to enhance the effectiveness of such organizations and their programs. NAHEFA's general purpose may be more fully effected by the following activities:

(1) encouraging and assisting the promotion of and more effective operation of higher educational facilities authorities via educational programs and research projects as determined by the board of directors;

(2) informing the public about the programs, activities and achievements of higher educational facilities authorities and acting as a clearinghouse of information among the authorities themselves;

(3) keeping members fully informed about federal and state administrative and legislative developments that affect the programs of higher educational facilities authorities and the growth and operation of such authorities and assisting the exchange of information and views among such authorities regarding such matters;

(4) assisting in the collection and presentation of information to various segments of the financial community, including rating agencies, for the purpose of assisting the financial community to better understand the role and purpose of higher educational facilities authorities;

(5) assisting in the formulation and implementation of effective governmental programs of assistance for meeting higher education financing needs;

(6) presenting to concerned parties the policies for views of NAHEFA or its members concerning public issues relevant to the programs and operations of higher educational facilities authorities; and

(7) performing such other activities as are necessary or proper to forward the interests of NAHEFA and its members.

Members and Agencies

California Educational Facilities Authority
Rose Sloan
Executive Director
304 S. Broadway, Suite 500
Los Angeles, California 90013-1209
(213) 620-4467
Fax: (213) 620-5384

Colorado Postsecondary Educational Facilities Authority
Mark Gallegos
Executive Director
1981 Blake Street
Denver, Colorado 80202-1272
(303) 297-2538
Fax: (303) 297-2615

Connecticut Health and Educational Facilities Authority
Roger H. Stephenson
Executive Director
10 Columbus Boulevard, 7th Floor
Hartford, Connecticut 06106-1976
(203) 520-4700
Fax: (203) 520-4706

Illinois Educational Facilities Authority
Thomas P. Conley
Executive Director
333 W. Wacker Drive, Suite 2600
Chicago, Illinois 60606-1218
(312) 781-6633
Fax: (312) 781-6630

Indiana Educational Facilities Authority
Dr. Robert E. Martin
Executive Director
8777 Purdue Road, Suite 102
Indianapolis, Indiana 46268
(317) 875-3395
Fax: (317) 875-3397

Iowa Higher Education Loan Authority
Linda Beaver
Executive Director
505 Fifth Avenue, Suite 1040
Des Moines, Iowa 50309-2315
(515) 282-3769
Fax: (515) 282-9508

Kentucky Development Finance Authority
Jeff Noel
Executive Director
Capital Plaza Tower, 24th Floor
Frankfort, Kentucky 40601
(502) 564-4554
Fax: (502) 564-7697

Louisiana Public Facilities Authority
Billy Gordan
Managing Director, Administration and Finance
8555 United Plaza Boulevard, Suite 100
Baton Rouge, Louisiana 70809
(504) 929-8560
Fax: (504) 929-8561

Maine Health and Higher Educational Facilities Authority
Robert O. Lenna
Executive Director
45 University Drive, 3rd Floor
P.O. Box 2268
Augusta, Maine 04338
(207) 622-1958
Fax: (207) 623-5359

Maryland Health and Higher Educational Facilities Authority
Donald P. Carter
Executive Director
22 E. Fayette Street, 4th Floor
Baltimore, Maryland 21202-1516
(410) 837-6220
Fax: (410) 685-1611

Massachusetts Health and Educational Facilities Authority
Edward M. Murphy
Executive Director
99 Summer Street, Suite 1000
Boston, Massachusetts 02110-1240
(617) 737-8377
Fax: (617) 737-8366

Michigan State Hospital Finance Authority
Roy Pentilla
Executive Director
P.O. Box 15128
Lansing, Michigan 48901
(517) 344-6560
Fax: (517) 334-6680

Minnesota Higher Education Facilities Authority
Dr. Joseph E. LaBelle
Executive Director
175 Fifth Street East, Suite 450
St. Paul, Minnesota 55101-2901
(612) 296-4690
Fax: (612) 297-5751

Missouri Health and Educational Facilities Authority
Melinda S. O'Shea
Executive Director
One City Centre, Suite 1310
St. Louis, Missouri 63101
(314) 231-3355
Fax: (314) 231-3019

Nebraska Educational Facilities Authority
Dr. Howard B. Dooley
Executive Director
2120 South 72nd Street, Suite 429
Omaha, Nebraska 68124
(402) 397-6482
Fax: (402) 397-6783

New Hampshire Higher Educational and Health Facilities Authority
David C. Bliss
Executive Director
P.O. Box 827
Concord, New Hampshire 03303-0827
(603) 224-0696
Fax: (603) 224-3058

New Jersey Educational Facilities Authority
Linda Lordi Cavanaugh
Executive Director
133 Franklin Corner Road, Suite 205
Lawrenceville, New Jersey 08648-2531
(609) 530-4377
Fax: (609) 530-4587

Dormitory Authority of the State of New York
Theodore A. Holmes
First Deputy Executive Director
161 Delaware Avenue
Delmar, New York 12054-1398
(518) 475-3050
Fax: (518) 475-3040

Ohio Educational Facilities Authority
Barry Keefe
Executive Director
1800 Huntington Building
Cleveland, Ohio 44115
(216) 479-8535
Fax: (216) 479-8787

Pennsylvania Higher Educational Facilities Authority
Donald W. Bagenstose
Executive Director
101 South 25th Street
P.O. Box 3161
Harrisburg, Pennsylvania 17105-3161
(717) 975-2203
Fax: (717) 975-2215

Rhode Island Health and Educational Building
Robert Donovan
Executive Director
400 Westminster Street, 2nd Floor
Providence, Rhode Island 02903
(401) 831-3770
Fax: (401) 421-3910

South Dakota Health and Educational Facilities Authority
Jerry D. Fischer
Executive Director
330 South Poplar Street
P.O. Box 846
Pierre, South Dakota 57501
(605) 224-9209
Fax: (605) 244-7177

Vermont Educational and Health Buildings Financing Agency
Malcolm S. Rode
Executive Director
Two Spring Street
P.O. Box 1219
Montpelier, Vermont 05601-1219
(802) 223-2717
Fax: (802) 229-4709

Virginia College Building Authority
Susan F. Dewey
Assistant Secretary
P.O. Box 1879
Richmond, Virginia 23215
(804) 225-4927
Fax: (804) 225-3187

Washington Health Care Facilities Authority
John H. Van Gorkom
Executive Director
1212 Jefferson Street, Suite 201
P.O. Box 40935
Olympia, Washington 98504-0935
(206) 753-6185
Fax: (206) 586-9168

Wisconsin Health and Educational Facilities Authority
Lawrence R. Nines
Executive Director
18000 West Sarah Lane, Suite 140
Brookfield, Wisconsin 53045-5843
(414) 792-0466
Fax: (414) 792-0649

APPENDIX C

Directories and Information

Bond Information

American Banker-Bond Buyer (A Division of Thomas Publishing Corporation)

The Bond Buyer and related documents assist individuals in obtaining information pertaining to the bond market. Listed below is a buy description of *Bond Buyer* publications, and how to gain access to them.

The Bond Buyer is a daily newspaper, printed Monday through Friday. It includes information on the bond market as well as financial news. To receive a subscription of *The Bond Buyer,* write: Subscription Services, The Bond Buyer, One State Street Plaza, New York, NY 10004. The telephone number is (800) 221-1809 or (212) 943-2988.

The Bond Buyer's Municipal Marketplace is a directory that is published semiannually. Also referred to as the Redbook, it contains listings for underwriters and dealers, financial and investment advisors, corporate trust departments, and municipal bond attorneys. The Redbook lists these groups by states, making it user friendly. To obtain a copy, write to The Bond Buyer's Municipal Marketplace, 4709 West Gulf Road, 6th Floor, Skokie, IL 60076-1253. The telephone number is (800) 321-3373.

The Bond Buyer Yearbook includes information on the years highlights in the bond market. To obtain a copy of *The Bond Buyer Yearbook,* write to: The Bond Buyer Yearbook, One State Street Plaza, New York, NY 10004. The telephone number is (212) 943-4845.

Higher Education Associations

National Association of College and University Business Officers (NACUBO)
One Dupont Circle, Suite 500
Washington, DC 20036
(202) 861-2500

NACUBO publishes material on debt financing and management and sponsors seminars on debt financing. NACUBO's Center for Institutional Accounting, Finance, and Management can provide information on debt financing and management.

Municipal Bond Industry Organizations

Government Finance Officers Association of the United States and Canada (GFOA)
180 N. Michigan Avenue, Suite 800
Chicago, IL 60601
(312) 977-9700

GFOA is a professional association of state and local government finance officers that holds conferences and sponsors activities on topics relating to public finance. GFOA publishes a wide variety of financing information and sponsors many seminars.

Rating Agencies

Fitch Investor Services, Inc. (Fitch)
One State Street Plaza
New York, NY 10004
(212) 908-0500

Fitch Investor Services, Inc., sold its rating system to S&P but retained rights to use it. Recently recapitalized, Fitch began rating colleges and universities in 1989.

Moody's Investors Service, Inc. (Moody's)
99 Church Street
New York, NY 10007
(212) 553-0470
Moody's publishes *Moody's Bond Record; Moody's Municipal & Government Manual; Moody's Bond Survey;* and other specialized publications.

Standard & Poor's Corporation (S&P)
25 Broadway
New York, NY 10004
(212) 208-8000
S&P publishes *CreditWeek* and holds occasional one-day seminars on higher education creditworthiness aimed at college and university financial and business officers and investment bankers.

Municipal Bond Industry Regulation

Municipal Securities Rulemaking Board (MSRB)
1818 N Street, NW, Suite 800
Washington, DC 20036-2491
(202) 223-9347
The Municipal Securities Rulemaking Board was established by Congress as part of the Securities Acts Amendments of 1975 to develop rules governing securities firms and banks involved in underwriting, trading, and selling municipal securities. The MSRB, which is composed of members of the municipal securities industry and the public, is a self-regulatory body that sets standards based on the expertise of industry members. The MSRB has a quarterly newsletter which provides information on current events affecting the MSRB.

National Federation of Municipal Analysts (NFMA)
P.O. Box 14893
Pittsburgh, PA 15234
(412) 341-4898
NFMA represents analysts who make credit recommendations for both issuers and buyers of municipal securities. NFMA has become more active in recent years in the publication of written documents which present its views.

Public Securities Association (PSA)
40 Broad Street
New York, NY 10004
(212) 809-7000
PSA is the national trade organization of dealers and dealer banks that underwrite, trade, and sell state and local government securities and U.S. government and federal agency securities. PSA prepares a variety of educational materials in written and video cassette form which may be helpful to business officers.

APPENDIX D

Other NACUBO Publications and Services

In addition to the *NACUBO Guide to Issuing and Managing Debt,* NACUBO also offers the following publications and services relating to higher education financing.

"Debt Financing and Management," chapter 12 of *College and University Business Administration,* fifth edition (1992). Available as an offprint, this publication provides solid background information on policies and terms relating to debt financing. NACUBO member price: $9.75; nonmember price: $17.95.

A Handbook of Debt Management for Colleges and Universities (1988). This reference manual covers managing and accounting for debt, debt accounting, and many other subjects not addressed in the *NACUBO Guide to Issuing and Managing Debt.* NACUBO member price: $9.95; nonmember price: $17.95.

Database on Rated Debt Issued in Higher Education, NACUBO NET. This database contains valuable information on colleges and universities that issued debt over the last ten years, such as date and amount of issuance, whether the debt is taxable or exempt, credit enhancer, bond rating, and lead underwriter. This information is updated quarterly and available at no charge to NACUBO members through NACUBO NET, the association's electronic information service.

Performance Indexes, NACUBO NET. Updated monthly, this NACUBO NET service features domestic and international common stock indexes, domestic and global fixed income indexes, bond financing indexes, fixed income yields, and much more. Available at no charge to NACUBO members.

State-by-State Capital Renewal Summaries (1992). This publication is a compilation of state higher education capital renewal and replacement policies, current through January 1992. Contains information on legislative appropriation and financing policies. An update, to be greatly expanded, is currently underway and scheduled for publication in fall 1994. Price: $10.

Financing Capital Maintenance (1989). This publication presents the proceedings from the Symposium on Financing Capital Maintenance held in April 1989. Covers approaches by different states in financing capital renewal and examples from three independent institutions. NACUBO member price; $9.95; nonmember price: $13.95.

Capital Formation Alternatives in Higher Education (1988). This book provides an overview of nontraditional methods of capital formation and features case studies of methods in practice at five colleges and universities. NACUBO member price: $13; nonmember price: $20.

For ordering information on any of the above publications, contact the NACUBO Publications Desk at (202) 861-2560. To find out more about NACUBO NET, call (202) 861-2535.

NACUBO Board of Directors

National Association of College and University Business Officers
One Dupont Circle, Suite 500
Washington, DC 20036
(202) 861-2500